Lacan, Language, and Philosophy

SUNY series, Insinuations:
Philosophy, Psychoanalysis, Literature

Charles Shepherdson, editor

Lacan, Language, and Philosophy

Russell Grigg

STATE UNIVERSITY OF NEW YORK PRESS

Published by
State University of New York Press, Albany

© 2008 State University of New York

For information, contact State University of New York Press, Albany, NY
www.sunypress.edu

Cover art courtesy of Rebecca Driffield. The painting is entitled "Spring
and Autumn."

Production by Diane Ganeles
Marketing by Michael Campochiaro

Library of Congress Cataloging-in-Publication Data

Grigg, Russell.
    Lacan, language, and philosophy / Russell Grigg.
        p. cm. — (SUNY series, insinuations: philosophy, psychoanalysis,
literature)
    Includes bibliographical references and index.
    ISBN 978-0-7914-7345-0 (hardcover : alk. paper)
    ISBN 978-0-7914-7346-7 (pbk. : alk. paper)
    1. Lacan, Jacques, 1901–1981.   2. Psychoanalysis.   3. Philosophy.
I. Title.

BF109.L23G75 2007
150.19'5092—dc22   2007016959

10 9 8 7 6 5 4 3 2 1

For KRM

Contents

Acknowledgments

Versions of the material contained in this book have been previously published as articles in various journals and books. Chapter 1 appeared in *Key Concepts of Lacanian Psychoanalysis*, edited by Dany Nobus (London: Rebus, 1998). An earlier version of Chapter 2 was published in *The Australian Journal of Psychotherapy* 5 (1986). Chapter 3 appeared in *Jacques Lacan and the Other Side of Psychoanalysis,* edited by Justin Clemens and Russell Grigg (Durham, NC: Duke University Press, 2006). An earlier version of Chapter 4 was published in *Lacan and the Subject of Language,* edited by Ellie Ragland-Sullivan and Mark Bracher (New York: Routledge, 1991). Chapter 5 first appeared in print as a contribution to Jacques-Alain Miller, *The Pathology of Democracy* (London: Karnac, 2005). Chapter 6 was published in the Slovenian journal *Filozofski Vestnik* 26:2 (2005). Earlier versions of parts of Chapter 7 appeared in *Afreudite: Portuguese Review of Pure and Applied Psychoanalysis* 1 (2005), *Analysis* 3 (1991), and the Belgian journal *Quarto* 43 (1991). Chapter 8 was originally published in *Cardozo Law Review* 24 (2003). An earlier version of Chapter 9 appeared in *Paragraph* 24 (2001). And Chapter 11 had its first iteration in French in *Ornicar?* 35 (1986).

Introduction

Whatever the subsequent developments came to be, the real break-through for Jacques Lacan came with the recognition that the uncon-scious is structured like a language. It was only once he had made this discovery that Lacan was able to scrupulously distinguish what in psychoanalysis is "symbolic," as he called the field of language, from the secondary and dependent register of the imaginary, a move that enabled him to better analyze the true place of language in the psy-choanalytic experience. The third register, that of the real, which be-came the focus of Lacan's late teaching, with particular reference to jouissance, only emerged against the background of the discovery of the central place that the symbolic plays in psychoanalysis.

How germane the study of language and logic is to psychoana-lytic theory and practice had not been recognized before Lacan, and it is reasonable to assume that it would have remained unrecognized in the absence of any explicit acknowledgment of the linguistic nature of the unconscious. Thus while the focus of much of the recent work on Lacan has been elsewhere, the study of language and logic remains of central interest to psychoanalysts, philosophers, and others who draw upon the insights that psychoanalysis has brought to the study of the human subject.

The chapters in this book examine a number of the ways in which Lacan draws upon studies of language and logic for the benefit of psychoanalysis, with the aim of clarifying and, where necessary, cri-tiquing linguistic, logical, and philosophical theses underpinning Lacan's work, whether his own or derived from his sources. These chapters also engage, often critically, with positions adopted not only by psychoanalysts but also by philosophers and linguists whom Lacan has written on, who have written on Lacan, or who simply hold views on the issues raised herein.

The first three chapters in Part 1 approach the question of the father in Lacan's work from different angles. Chapter 1, "Foreclo-sure," argues that it is the study of psychosis that most convincingly demonstrates the significance of the discovery of the place of the symbolic in analytic experience. Drawing on the distinction between repression and foreclosure introduced by Lacan to open up a new psychoanalytic approach to neurosis and psychosis, the chapter details the ways in which the foreclosure of the signifier the Name-of-the-Father ramifies through all psychotic phenomena, ranging from delusions to relations with others, passing via "verbal" hallucinations, paranoia, and the bodily devastation so graphically portrayed by President Schreber's *Memoirs*.

While "Foreclosure" concerns psychosis, Chapter 2, "The Father's Function," addresses the interplay in neurosis between imaginary and symbolic figures of the paternal function. This chapter touches on issues of identification, a largely ignored and still unresolved issue over identification in Freud's work, and on the place in neurosis of the paternal function. This itself raises a question about the end of analysis and also has implications for the tendency of Lacan's contemporaries in psychoanalysis, one thinks of Melanie Klein, to reduce the death drive to a simple instinct of aggression.

Chapter 3, "Beyond the Oedipus Complex," includes a discussion of Lacan's critique of the complex that Freud considered the cornerstone of psychoanalysis and reveals the way in which Lacan makes use of the Oedipus complex even as he goes beyond it. The chapter discusses Lacan's argument for distinguishing analysis of myth à la Lévi-Strauss from analysis of dreams, symptoms, and other "formations of the unconscious," thereby laying the ground for a critique of the Oedipus complex as a myth of Freud's. In a radical departure from earlier views, Lacan henceforth regards the Oedipal story as Freud's attempt to maintain the position of the father in the face of his crumbling authority and the response to the decline in the paternal figure coming from Freud's hysterics. Some intriguing aspects to Freud's writings on the father emerge when one compares the Oedipus complex and the primal horde myth, leading to questions about the relationship between Freud's Oedipal father, in both senses of the term, and the father of excess and *jouissance* as portrayed in the father of the primal horde.

Chapter 4, "Signifier and Object in the Transference," in Part 1, brings out the ethical responsibility that the transference places upon the analyst in his or her interventions. Lacan's subject supposed to know is a unifying concept for the different ways in which Freud describes the transference, one that brings out clearly the paradox of the analyst's position: a position of power that should not be used, even in the interests of the analysand.

Chapter 5, "Regulating Psychoanalysis," which completes Part 1, takes up the ethical place of the psychoanalyst in relation to a concrete issue for psychoanalysis in the contemporary world, namely, recent moves to regulate psychoanalysis. The events that unfolded in France when in 2005 a sudden and unexpected push for regulation emerged apparently from nowhere are of wider interest given the moves in many jurisdictions towards a much greater control over the practice of psychoanalysis and psychotherapy and the rise and rise of competing therapies such as cognitive-behavioral therapy, or CBT. I discuss what in psychoanalysis resists regulation and would be compromised or even lost if it were subject to state control.

The six chapters in Part 2 are of a more philosophical kind, exploring as they do either the way Lacan makes use of the philosophy of Kant and Descartes or the responses of philosophers Alain Badiou and Slavoj Žižek to Lacan's work. The concluding chapter addresses Lacan's relationship to Jakobson via his work on metaphor and metonymy.

Chapter 6, "Lacan and Badiou: Logic of the *Pas-Tout*," both clarifies how this Lacanian concept of the "not all" or the "not all of" developed in his *Seminar XX* in relation to feminine sexuality is to be understood and offers a critique of Badiou's criticism of Lacan, which relies upon a view about the infinite in mathematics that is controversial, to say the least.

Philosophy and psychoanalysis share common ground when it comes to the major Lacanian concept, that of the Name-of-the-Father. This concept, with its roots in the Freudian Oedipus complex, also sends shoots off into not just philosophical but also religious, historical, and cultural questions. Two chapters here, one on Kant and Freud and the second on guilt and transgression, both reveal Lacan's new perspective on the Freudian superego and throw new light on Kant's moral philosophy. Chapters 7 and 8, "Kant and Freud" and "Guilt, the Law, and Transgression," are both concerned with the connections between Kant's ethics and the Freudian superego. The first discusses the connection in Kant's philosophy between the recognition of the moral law and the mortification of desire. The second explores this same relationship through the link that psychoanalysis (since Freud) has made between unconscious guilt and the drive towards transgression.

Slavoj Žižek has produced an influential philosophical position derived from Lacan's work, which one cannot do justice to in a brief space. Chapter 9, "Absolute Freedom and Radical Change: On Žižek," takes a critical approach to one of Žižek's claims about various kinds of highly radical acts. Žižek argues that an agent who performed a truly radical act is radically transformed as a result. I remain unconvinced by

the argument and try to show in this chapter that each of the cases
Žižek discusses is open to a more conservative reading, one moreover
that is consistent with the clinical experience of psychoanalysis.

Chapter 10, "Descartes and the Subject of Science," addresses
Descartes' role in the emergence of science in the seventeenth century.
Lacan's view is that the emergence of the *cogito* and the mathematization of the empirical world were necessary metaphysical preconditions
for the appearance of modern science. This is a position that implies a
rejection of empiricist accounts that attribute the emergence of modern
science to observation and experiment. Lacan, joining company with
Alexandre Koyré, stresses the significance of Descartes' ontological shift
for modern science, to the point where he identifies the Cartesian cogito,
this "empty subject," with the subject of science itself.

In Chapter 11, "Lacan and Jakobson: Metaphor and Metonymy,"
I construct a theory of metaphor based on, and I think faithful to,
Lacan's own. Although Lacan gives a prominent role to metaphor in
his work, it is striking that his own theory of what metaphors are is
neither clearly elaborated by him nor satisfactorily developed in the
literature. Not only does my construction detail an account of metaphor that is Lacanian, but I also discuss why it is preferable to other
well-known views such as those of Davidson and Black.

Some of the chapters differ only slightly from their original publication. Others have been reworked for this book. Most originally
appeared in publications that are out of print or difficult to obtain.

Part 1

Psychosis, Neurosis, and the Name-of-the-Father

Chapter 1

Foreclosure

Lacan introduces the term *foreclosure* to explain the massive and global differences between psychosis and neurosis; neurosis operates by way of *repression*, while psychosis operates by way of *foreclosure*. This distinction is complemented by a third category, though arguably less secure and more problematic than the first two, of *disavowal,* as a mechanism specific to perversion. These three terms, which correspond, respectively, to Freud's *Verdrängung, Verwerfung,* and *Verleugnung,* along with the three-part division of neurosis, psychosis, and perversion, form the basis of what is effectively a differential diagnosis in Lacan's work, one that aspires to being truly psychoanalytic, deriving nothing from psychiatric categories. Thus underlying the elaboration of the notion of foreclosure is a clear and sharp distinction between three separate subjective structures.

Two features of this psychoanalytic nosology worthy of note are first that it assumes a structural unity behind often quite different symptoms that are expressions of the one clinical type, and second that there is no continuum between the various clinical types uncovered. A corollary is that in the case of psychosis this structure, a quite different structure from that of neurosis, is present even before the psychosis declares itself clinically.

ORIGIN OF THE TERM

While the term *foreclosure* is a common French legal term with a meaning very close to its English equivalent, for Lacan's purposes it clearly derives more directly from the work of French linguists Jacques Damourette and Édouard Pichon, *Des Mots à la Pensée.*[1] In their *Grammaire*, these authors speak of "foreclosure" in certain circumstances when an utterance repudiates facts that are treated as either true or merely possible. In their words, a proposition is "foreclosed" when "expelled from the field of possibility" as seen by the speaker who thereby "scotomizes" (a term they adopt from René Laforgue) the possibility of something's being the case. They take the presence of certain linguistic elements as an indication of foreclosure, so that when it is said that

Mr. Brook is not the sort of person who would *ever* complain,

on Damourette and Pichon's analysis the word "ever" would flag the foreclosure of the very possibility of Mr. Brook's complaining; that is, that Mr. Brook should complain is expelled, foreclosed, from the field of possibility.

Whether this analysis is correct or not is largely irrelevant as far as Lacan is concerned since, although he derives the term from Damourette and Pichon, he puts it to quite a different use. For Lacan, what is foreclosed is not the possibility of an event's coming to pass but the very signifier, or signifiers, that makes the expression of impossibility possible in the first place. Thus "foreclosure" refers not to the fact that a speaker makes a statement that declares something impossible—a process closer to disavowal—but to the fact that the speaker lacks the very linguistic means for making the statement at all.

This is where the difference between repression and foreclosure lies. On Lacan's analysis of Freud's classic studies on the unconscious—*The Interpretation of Dreams, The Psychopathology of Everyday Life, Jokes and Their Relation to the Unconscious*—the mechanisms of repression and the return of the repressed are linguistic in nature. His thesis that the unconscious is structured like a language implies the claim that for something to be repressed it has first of all to be registered in the symbolic. Thus repression implies the prior recognition of the repressed in the symbolic system or register. In psychosis, on the other hand, the necessary signifiers are lacking altogether, and so the recognition required for repression is impossible. However, what is foreclosed does not simply disappear altogether but may return, albeit in a different form, from outside the subject.

Lacan chooses "foreclosure" to translate Freud's "*Verwerfung*," a term that though it is difficult to chart through the *Standard Edition* because it is not indexed is there usually given the more literal translation, "rejection" or "repudiation." For a number of years Lacan also employed more literal French translations, "*rejet*," or, on occasion, "*retranchement*." It was not until the very last session of his seminar on psychosis in 1955–1956 that he finally opted for the term that has since become so familiar: "I shan't go back over the notion of *Verwerfung* I began with, and for which, having thought it through, I propose to you definitively to adopt this translation which I believe is the best—*foreclosure*."[2]

It is reasonable to regard this choice as implying an acknowledgment that through his work Lacan raised to the level of a concept what in Freud had remained less clear in its meaning and more ambiguous in its employment. Freud does not use only the term *"Verwerfung"* in connection with psychosis, since at times, especially late in his work, he prefers to speak in terms of the *disavowal* of reality in psychosis. On a number of occasions Freud appeared to be grasping for a way of characterizing different mechanisms underlying neurosis and psychosis, without ever coming to any satisfactory conclusion. It is fair to say that with the work of Lacan the mechanism of foreclosure and the structure of psychosis are understood in a new way, one that has given the psychoanalytic treatment of psychosis a more secure basis.

Indeed, on more than one occasion Lacan declared that psychoanalysts must not back away from psychosis, and the treatment of psychotics is a significant feature of analytic work in the Lacanian orientation.[3] It should be noted, though, that Lacan's remark is not to be taken as a recommendation to shoulder fearlessly the clinical burden imposed by the psychotic patient. It rather reflects Lacan's belief that the problems the psychotic raises are central to psychoanalysis and not a mere supplement to any supposed primary concern with neurosis.

Lacan observed that Freud's breakthrough in his examination of President Schreber's *Memoirs* was discovering that the discourse of the psychotic and other bizarre and apparently meaningless phenomena of psychosis could be deciphered and understood, just as dreams can. Lacan compares the scale of this breakthrough with that obtained in the interpretation of dreams; indeed, he is inclined to regard it as even more original than dream interpretation, arguing that while Freudian interpretation of dreams has nothing in common with previous interest in the meaning of dreams, the claim that dreams have meaning was itself not new.

However, Lacan also points out that the fact that the psychotic's discourse is just as interpretable as neurotic phenomena such as dreams leaves the two disorders at the same level and fails to account for the major, qualitative differences between them. Therefore, if psychoanalysis is to account for the distinction between the two, it cannot do so on the basis of meaning alone.

It is on this issue of what makes psychosis different from neurosis that Lacan focuses: How are we to explain the massive, qualitative differences between the two disorders? It is because Lacan is convinced that the delusional system and the hallucinations are so invasive for the subject, have such a devastating effect upon his relations with his world and with his fellow beings, that he regards as inadequate prior psychoanalytic attempts to explain psychosis, ultimately including Freud's own.

Freud explains psychosis in terms of a repressed homosexual relationship to the father. In the Schreber case, Freud argues that it was the emergence of an erotic homosexual relationship towards his treating doctor, Professor Flechsig, and the conflict this desire produced in him that led in the first instance to the delusion of persecution and ultimately to the fully developed delusional system centered on Schreber's special relationship to God.

Freud also compares and contrasts the mechanisms of neurosis and psychosis in the following terms: in both there is a withdrawal of investment, or object-cathexis, from objects in the world. In the case of neurosis this object-cathexis is retained but invested in fantasized objects in the neurotic's internal world. In the case of psychosis, the withdrawn cathexis is invested in the ego. This takes place at the expense of all object-cathexes, even in fantasy, and it is this turning of libido upon the ego that accounts for symptoms such as hypochondria and megalomania. The delusional system, the most striking feature of psychosis, arises in a second stage. Freud characterizes the construction of a delusional system as an attempt at recovery, one in which the subject reestablishes a new, often very intense relation with the people and things in the world by his or her delusions.

One can see that despite the differences in detail on Freud's account between the mechanisms in neurosis and psychosis, both still operate essentially by repression: withdrawal of libido onto fantasized objects in neurosis, withdrawal of object libido onto the ego in psychosis. It is basically for this reason that Lacan finds it inadequate:

> It is difficult to see how it could be purely and simply the suppression of a given [homosexual] tendency, the rejection or repression of some more or less transferential drive he would have felt toward Flechsig, that led President Schreber to construct his enormous delusion. There really must be something more proportionate to the result involved.[4]

THE FORECLOSURE OF CASTRATION IN THE WOLF MAN

However, it is apparent in his work prior to *Seminar III* that Lacan was already thinking about a mechanism in psychosis that is different from repression. In his "Response to Jean Hyppolite's Commentary on Freud's 'Verneinung,' " published in 1956 but dating back to a discussion in his seminar in early 1954, Lacan refers to Freud's use of the term *"Verwerfung"* to characterize the Wolf Man's attitude towards castration.[5] The discussion focuses on a series of comments in this case study where Freud first contrasts repression and foreclosure in categorical terms, stating, "A repression is something very different from a foreclosure."[6] Freud then observes:

> [The Wolf Man] rejected [*verwerft*] castration. . . . When I speak of his having rejected it, the first meaning of the phrase is that he would have nothing to do with it in the sense of having repressed it. This really involved no judgment upon the question of its existence, but it was the same as if it did not exist.[7]

Lacan considers that the Wolf Man's attitude towards castration shows that, at least in his childhood, castration is foreclosed; it lies outside the limits of what can be judged to exist because it is withdrawn from the possibilities of speech. While no judgment can be made about the existence of castration, it may nevertheless appear in the real in an erratic and unpredictable manner that Lacan describes as being "in relations of resistance without transference" or, again, "as punctuation without a text."[8] While clearly indicating that a difference of register is at stake here, these formulations remain metaphorical. They will subsequently be developed into a more complex position concerning the vicissitudes of the foreclosed.

The implication in Freud is, then, that foreclosure is a mechanism that simply treats the foreclosed as if it did not exist, and as such it is distinct from repression where the repressed manifests itself in symptomatic formations. Pursuing this line of thought farther, Lacan turns to Freud's paper "Negation," a topic of his discussion with Jean Hyppolite at Lacan's seminar at the Sainte Anne Hospital on February 10, 1954. In this paper Freud distinguishes between *Einbeziehung ins Ich* and *Ausstossung aus dem Ich*. Regarding these, respectively, as "introduction into the subject" and "expulsion from the subject," Lacan argues that the latter constitutes the domain of what subsists outside of symbolization—that is, as what is "foreclosed." This initial, primary expulsion constitutes a domain that is external to, in the sense of radically alien or foreign to, the subject and the subject's world. Lacan calls this domain the "real." He regards it as distinct from reality, since reality is to be discriminated within the field of representation (Freud's *Vorstellung*), which Lacan, in taking Freud's *Project* as his point of departure, considers to be constituted by the imaginary reproduction of initial perception. Reality is thus understood to be the domain within which not only the question of the possible existence of the object of this initial perception can be raised, but also and moreover within which this object can actually be refound (*wiedergefunden*) and located. The distinction between "introduction into" and "expulsion from" the subject amounts, as Lacan construes it, to the distinction between reality and the field of representation—what Kant called the "world of appearances"—and a second realm, the real, which one could compare to Kant's thing in itself, were it not for the fact that this real is capable of intruding into the subject's experience in a way that finds him or her devoid of any means of protection. So although the real is excluded from the symbolic field within which the question of the existence of objects in reality can be raised, it may nevertheless appear in reality. It will do so, for instance, in the form of a hallucination, thus Lacan's remark, "That which has not seen the light of day in the symbolic appears in the real."[9]

Though there is no explicit statement to this effect, it is clearly implied in Lacan's "Response to Jean Hyppolite's Commentary on Freud's 'Verneinung'" that it is castration that is foreclosed. This is an issue that is taken up again in *Seminar III*.

> What is at issue when I speak of [foreclosure]? At issue is the rejection of a primordial signifier into the outer shadows, a signifier that will henceforth be missing. . . . Here you have the fundamental mechanism that I posit as being at the basis of paranoia. It's a matter of a primordial process of exclusion of an original within, which is not a bodily within but that of an initial body of signifiers.[10]

However, Lacan shifts ground in this seminar and comes to the conclusion that foreclosure of castration is secondary to the original foreclosure of the primordial signifier, the Name-of-the-Father.

SCHREBER'S WAY

Lacan devoted his seminar in 1955–1956 to a reexamination of Schreber's *Memoirs* and Freud's discussion of the case. Already armed with the distinction between *Verdrängung* and *Verwerfung*, Lacan's intention was to explore the clinical, nosographical, and technical difficulties the psychoses raised.

In further examining the nature of foreclosure in *Seminar III*, the earlier views outlined previously undergo a number of modifications. While it seems to be a common assumption that foreclosure entails psychosis, there in fact appears to be nothing to rule out the possibility that foreclosure is a normal psychic process. Indeed, although he does not do this systematically, Lacan does not hesitate to speak of the foreclosure of femininity, or, later and in a different context, of the foreclosure of the subject of science. Foreclosure in psychosis is the foreclosure of the Name-of-the-Father, a key signifier that "anchors" or "quilts" signifier and signified. Thus it is only when what is foreclosed is specifically concerned with the question of the father, as in Schreber's case, that psychosis is produced. The term "Name-of-the-Father" indicates that what is at issue is not a person but a signifier, one that is replete with cultural and religious significance.[11] It is a key signifier for the subject's symbolic universe, regulating this order and giving it its structure. Its function in the Oedipus complex is to be the vehicle of the law that regulates desire—both the subject's desire and the omnipotent desire of the maternal figure. It also should be noted that since foreclosure of the Name-of-the-Father is one possible outcome of the Oedipus complex, neurosis and perversion being the others, these structures are laid down at the time of negotiating the Oedipus complex.

In contrast with Freud and also, in part, with his own earlier views, Lacan sees both the foreclosure of castration and the homosexual identification as effects and not causes of psychosis. In fact, he claims that Schreber's symptoms are not really homosexual at all and that it would be more accurate to call them "transsexual." These transsexual and other phenomena, for which Lacan will later coin the phrase "push towards woman," *pousse à la femme*, are the result of the initial foreclosure of the Name-of-the-Father and the corresponding lack in the imaginary of phallic meaning. The paternal metaphor is an operation in which the Name-of-the-Father is substituted for the mother's desire, thereby producing a new species of meaning, phallic meaning, which heralds the introduction of the subject to the phallic economy of the neurotic and, therefore, to castration. This phallic meaning, as both the product of the paternal metaphor and the key to all questions of sexual identity, is absent in psychosis. The operation of the paternal metaphor is expressed in the following formula[12]:

$$\frac{\text{Name-of-the-Father}}{\text{Mother's Desire}} \cdot \frac{\text{Mother's Desire}}{\text{Signified to the Subject}} \rightarrow \text{Name-of-the-Father} \left(\frac{A}{\text{Phallus}} \right)$$

In psychosis, then, the foreclosure of the Name-of-the-Father is accompanied by the corresponding absence, foreclosure, of the phallic meaning that is necessary for libidinal relations. Without this phallic meaning the subject is left prey to—"left in the lurch," as President Schreber puts it—the mother's unregulated desire, confronted by an obscure enigma at the level of the Other's jouissance that the subject lacks the means to comprehend. It is not that the absence of this signifier, the Name-of-the-Father, prevents the symbolic from functioning altogether. Schreber is, after all, within the symbolic; indeed, he is a very prolix author, as his *Memoirs* so clearly demonstrates. Yet his entire literary output revolves around two connected, fundamental issues that he is unable to resolve: The question of the father and the question of his own sexual identity, two dimensions of his being that concern the symbolic and his embodiment.

The difference between Schreber and the neurotic here is striking: The neurotic finds a response, in the form of a neurotic compromise, a more or less satisfactory solution to the questions of the law and of sexual identity. Schreber, on the other hand, finds himself completely incapable of resolving them because the materials he needs to do so, the requisite signifiers, are missing.

Yet what is foreclosed from the symbolic is not purely and simply abolished. It returns, but, unlike the return of the repressed, it returns from outside the subject, as emanating from the real. As Lacan henceforth puts it: What has been foreclosed from the symbolic reappears in the real. It is important to recognize not only that what in the real returns is actual bits of language, signifiers, but also that the effects of this return are located at both the symbolic and imaginary levels.

With the emphasis upon the function of speech in *Seminar III*, where the Other is understood as the Other of speech and of subjective recognition, Lacan pays very close attention to the imaginary means by which the subject makes good the lack in the symbolic. For instance, Lacan considers that in psychosis there is a form of regression involved; there is regression, which is topographical rather than chronological regression, from the symbolic register to the imaginary. Thus when he declares that what has been foreclosed from the symbolic reappears in the real, it is marked by the properties of the imaginary.

Whereas the symbolic is linguistic in nature, the imaginary groups together a series of phenomena the cornerstone of which is the mirror stage. The mirror stage, which refers to the infant's early experience of fascination with its own image in a mirror, relates how the child responds with jubilation and pleasure to seeing a reflection of its own image. Lacan claims that the child is fascinated with its image because it is here that the child experiences itself as a whole, as a unity, for the first time. Furthermore, the experience of a self-unity lays the basis for the ego, which is formed through the subject's identification with this image. Of course, the reference to the mirror is not essential but is intended to capture the fact that the ego and the other both come into existence together, and, moreover, that the ego and other (or, more strictly speaking, the image of the other, *i(a)* in Lacan's writing) are dependent upon one another and indeed are not clearly differentiated. The reference to the mirror captures this ambiguity by emphasizing that the ego is built upon an image of one's own body as it would be perceived from another's point of view.

The ego and its other are locked together in the sense that they come into existence together and depend upon one another for their sense of identity. For Lacan this dual relationship epitomizes the imaginary relationship, characterized as it is by imaginary identification and alienation and marked by an ambivalent relationship of aggressive rivalry with and erotic attachment to the other. In psychosis this means that relations with the other are marked by the erotic attachment and aggressive rivalry characteristic of the imaginary. Thus Professor Flechsig becomes an erotic object for Schreber but also the agent of Schreber's persecution.

In "On a Question Prior to any Possible Treatment of Psychosis" there is a shift away from the function of speech to the laws of language, which is accompanied by a simultaneous shift away from "intersubjectivity" to the relationship with the Other as the Other of language. As a consequence there is a somewhat more detailed analysis of language phenomena and language disorders in psychosis. This appears very clearly in Lacan's analysis of the psychiatric term "elementary phenomena," introduced by French psychiatrist de Clérambault, described by Lacan as his "only master" in psychiatry.

Throughout his work Lacan makes repeated references to these elementary phenomena, a term that embraces thought-echoes, verbal enunciations of actions, and various forms of hallucination. In *Seminar III* Lacan uses it as a general term for the phenomena produced in psychosis by the appearance of signifiers in the real. These are classically referred to as "primary phenomena," considered instrumental in the onset of the psychosis, while they themselves lack any apparent external cause. Lacan's use of the term dates back to his 1932 thesis in medicine, where he observes:

> By this name, in effect, according to a schema frequently accepted in psychopathology, . . . authors designate symptoms in which the determining factors of psychosis are said to be primitively expressed and on the basis of which the delusion is said to be constructed according to secondary affective reactions and deductions that in themselves are rational.[13]

In *Seminar III* his task is to explain how these elementary phenomena result from the emergence of signifiers in the real. Lacan claims that if they are to be called elementary this has to be understood in the sense that they contain all of the elements of the fully developed psychosis.[14] This approach is made possible by the recognition that all psychotic phenomena can in fact be analyzed as phenomena of speech, rather than as a reaction by the subject, in the imaginary, to a lack in the symbolic.

In "Question," elementary phenomena (though no longer called this) are analyzed as reflecting the structure of the signifier, resulting in an analysis of hallucinations that divides them into code phenomena and message phenomena.[15]

The code phenomena include the following:

- Schreber's *Grundsprache,* or basic language, and its neologisms and "autonyms." "Autonymous" is Jakobson's term for contexts in which expressions are mentioned rather than used—the first word in this sentence is an example. Jakobson describes this as a case of a message referring to a code. It is a common occurrence in ordinary language, but in Schreber's case there is a highly developed code-message interaction, moreover, one that also is reflected in the relationships between the "rays" or "nerves" that speak. These rays, Lacan says, are nothing but a reification of the very structure and phenomenon of language itself.[16]

- The frequently encountered phenomenon in psychosis of the enigma, along with psychotic certainty, which according to Lacan develops out of it.[17] Lacan claims that there is a temporal sequence between these phenomena. First, there is an initial experience of an enigma, arising from an absence or lack of meaning that occurs in the place where meaning should be. The enigma arises because the expectation of meaning that the signifier generates is radically disappointed. An enigma is not just the absence of meaning but its absence there where meaning should be present. Thus in a second stage what was already implicit in the first comes to the fore, namely, the conviction, which by its very nature the signifier generates, that there is a meaning, or as Schreber's rays put it, that "all nonsense cancels itself out."[18]

One should note that in both sorts of case there is effectively a failure of language ("the code") to produce meaning ("the message").

In the first there is a communication of the structure of language, but no meaning is conveyed; in the second the absence of meaning gives rise to the conviction of the psychotic.

As examples of message phenomena Lacan gives the interrupted messages that Schreber receives from God, to which Schreber is called upon to give a reply that completes the message—for instance, "Now I will . . . myself . . . ," to which Schreber replies, ". . . face the fact that I am an idiot." In calling these "message phenomena," on the grounds that the sentence is interrupted at a point at which the indexical elements of the sentence have been uttered, Lacan appears to have in mind Jakobson's observation that the "general meaning of a shifter cannot be defined without a reference to the message."[19]

Both types of phenomena are examples of the return of the signifier in the real. Both indicate the appearance, in the real, of the signifier cut off from its connections with the signifying chain, that is, S_1 appears in the real without S_2 and, as a consequence, the "quilting" that would normally produce meaning cannot occur. This does not, however, result in the complete extinguishment of meaning but rather in the proliferation of a meaningfulness that manifests itself in the real in the form of verbal hallucinations, as well as in the enigma and the conviction the psychotic experiences.

Of special note as examples of the return of the signifier in the real are those verbal hallucinations, often persecutory, of the psychotic, such as the case of the hallucinated insult "Sow!" discussed in both *Seminar III* and "On a Question Prior to Any Possible Treatment of Psychosis," where both imaginary and symbolic disturbances can be detected. On Lacan's analysis the example displays disturbances of the code, but it also reveals the appearance in psychotic form of the same content that one finds expressed in different ways in neurotic formations of the unconscious—the utterance expresses the imaginary meaning of fragmentation of the body. What is perhaps different is that this emerges in the place from which phallic meaning has been foreclosed.[20]

Given that the foreclosure of the signifier the Name-of-the-Father entails the corresponding absence of phallic meaning, it is to be expected that this will have particular consequences for the psychotic subject's sexual identity. Lacan speaks of a push towards woman to describe the gradual transformation of sexuality in Schreber's delusion as well as in other cases of psychosis. Prior to his psychosis Schreber lived as a heterosexual man with no apparent trace of feminization. The first intimation of this push towards woman is given in Schreber's conscious fantasy just prior to the onset of his psychosis, "How beautiful it would be to be a woman undergoing sexual intercourse." Subsequently Schreber's "manly honor" struggles against the increasingly desperate attempts by God to "unman" him and transform him into a woman. But he finally becomes reconciled to this transformation, recognizing as he does that his emasculation is necessary if one day he is to be fertilized by God and repopulate the world with new beings. In the meantime he will adorn his naked body with trinkets and cheap jewellery to enhance and promote this unavoidable feminization.

Lacan sees in this development two separate aspects to the restoration of the imaginary structure. Both were detected by Freud and both are, for Lacan, linked either directly or indirectly to the absence of phallic meaning in the imaginary. The first aspect has already been mentioned. It is Schreber's "transsexualism." The second aspect links "the subject's feminization to the coordinate of divine copulation."[21] This psychotic drive to be transformed into a woman is an attempt to embody the woman in the figure of the wife of God. Lacan notes that transsexualism is common in psychosis where it is normally linked to the demand for endorsement and consent from the father.

What triggers a psychosis? Lacan argues that even though the onset of psychosis is largely unforeseeable, the psychotic structure will have been there all along, like an invisible flaw in the glass, prior to the appearance of the clinical psychosis, when it suddenly and dramatically manifests itself. And we can see this in Schreber, who had up until the age of fifty-one led a relatively normal life, enjoying a successful career and carrying out the demanding duties of a senior position in the judiciary.

Lacan holds that it is a certain type of encounter, in which the Name-of-the-Father is "summoned to that place [the Other] in symbolic opposition to the subject," that is the trigger, the precipitating cause, of a psychosis.[22] What does this "symbolic opposition to the subject" mean? The issue is explored in the seminar on psychosis in a lengthy discussion that continues over a number of sessions of the function of what Lacan calls "l'appel," "the call," "the calling," "the appeal," or even "the interpellation." The discussion is not related specifically to psychosis but rather to a quite general function of language.

Lacan takes a number of examples from everyday French, drawing on the difference between "Tu es celui qui me suivras" and "Tu es celui qui me suivra," where the subordinate clause is in the second and third person, respectively. The basic idea can be hinted at by the English distinction between "shall" and "will." Consider these two statements:

You are the one who will follow me.

You are the one who shall follow me.

It is possible here to take the first as a description of or prediction about something that will come to pass: "I predict that you will follow me." The second, on the other hand, can serve as an appeal, where the interlocutor, the one who is being addressed, is called upon to make a decision, to pursue a course of action that he or she must either embrace or repudiate. This latter case is, for instance, exemplified by Jesus of Nazareth's invocation, his appeal, to his disciples-to-be. "I say to you, 'You are the ones who shall follow me.' Now, tell me, what is your reply, what do you say to this? Give me your answer, for now is the time to choose." In this example we could say that Jesus is "in symbolic opposition to" his disciples, or, we could equally well say he is asking them for "symbolic recognition," since his speech calls upon them to respond in a way that engages them in, commits them to, a decision, one loaded with practical consequences, as to whether they are to recognize him as the Messiah.

For Schreber, then, there is a moment when he is called, interpellated, by—or perhaps better "in"—the Name-of-the-Father. This is when the lack of the signifier declares itself, and it is sufficient to trigger the psychosis.

How is this symbolic opposition, this call for symbolic recognition, brought about in psychosis? Lacan gives this response: by an encounter with "a real father, not at all necessarily by the subject's own father, but by One-father [*Un-père*]."[23] This is a situation that arises under two conditions: when the subject is in a particularly intense relationship involving a strong narcissistic component; and when, in this situation, the question of the father arises from a third position, one that is external to the erotic relation. For instance, and the examples are Lacan's, it presents itself "to a woman who has just given birth, in her husband's face, to a penitent confessing her sins in the person of her confessor, or to a girl in love in her encounter with 'the young man's father.' "[24] And, as is well known, it also can occur in analysis, where the development of the transference can sometimes precipitate a psychosis. Lacan puts it thus:

> It sometimes happens that we take prepsychotics into analysis, and we know what that produces—it produces psychotics. The question of the contraindications of analysis would not arise if we didn't all recall some particular case in our practice,

or in the practice of our colleagues, where a full-blown psychosis . . . is triggered during the first analytic sessions in which things heat up a bit.[25]

Indeed, at issue in the treatment of a subject in analysis is the unpredictability of psychosis, the uncertainty of knowing in whom a psychosis may be triggered and the lack of diagnostic criteria for psychosis prior to its onset. And yet if Lacan's views on the structure of psychosis are right, then it makes sense to speak of "prepsychosis" in the case of subjects with a psychotic structure who are not clinically psychotic.

Once the psychosis is triggered, everything will have changed for good, but what about before the onset? It is in pursuing this question that the work of Maurits Katan on prepsychosis and that of Helene Deutsch on the "as if" phenomenon is discussed.[26] While Lacan finds Katan's characterization of the prepsychotic period unconvincing, facetiously remarking that nothing resembles a prepsychosis more than a neurosis does, he finds more of interest in Deutsch's work, and especially in what she refers to as the "as if" phenomenon, where, for example, an adolescent boy identifies with another youth in what looks like a homosexual attachment but turns out to be a precursor of psychosis. Here there is something that plays the role of a *suppléance,* a suppletion, that is, a substitute or a stand-in for what is missing at the level of the symbolic. Lacan uses the analogy of a three-legged stool:

> Not every stool has four legs. There are some that stand upright on three. Here, though, there is no question of their lacking any, otherwise things go very badly indeed. . . . It is possible that at the outset the stool doesn't have enough legs, but that up to a certain point it will nevertheless stand up, when the subject, at a certain crossroads of his biographical history, is confronted by this lack that has always existed.[27]

Suppletion can take various forms. The case of Deutsch's is a good example of imaginary suppletion, where the support derived from an identification with the other is sufficient to compensate for the absence of the signifier. The psychosis is thus triggered at the moment at which the imaginary suppletion with which the subject has until then been able to make do proves inadequate. It is not uncommon for this to occur at the beginnings of adult life when the subject loses the protective support of the family network—indeed, Lacan even goes so far as to evoke the imaginary identification with the mother's desire as a means of maintaining the stability of the "imaginary tripod."

Lacan also considers that the delusion itself can provide the psychotic with a degree of stability, and this can be regarded as a second form of suppletion.[28] Considered by Freud as an attempt at cure, the stability of the delusional metaphor is seen by some in Lacan's school as the aim of the treatment of psychotics—an important consideration in light of the claim that psychosis is a discrete subjective structure that no treatment will cure.

A third form of suppletion is, despite the air of paradox, best called symbolic suppletion. It is an intriguing fact that some psychotics have been capable of making important scientific or artistic contributions. Cantor, the mathematician, is a famous example, but there are numerous such cases. We know about them because of the documented psychotic episodes these people underwent. But it is also interesting to speculate that there may be cases where the psychosis never declares itself and the clinical phenomena never eventuate. Perhaps in these cases the (pre)psychotic subject may find a form of substitute for the foreclosed signifier that enables the subject to maintain the fewest symbolic links necessary for normal, even for highly original and creative, functioning. In his 1975–1976 seminar, Lacan argues that James Joyce was such a case.[29] And, indeed, there are a number of indications that one can point to in support of the claim that Joyce was probably a psychotic who was able to use his writing as an effective substitute that prevented the onset of psychosis. This is an interesting thought, and I return to it later. There is something necessarily speculative about such cases, and Joyce himself is obviously such a special case that he can hardly serve as a model for others. Still, there are important issues here to do with the diagnosis of psychosis—could, for example, the so-called borderlines be situated here? Are they to be regarded as undeclared psychoses? Clearly the Lacanian model implies a search for indications of psychosis independent of and prior to the onset of a full-blown clinical psychosis.

What causes foreclosure of the Name-of-the-Father? Assuming the psychotic structure is laid down at the moment of the Oedipus complex, under what conditions is this foreclosure produced? Lacan does not have much to say about this issue, though he does make a criticism of certain views and offers some positive observations of his own. The criticism is that it is not enough to focus on the child-mother or child-father relationship alone; one must look at the triadic, Oedipal structure. Thus in looking at child, mother, and father, it is not enough to think in terms of "frustrating" or "smothering" mothers, any more than in terms of "dominating" or "easygoing" fathers, since these approaches neglect the triangular structure of the Oedipus complex. One needs to consider the place that the mother, as the first object of the child's desire, gives to the authority of the father or, as Lacan puts it, one needs to consider "the place she reserves for the Name-of-the-Father in the promotion of the law."[30] Lacan adds (and this is the second point) that one also needs to consider the father's relation to the law in itself. The issue here is whether or not the father is himself an adequate vehicle of the law. There are circumstances, he says, that make it easier for the father to be found undeserving, inadequate, or fraudulent with respect to the law and therefore found to be an ineffective vehicle for the Name-of-the-Father. This leads him to remark that psychosis occurs with "particular frequency" when the father "functions as a legislator," whether as one who actually makes the laws or as one who poses as the incarnation of high ideals.[31]

HEAVENLY JOYCE

The discussion of Joyce some twenty years after the seminar on Schreber was not as it happens merely an occasion to explore further the issue of suppletion in relation to foreclosure. It resulted in nothing less than a reformulation of the way in which the differences between neurosis and psychosis should be approached and also contributed to an understanding of the difference between paranoia and schizophrenia.

From the discussion so far it can be seen that initially neurosis is taken as the model for the formation of symptoms and the construction of the subject. When, in 1959, Lacan writes that "the condition of the subject . . . depends on what unfolds in the Other," it is clear that the structure of psychosis is conceptualized as a variant of the structure of neurosis.[32] If one examines the R schema and Lacan's comments on it, it is apparent that the Name-of-the-Father underpins the phallic signification, ϕ, and all object relations as a consequence.

The psychotic structure is then a transformation produced by the foreclosure of the Name-of-the-Father and the corresponding *lack* of phallic meaning of the neurotic structure. This thesis is apparent in the transformation of the R schema into the I schema.

Lacan's approach in his seminar on James Joyce offers a different perspective, one from which what Colette Soler, following Jacques-Alain Miller, has called a "general theory of the symptom" can be extracted.[33] This general theory is applicable to both neurosis and psychosis, whereas the theory of neurotic metaphor becomes a special case, one created by the addition of the function of the Name-of-the-

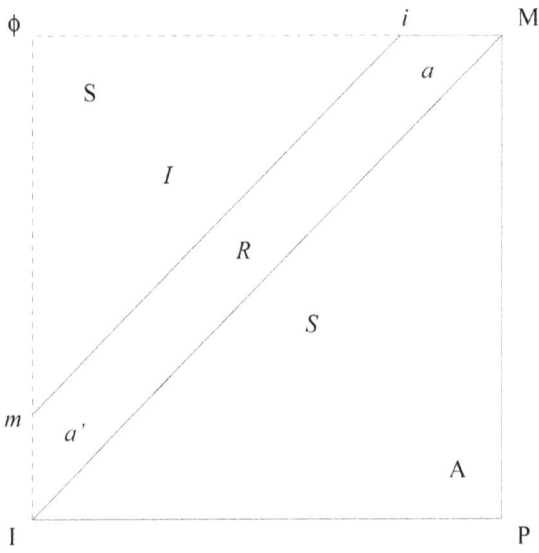

Figure 1.1 R schema

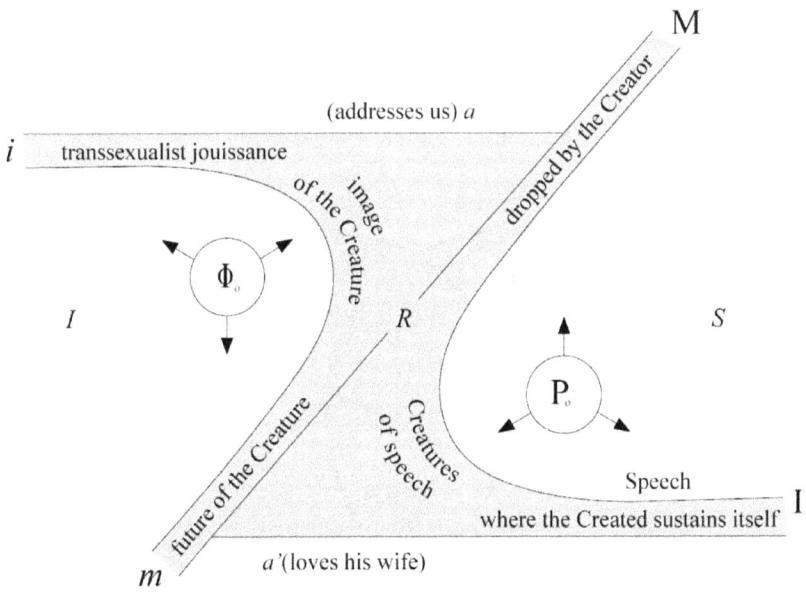

Figure 1.2 I Schema

Father. Thus rather than taking neurosis as the primary structure and considering psychosis to be produced by the foreclosure of the Name-of-the-Father, neurosis is henceforth considered as a special case created by the introduction of a specific signifier. This step effectively generalizes the concept of foreclosure. The delusional metaphor of psychosis is *one* response to this foreclosure; the symptom-metaphor of neurosis is another.

Developing these views by way of topology Lacan revises his earlier thesis that the symbolic, the imaginary, and the real are linked like the rings of a Borromean knot—in such a way, that is, that severing any one link will untie the other two. (See Figure 1.3.)

However, in this seminar, he declares that it is incorrect to think that the three-ring Borromean knot is the normal way in which the three categories are linked. It is therefore not the case that the separation of the three rings is the result of some defect, because the three are already separate. Where they are joined, they are connected by a fourth link, the *sinthome,* which Lacan writes as Σ. (See Figure 1.4.)

The Name-of-the-Father is henceforth but a certain form of the *sinthome:* "The Oedipus complex is, as such, a symptom. It is insofar as the Name-of-the-Father is also the Father of the Name that every-

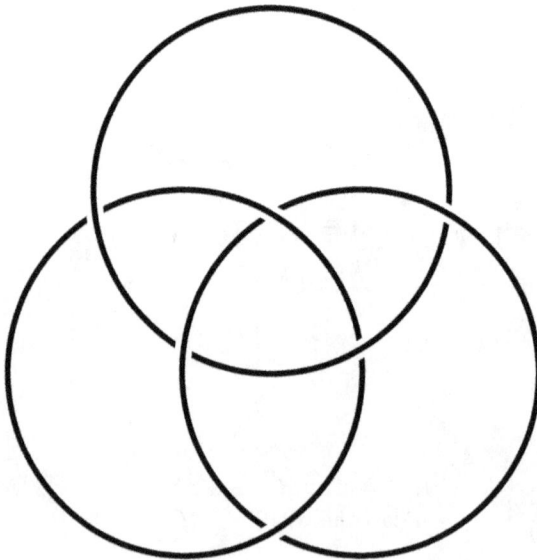

Figure 1.3 Borromean knot

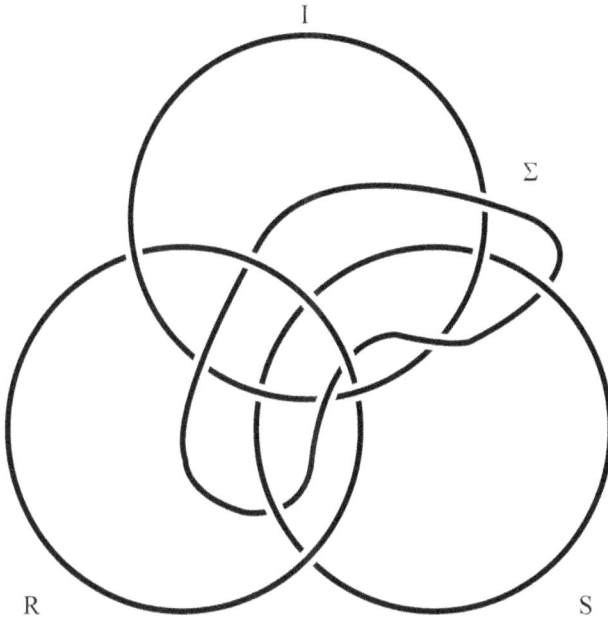

Figure 1.4 Four-ring Borromean knot

thing hangs together, which does not make the symptom any the less necessary." In *Ulysses* this father has to be "sustained by Joyce in order for the father to subsist."[34]

    Lacan's thesis, then, is that although Joyce was psychotic, he succeeded in avoiding the onset of psychosis through his writing, which thus plays the role for Joyce of his sinthome. Indeed, Lacan says, through his writing Joyce went as far as one can in analysis.[35] Joyce's achievement in preventing his own psychosis means that in him the psychotic phenomena appear in a different form both from neurosis and from a declared psychosis. Lacan locates the elementary phenomena and the experience of enigma, for instance, in Joyce's "epiphanies," fragments of actual conversations overheard, extracted from their context, and carefully recorded on separate sheets.[36] All of this was completed even before Joyce's first novel, and many of the fragments were subsequently reinserted unannounced into later texts. Torn from their context, the epiphanies remain nonsensical or enigmatic fragments and are striking for their qualities of incongruity and insignificance:

Joyce—I knew you meant him. But you're wrong about his age.

Maggie Sheehy—(*leans forward to speak seriously*). Why, how old is he?

Joyce—Seventy-two.

Maggie Sheehy—Is he?[37]

What is so striking is not so much that the epiphanies do not make much sense, which is what one might expect of such fragments taken out of their context, but rather that Joyce, or Stephen, should describe these meaningless and enigmatic fragments, outside of discourse and cut off from communication, as a "sudden spiritual manifestation." Lacan claims that this process, in which the absence of meaning of the epiphany is transformed into its opposite, the certainty of an ineffable revelation, is comparable to the enigmatic experience and its conversion into psychotic conviction in Schreber. Joyce of course differs from Schreber, and differs in that he cultivates the phenomenon and transforms it into a creative work. In *Finnegan's Wake*, Joyce the craftsmen transforms linguistic meaning into "non-sense" and vice versa, so that what corresponds to the enigmatic experience of a Schreber is thereby raised to the level of an artistic process.

It is therefore to be expected that the question of jouissance in psychosis should be treated somewhat differently in the seminar on Joyce. In the case of Schreber the foreclosure of phallic meaning leads to homosexual and transsexual impulses. For Freud, as we have seen, this is to be regarded as the consequence of a repressed passive homosexuality, whereas Lacan does not think that this will adequately account for the psychosis—it is more accurate to say that Schreber's virility itself is attacked by the return in the real of the castration that is foreclosed from the symbolic. In Schreber the barrier to jouissance is surmounted, and jouissance is no longer located outside of the body. Schreber's body is thus no longer the desert it is for the neurotic and is therefore besieged by an ineffable, inexplicable jouissance, which is ascribed to the divine Other who seeks his satisfaction in Schreber.[38]

Joyce's writing transforms the "enjoy-meant" that literature normally conveys into jouissance of the letter, into an enjoyment that lies outside of meaning. But what is even more astonishing is that in a secondary way, through imposing or introducing this strange literature that is outside of discourse, he manages to restore the social link that his writing abolishes and to promote himself to the place of the exception. Furthermore, he has the responsibility, which is usually assumed by the work of the delusion, for producing sense out of the opaque work, passed down to his commentators—thereby assuring the survival of his name.

One final important consideration is the particular prominence given in *Seminar XXIII* to the function of the letter in psychotic experience. In earlier work, in which Lacan spoke of the symptom as a formation of the unconscious on a par with dreams, jokes, and parapraxes, the symptom is taken to be a knot of signifiers excluded from discourse and therefore unable to be included in any circuit of communication. However, alongside this emphasis placed upon the signifier as such there are a number of important observations on the function of the letter. In fact, as early as 1957 Lacan had stated that the symptom is "already inscribed in a writing process."[39] The materiality of the letter is discussed in "The Agency of the Letter," while an important thesis of "The Seminar on *The Purloined Letter*," in which Lacan makes his first reference to Joyce's "a letter, a litter," is that the letter is not just a signifier but also an object. As such, it may become a remainder, a remnant, a vestige left in the wake of the message it conveys. The letter may occupy a status not unlike a fetish object, as was the case with André Gide, whose letters were burned by his wife when confronted with evidence she could no longer ignore of his sexual exploits with young boys. Gide's collapse belies the fact that the letters were the vehicle of a jouissance supplementary to the message they conveyed.[40] Similarly, the assumption in the seminar on Joyce is that the symptom is no longer to be regarded simply as a message excluded from the circuit of communication but also as a site of jouissance—while this does not make the theory of the signifier redundant, it stresses the localized effects of the materiality of the letter.

The thought that something fundamental may be excluded from the symbolic, and the role that this may play in understanding psychosis, was immediately grasped by Lacan, even prior to the discussion of Schreber in *Seminar III*, as a corollary of the thesis that the unconscious is structured like a language. Not only did this thought offer Lacan, with his psychiatric grounding, the means to develop a better theory of psychosis than psychoanalysis had previously managed to do, but the detailed work on the Schreber case also can be seen as a verification of the theoretical position Lacan had until then been developing in the context of neurosis alone. The Schreber case highlighted the nature of what it was that was foreclosed—the Name-of-the-Father. But it also brought the category of the real into much sharper focus than was apparent in earlier seminars, where the demarcation between the imaginary and the symbolic was more pressing—no doubt as the result of a focus on neurotic structures. In this context the return to a discussion of psychosis and foreclosure in the seminar on Joyce is quite important, with the real taking on a new and more ramified role in the overall explanation of psychosis. What is of particular interest in the discussion of Joyce is that it presents a new theory according to which foreclosure is the universal condition of the symptom.

Chapter 2

The Father's Function

It is widely assumed that the Oedipus complex recounts what happens to each human child at around the age of eighteen months or so. On this view the child and the child's actual mother and father are the three persons involved in a triangular relationship whose dynamics are set out in various places in Freud's writings. If one shares this view that the Oedipus complex describes essentially what happens to children born into nuclear families, then it follows fairly naturally that works such as *Totem and Taboo* or *Moses and Monotheism*, in dealing with the primal horde, the killing of the primal father, and all subsequent development of social and cultural institutions, are not just unnecessary but somehow illegitimate.[1] After all, if the question of, say, what a father is is exhausted by the dynamics of the family constellation, then why enter into dubious and unscientific speculation about the prehistory of mankind? It would be entirely justified to criticize Freud, as many have done, for the way he extrapolates from his explorations on the couch of the infantile fantasy world of *fin-de-siècle* Viennese neurotics to the social organization of *homo sapiens* at the very dawn of civilization.

But this would be a disservice to Freud. *Totem and Taboo* and *Moses and Monotheism* must be regarded not as applied psychoanalysis but rather as a prolongation of the question of what a father is, a question far from exhausted by the events of the Oedipus complex as they relate to object love, rivalry, and the threat—or acknowledgment—of castration.

The second fairly natural consequence of taking the father of the Oedipus complex as the father of the nuclear family is that there seems little to add to what has already been said about the father in psychoanalytic theory. It was natural, then, to turn from Oedipal structures and look at various issues that were relatively unexplored. Thus it is possible to turn, for instance, to pre-Oedipal structures and to the question of the mother, as the Kleinians did. Or, again, ego psychology looked increasingly outside of the Oedipus complex for explanations of such phenomena as aggression. So if Lacan returns to the question of the father in psychoanalysis as part of his "return to Freud," then it is because in his opinion the final word has *not* been said on this issue and also because the import of Freud's views themselves was either lost, or maybe never fully realized, in the post-Freudian era of the 1950s and 1960s. Lacan follows his own trajectory over this period. Initially making the Oedipus complex and the father's function—the "paternal function," as he calls it—within it central to his psychoanalytic doctrine, by the end of the 1960s he had become a sometimes scornful critic of this aspect of Freud's legacy.

It also is frequently believed that the father's function within the Oedipus complex is to regulate desire—a view that while not incorrect is nevertheless incomplete, for it is equally true to say that the father functions to deregulate desire: Lacan's *père-version*.

The most significant function the father has relates to what Freud calls the superego and the ego ideal. Both can lay claim to being heirs to the Oedipus complex by a process to which identification is central. There is an issue here, though, which is the unclarity over the way the process of identification is understood; Freud at one point distinguishes three types of identification, and the distinction is not always carefully drawn.

Lacan draws a sharper distinction between symbolic and imaginary identification, situating the latter in the context of the mirror stage, and thus the formation of the ego. The former is central to the father's function.

SYMBOLIC IDENTIFICATION

Thus this term *symbolic* identification distinguishes the function of identification to which psychoanalytic theory gives a central place in various places from the "imaginary identification" theorized by Lacan in his writings on the mirror phase.

Let us revisit the three different forms of identification that Freud describes in the chapter on "Identification" in *Group Psychology and the Analysis of the Ego*.[2]

The first is the primordial identification that Freud describes as the earliest form of emotional tie with an object; it is a tie that retroactively emerges in the dialectic of the Oedipus complex as a fundamentally ambivalent mix of hostility and tenderness.

It is unclear whether we should regard this primordial identification as an identification with the father or with the mother. Certainly there is no consistency in Freud on this point, as he sometimes speaks of an identification with the father as bearer of the phallus, sometimes of an identification with both the father and the mother. On the one hand, it could be argued that, because of his subsequent realization in his 1925 paper "Some Psychical Consequences of the Anatomical Distinction between the Sexes" that the Oedipal situation was neither symmetrical nor reciprocal as to the dynamics of male and female sexuation, the situation is best viewed as one in which identification is an identification with the father, and the mother is taken as the child's love object. On the other, in "Group Psychology," Freud describes identification as "the earliest expression of an emotional tie with another person," and then adds in a later (1931) discussion of female sexuality that an intense identification on the part of a woman with her father is preceded by a "phase of exclusive attachment to her mother." And, as we shall see later, there are further obscurities in Freud's account.

Lacan points out Melanie Klein's discovery, that no matter how young the subjects of her investigations, the father is invariably present in the form of fantasies containing the phallus as imaginary object. Even in Klein's experience, however "far back" one goes, the presence of the father is never circumvented: "The father's penis" is an "object of the boy's oral-sadistic tendencies inside the mother."[3]

The second form of identification occurs at the decline or dissolution of the Oedipus complex and results in the formation of both the ego ideal and the superego—I return to the importance that Lacan attributes to the distinction between these two formations. This second form is crucial in the construction of masculine and feminine sexuality, the differences between them, and the structures of the three most general categories of differential clinical diagnosis: neurosis, psychosis, and perversion. Moreover, this second form is also crucial in the differential clinical diagnosis of the neuroses themselves in the two general forms of hysteria and obsessional neurosis.

Lastly, the third form of identification plays an important role in diagnosis, characterizing as it does the specific mechanism of hysterical identification. This is the identification by which a person identifies with another in relation to a third, generally libidinal, object. This third form of identification is well illustrated by hysterical phenomena, in which it is particularly prominent, by identification with another person over that person's sexual object. This is quite clear in the case of Dora, Freud's fullest account of a case of hysteria, even though, at the time of his analysis of Dora, Freud did not really understand hysterical identification very well, and it was not until this third type of identification detailed in *Group Psychology* that Freud corrects this.

Lacan's "Intervention on the Transference" details why it is that Dora can take an interest in relations between man and woman, on condition that she can escape from them herself as object, and thus to the detriment of her desire *for* the sexual partner.[4] Freud slides from an imaginary identification to a symbolic one when he fails to distinguish object choice (Frau K) from the object of the hysteric's identification (Herr K). The symbolic identification extends beyond the subject's purely libidinal cathexes, the true source of relations of love and hate, to establish the ego ideal. In the case of Dora, this means designating a place from which she can see herself as lovable and identify herself with the signifiers that have given rise to the ego ideal.

This identification of Dora's with Herr K is an identification with a masculine object, and for this reason it can easily but mistakenly be thought that she is in love with him, an error that Freud failed to avoid. However, in the dynamics of Dora, Herr K occupies this position for her only so long as she herself is not his object. It is in fact possible to see here Lacan's formula that desire is the desire of the Other, since what Dora desires is not Herr K but his desire—provided she can avoid being its object.

This identification is a "virile" identification with Herr K as her ego ideal, and it leads to a formation of her ego that provides her with the means by which she can "act like a man" in relation to her love object, Frau K. This identification with the ideal is her attempt to symbolize an exit from the Oedipus complex. As well, she is competing with men in an imaginary rivalry that expresses her outrage at being treated as a love object and phallic signifier.

That is the essence of her relationship with Herr K. If we turn now to Frau K, just as Dora maintains her own desire unsatisfied, so she solicits a man to desire the woman who can unlock the mystery of her own femininity, Frau K.[5] And in fact it is Frau K who is her true love object, whom she loves "by proxy" through her own father. She arranges things so as to procure Frau K for her father, thereby, through her intrigues, acting as a support for *his* desire.

The relatively stable equilibrium that had been established is ruptured by the incident with Herr K that ended in her slapping his face. From his saying to her that his wife meant nothing to him, Dora concluded that he had sacrificed his wife to Dora's father in return for Dora herself, and it is this that leads Dora to see herself as an object of "odious exchange," of barter.[6]

Freud's error in the case of Dora, as he himself later came to realize, was what Lacan calls his "prejudice that girls are made for boys." That is, Freud assumes that it is natural for the girl to be amorously inclined towards her father and therefore towards the man that becomes his substitute. It was not until 1925 that Freud came to the full realization that the Oedipal phase for the girl has to be understood in terms of the phallic signifier that her mother has deprived her of and that she must seek elsewhere.[7]

It was in this 1925 paper that Freud first clearly spelled out the vicissitudes of the turn towards the father and away from the mother as primordial object. This turn towards the father and the subsequent identifications play a *causal* role in later neurotic formations. The identification for the woman with what, after all, was originally for her as much as for the man the Other sex is a critical point for the determination of hysteria. On the male side, the identification with the vehicle of the Name-of-the-Father and the source of the imaginary effects of the castration complex will leave him, on the other hand, particularly susceptible to obsessional neurosis.[8]

It is noticeable that in Freudian theory all *three* forms of identification have to do with the father. And in relation to identification and other phenomena Lacan saw that the question of the father in Freud was far from settled. Indeed, he came to recenter the psychoanalytic debate upon what was originally Freud's question: What is a father? But what grounds are there for calling this question an unresolved one in Freud? I shall discuss this and then turn to how Lacan throws light on what is left unthought in Freud.

THE FATHER: AN UNRESOLVED QUESTION IN FREUD

If we look at Freud's work on the father from the Oedipal father, through the father of the primal horde in *Totem and Taboo*, to the father of *Moses and Monotheism*, we find first of all an ambiguity in his function. On the one hand, the Oedipal father has a normative function. As possessor of the phallus, his function is to regulate the desire of the mother as omnipotent Other; he acts as the support of the subject's identification, producing the ego ideal. The price one pays for this is an imaginary rivalry with the father over the mother and consequently a desire for his death. On the other hand, there is the function of the father as pathogenic, playing as he does a causal role in subsequent neuroses.

There is nothing fundamentally surprising in this ambiguity of the father in his normative and pathogenic functions. There are, after all, many such phenomena in the theory of psychoanalysis. What is striking, though, in Freud's writings on the father is the increasingly strong emphasis placed upon the ambivalence of the function of the father alongside the important differences, which are not just differences of detail, in the various versions of the myth of the father. In *Totem and Taboo*, for example, in contrast to the father of the Oedipus complex who himself is subject to the law he transmits to his children, we find a figure of the father who is *an exception* to this same law. The father of the primal horde is the *père sévère*, who is egotistical and jealous, the sexual glutton who also keeps his sons in check by the threat of castration. This is the figure of the father of jouissance, who is not limited by any submission to the law of an order transcendent to him. Moreover, his death is no liberation for the sons, for his power to prohibit is only increased by his disappearance. Through his death the sons are even more strongly bound to the law of prohibition that returns in the form of his son's identification with him.

The development from the Oedipus complex to the myth of the father of *Totem and Taboo* and later of *Moses and Monotheism* is very striking. At the outset the father's function is clearly to pacify, regulate, and sublimate the omnipotence of the figure of the mother, called by Freud "the obscure power of the feminine sex." But by the end the father himself has assumed the power, obscurity, and cruelty of the omnipotence his function was supposed to dissipate in the first place.

REAL, SYMBOLIC, AND IMAGINARY

It is Lacan who by continuing Freud's question of the father has brought the aforementioned observations to our attention. In "The Neurotic's Individual Myth," he points to the pathogenic *and* normative roles of the father.[9] But he does much more than this. By introducing the symbolic-imaginary-real distinction, he accomplishes a thoroughgoing clarification of the question of the father.

The *symbolic* father, according to Lacan, is the dead father—the dead father of the primal horde, who is also embodied in the fantasies of the obsessional neurotic. Through the symbolic debt, the subject comes to be bound to the law as a result of the murder of the father, of which *Totem and Taboo* is the mythical expression. As Lacan puts it, "The symbolic Father, insofar as he signifies this Law, is truly the dead Father."[10]

The symbolic father is also designated as the Name-of-the-Father, where Lacan insists upon the fact that the symbolic father is a *pure* signifier in the sense that there is no representation correlative to it. In this respect, the Name-of-the-Father is one of the minimal elements of any signifying network whatsoever—Lacan, like Freud, situates the Name-of-the-Father in "prehistory." At one point he calls it "transcendent," in the Kantian sense of a condition for the possibility of any signifying chain. In calling this signifier transcendent, he is claiming that while it has no correlate in any representation it is nevertheless a condition for the possibility of any representation. Just as the dream that Freud recounts, "My father don't you see I'm burning?," is the dream of a son and not of a father, so there is no subjective representation of paternity. As a pure signifier, the Name-of-the-Father supports the entire symbolic system; it is its keystone, its *point de capiton,* or quilting point. It is pure also in the sense of the opposite of applied. A pure signifier in this sense is one whose identity is established by its position within a formal system, without implying that any particular signification is associated with it. It is then a further question whether and in what way it applies to reality. This is similar to the case with the term *line,* or *point* in post-Euclidean geometry, say, which is given a certain definition, it being a further "empirical" question whether, and if so, how, "line" or "point," so defined, actually applies to psychical space.

A close relation exists between the Name-of-the-Father and the phallic signifier, Φ. Whereas the Name-of-the-Father is a pure signifier, the vicissitudes of the Oedipus complex show that the phallus is "impure," never clearly distinguished from its imaginary connections. The imaginary object that the subject in the Oedipal situation wants to be, namely, the phallus that will satisfy the mother's desire, is transformed into a signifier by the operation of the paternal metaphor when the paternal signifier is substituted for the signifier of the mother, thereby producing a new signification or meaning, *Bedeutung,* which is the meaning of the phallus.[11]

The passage from imaginary phallus to phallic signifier results from the paternal metaphor that is brought about by symbolic castration. While there are clear imaginary effects of symbolic castration, which are described in detail by Freud in his account of the Oedipus complex, at the same time symbolic castration allows access to the phallic signification necessary for the assumption not only of the question of one's sex (am I man or woman?) but also of the question of one's existence (am I dead or alive?). These questions reappear in hysteria and obsessional neurosis as questions to which the answer provided by the neurotic subject in his very being is, as Lacan puts it, "a sort of response."[12]

The *imaginary* father appears in various guises as what Lacan calls "figures of the father." These emerge as a result of the discordance or disagreement between the real father and his symbolic role of assuring the correct functioning of the Name-of-the-Father in the paternal metaphor, that is, in the relation between the Other as primordial object, or Mother, and the subject. The paradigmatic expression of the imaginary father figure is the *carence,* or defaulting, of the father, and it is the expression of this figure that gives the father of the Oedipus complex a role that is also pathogenic and not merely normative.

This sketch of the relation between the Name-of-the-Father, the function of the real father in the desire of the mother, and the imaginary figures of the father gives some idea of the way in which these fundamental distinctions drawn by Lacan continue and considerably clarify the Freudian debate around the father's function.

EGO IDEAL AND SUPEREGO

What I have said also helps to understand the particular way in which Lacan construes the distinction between ego ideal and superego. The ego ideal is the outcome of the identification with the father produced by the paternal metaphor—produced, that is, as an effect of the symbolic father. It is a precipitate of the "internalization of the law" described by Freud in *Totem and Taboo.*[13] The superego, on the other hand, results from slightly different dynamics. We know that Freud became increasingly preoccupied by superego phenomena in his later work. In a celebrated passage in *Civilization and Its Discontents,* Freud denies that there is a proportional relation between guilt feelings and acts of which one is actually guilty and he evokes, on the contrary, the paradox of conscience: "The more virtuous a man is, the more severe and distrustful is [the superego's] behavior, so that ultimately it is precisely those people who have carried saintliness furthest who reproach themselves with the worst sinfulness."[14]

Although phenomenologically this view may not be entirely valid, there is a theoretical point here that is worthwhile disengaging for discussion—that the inhibition of aggression turns the aggression around against the ego so that there is manifested with respect to the ego the same aggressiveness that the ego would have liked to satisfy against others.[15] This has particular bearing upon the Oedipus complex and the place of the father—the imaginary father—within it. Again, in *Civilization and Its Discontents,* there is a passage where Freud contradicts a view beginning to find favor that had been proposed by Jones and Klein. Both had proposed that the frustration or thwarting (*Versagung* is Freud's term) of any drive satisfaction *whatsoever* would result in an increase in feelings of guilt. At a time when attention was already being paid to the possibility of pre-Oedipal structures, this view was not without interest, suggesting as it does that the drives were subject to vicissitudes that could be considered independently of any relation to the dynamics of the Oedipal situation. Freud explicitly contradicts this view, maintaining instead that the aggression, which when suppressed is given over to the super-ego and turned against the subject to exacerbate feelings of guilt, is directed towards the person responsible for the prohibition of an erotic satisfaction. In what he describes as an "average approxima-tion," he says, "When an instinctual trend undergoes repression, its libidinal elements are turned into symptoms, and its aggressive com-ponents into a sense of guilt."[16]

This view and ones similar to it elsewhere where Freud explicitly links the aggression towards the father to the internalized aggression at the heart of the severity of the superego indicate, as has been pointed out, that the death drive increasingly appears linked to the phenom-enon of aggression and less frequently with the compulsion to repeat of *Beyond the Pleasure Principle*. But, further, these views seem to con-tradict the position I have been presenting as Lacan's, whereby the symbolic father, who unites rather than opposes desire to the Law, is *not* the privative father who incurs the aggression of the subject through the frustration of his drive satisfactions and who is rather an imagi-nary figure of the father.

Certainly this privative father is crucial to the etiology of neuro-sis, particularly of obsessional neurosis. The privative father is upper-most in the history of the Rat Man, for example, and yet Lacan insists that this figure of the father is a figure of the imaginary father.

As a matter of fact, if we look at Freud's texts a bit more closely, we see that Lacan's distinction between symbolic father and various imaginary figures of the father is no mere elegant innovation but is rather a distinction that is necessary if we wish to overcome a theoreti-cal difficulty at the heart of Freudian theory itself.

I will give two examples to illustrate this. First, the mechanism Freud suggests for mourning in *Mourning and Melancholia* is that ob-ject loss produces a regression and then an ego identification with the lost object, so that the reproaches of the superego are henceforth di-rected against the ego.[17] The shadow of the object, as Freud says, falls upon the ego and the self-reproaches to which the ego is now subject have their origin in the suppressed aggression directed towards the former object. However, turning to Chapter 3 of *The Ego and the Id*, we find the following account of identification with the father: The disso-lution of the Oedipus complex is accompanied by the child's renuncia-tion of the mother as object choice and a concomitant *intensification* of the identification with the father. Freud himself quite rightly observes that this is not what we should expect, given psychoanalytic theory, since we are led to assume that the *abandoned* object is the one that would be introduced into the ego (i.e., identified with) rather than the father, who is, after all, the agent of the frustration.[18]

Second, according to *Totem and Taboo* and *Moses and Monotheism* the consequences for the sons of murdering the father of the primal horde are not the ones expected by the sons—principally access to a jouissance without limit—since no one accedes to the omnipotence of the vacated position. The prohibitions prior to the murder continue just as strongly afterwards, because the sons agree upon them amongst themselves so that total and mutual destruction does not ensue. As Freud writes in *Moses and Monotheism*, "Each individual renounced his ideal of acquiring his father's position for himself and of possessing his mother and sisters. Thus the taboo on incest and the injunction to exogamy came about."[19]

The reference to the son's identification with the father, in relation to the ideal of acquiring his father's position, suggests that an answer to the question how in this myth the incest taboo arises should be sought in terms of an identification with the father and not merely in terms of a vaguely sociological theory of a social contract between equals. Further, Freud also attributes a crucial role in the setting up of prohibitions to the son's love for the primal father: "[The primal father] forced [the sons] into abstinence and *consequently* into the emotional ties with him and with one another which could arise out of those of their impulsions that were inhibited in their sexual aim."[20] Here again we need to make a similar observation to the one in the first example. Freud's views on aim-inhibited drives that lead to tenderness and empathy in object relations are that the renunciation of direct sexual satisfaction with an object leads to idealization of the object and to the appearance of a relation of tenderness with it, whereas the actual vehicle of the frustration draws the subject's hatred and aggression upon himself.[21] However, here as before, "forced abstinence" produces an emotional tie with the agent, in a way that runs counter to what we should expect on the theory.

I think these two examples clearly illustrate a theoretical hiatus in Freud's views on identification, that is, in his views concerning the identification with the father at the very moment at which he is also the agent who deprives the subject of his erotic satisfactions. And the importance of this for the Oedipus complex is of course obvious. Lacan says, "Love relates to the father by virtue of the father's being the vehicle of castration. This is what Freud proposes in *Totem and Taboo*. It is insofar as the sons are deprived of women that they love the father—a bewildering remark that is sanctioned by the insight of a Freud."[22]

The way in which Lacan situates Freud's views on the function of the father is not just enlightening, it is also a necessary innovation. And like any real innovation, its ramifications penetrate deep into different aspects of the theory, such as here into the question of identification, just as they extend deep into different clinical aspects.

This innovation has ramifications, for instance, concerning the end of a psychoanalytic cure. Recall Freud's pessimism expressed in *Civilization and Its Discontents* and elsewhere concerning the chances of bringing a cure to a successful end. Acting against this is the negative therapeutic reaction and also the apparently insurmountable obstacles of the threat of castration and penis envy.

The hatred of the father and the guilt of the sons are the principal themes of *Civilization and Its Discontents*. The hatred of the father, when transferred onto the superego, becomes here *the* major obstacle to the efficacy of psychoanalytic treatment by bolstering those symptoms that are the most difficult to conquer in the form of the negative therapeutic reaction.

Serge Cottet has pointed out that since this negative therapeutic reaction originates in the fact that the prospect of a cure is experienced as a new danger, the source of this danger is clearly the refusal to accept castration.[23] The analyst is experienced as a substitute for the father, so that the refusal to be cured signifies the refusal to bow before him. Freud considered this the final and perhaps insurmountable obstacle to the efficacy of a psychoanalytic cure, and indeed the alternatives appear unattractive. *Either* one admits that aggressiveness is in fact linked to the Oedipus complex and castration and is directed at the father. In this case, Freud's view that this may be insurmountable appears warranted, even inescapable. Or, take full account of this aggressiveness but rather than link it to the castrating father, derive it from elsewhere. This is the line taken by many in the British school.

Lacan, however, follows Freud in insisting that the aggressiveness in question has its origins in the Oedipus complex, but of course once the Oedipus complex is seen in light of the symbolic-imaginary-real distinction, it emerges that the superego is not derived from the relation to the symbolic father but from the relation to the privative imaginary father. This is given further support by the distinction between the ego ideal, which is the product both of the "internalization of the law" and of identification supported by the symbolic father, and the superego, which is the heritage of what in *Freud's Papers on Technique* Lacan calls a fault in the transmission and comprehension of the law, the heritage of a perception of the law as arbitrary and senseless.[24]

Therefore, rather than regarding the superego as the agency by which the subject acquires the "moral law within," as certain culturalist interpretations would have it, Lacan insists upon the superego as being "obscene and ferocious," as well as upon the fact that the ravages of the superego are not wrought by the symbolic father but by an imaginary figure of the father that may indeed, as Freud's case of the Wolf Man shows, bear little relation to the real father.

Chapter 3

Beyond the Oedipus Complex

It is well known that the Oedipus complex plays a central role for Lacan. In his early seminars, including *The Psychoses*, *The Object Relation*, and *Formations of the Unconscious*, he refers to the Oedipus complex constantly, recurrently, and persistently. Indeed, his conceptual edifice revolves around it. The mother's desire, the phallus as object of the mother's desire, the child that initially wants *to be* the phallus and then comes to accept *to have* the phallus, the Name-of-the-Father—none of this would make any sense outside of its reference to the function of the Oedipus complex. This is all so much magnificent and complex machinery that depends upon, indeed is a part of, the Oedipus complex which, for Lacan, it is necessary to invoke if we are to explain pretty well anything that is at all relevant to psychoanalysis, whether a phobia in a child, the nature of hysteria and obsessional neurosis, why psychosis and not neurosis, the conditions for fetishism and transsexualism to be set in place, and, of course, the engendering of masculinity and femininity. In all of this, the particular dynamics of the Oedipus complex in each particular case are invoked, in the constant belief that this is where we have to look to understand the origin and nature of the different clinical structures that are the psychoanalyst's daily fare. Without the Oedipus complex, there is no possibility of understanding neurosis, psychosis, or perversion, no way of thinking about sexuation. The constant return to the Oedipus complex indicates Lacan's belief that nothing can be understood in the absence of a reference to it as the cornerstone of psychoanalysis. Whereas Freud called it the "nucleus of the neuroses," Lacan went even further, declaring that the Oedipus complex covers the entire field of analytic experience, marking the limit that our discipline assigns to subjectivity.[1]

Lacan discusses, elaborates, and develops Freud's theory of the Oedipus complex at great length in his early seminars. See, for instance, his discussion of the "three moments" of the Oedipus complex in *Seminar V*; or, in *Seminar IV*, the detailed breakdown of the Oedipus complex in terms of the real father, the imaginary father, and the symbolic mother; symbolic castration, imaginary frustration, and real privation; the imaginary phallus, the symbolic phallus, and the real breast. All of this is discussed and elaborated in the 1950s and in a way, it must be said, that is very compelling, clarifies a great number of issues in psychoanalysis, and is clinically useful.

CRITIQUE OF THE OEDIPUS COMPLEX

Then something unexpected happens. At about the time of *Seminar XVI, Seminar XVII,* and *Seminar XVIII* (that is 1968–1971), Lacan gradually dismisses the Oedipus complex as being, at best, useless and irrelevant and, at worst, liable to lead us into significant errors of judgment in the clinical setting. Most analysts ignore it altogether, he says, even those trained in his school. And those who make it a point of reference for their work get into all sorts of bother—one need look no farther than Freud's own cases. This turnaround is particularly apparent in *Seminar XVII, The Other Side of Psychoanalysis,* and *Seminar XVIII, D'un Discours qui ne Serait Pas du Semblant,* where Lacan adopts a surprisingly new approach to the Oedipus complex and to what till then had been the key signifier, the Name-of-the-Father. Quite suddenly Lacan starts referring to the Oedipus complex as "Freud's dream." And, if it is a dream, he says, it can no longer be a theoretical construction to be unpacked, dissected, and rebuilt; it can no longer be the bedrock of psychoanalysis. If it is Freud's dream, it is a formation of the unconscious, which implies that it calls for interpretation.[2]

Why this turnaround from seeing the Oedipus complex as the bedrock of psychoanalysis to the judgment that it is a dream of Freud's? While there are probably a number of reasons, there is one factor that is absolutely crucial: the introduction, in the late 1960s, of the theory of the four discourses and, in particular, the role played within the four discourses of the concepts of master, master signifier, S_1, and master's discourse.

$$\frac{S_1}{\$} \quad \rightarrow \quad \frac{S_2}{a}$$

The master's discourse

Many things follow from this, in particular, the hysteric's discourse, the analyst's discourse, and the university discourse, which are derivatives of the principal discourse, the master's discourse.

When Lacan calls the Oedipus complex Freud's dream, we have to understand that one of the things he is doing is distinguishing it from myth. It is *also* a myth, one that takes two forms in Freud's work: the Oedipus complex that derives from Sophocles' play and a myth of Freud's own invention, which is the myth of the primal father that is advanced for the first time in *Totem and Taboo*. But by calling it a dream he is implying that there is a place for it to be treated psychoanalytically and not anthropologically.

The difference between anthropology and psychoanalysis is important and, even though Lacan always appreciated it, it took some time for him to realize its full significance. Lacan initially thought that psychoanalysis could draw upon Lévi-Strauss's anthropology of myths and engaged in some serious efforts to make use of Lévi-Strauss's work in his own work on individual analytic cases. His approach in *Seminar IV* in 1957 to the analysis of Little Hans draws heavily upon Lévi-Strauss's study of myths and analysis of the Oedipus myth, or myths, in particular. He takes a similar approach in "The Neurotic's Individual Myth," conceived analogously to Freud's thesis on religion when he takes obsessional neurosis to be an individual religion of the neurotic. Here, it seems, the analyst has much to learn from the anthropologist's method for the analysis of myths, which comprises a comparative study of all the different versions of the myth that are known to exist. If one applies this method to Little Hans, as Lacan does, then the evolution of his phobia can be regarded as exhibiting a number of versions of the key Oedipal myth, as the young boy grapples with the questions of his existence and his sexual identity.

In "The Structural Study of Myth," Lévi-Strauss develops a method for uncovering the underlying structure of myths and takes the myth of Oedipus as a case study.[3] Noting that the myth can be found all around the world, though disguised in various ways, he gathers together all of its known variants for analysis. For Lévi-Strauss, the meaning of the myth resides not in the story narrated but in the way in which the elements of the myth, the "mythemes," are combined. A mytheme is a phrase or proposition, not unlike a fantasy, at least as Lacan understands it, such as, for example, "A child is being beaten."

Lévi-Strauss's method consists of writing out the themes of a myth from left to right, with different myths located one above the other, as if they were each the parts of the one orchestral score. When the elements from different myths express the same theme or idea, one locates them one above the other, without taking any account of the order in which the elements occur in the original myth. Take, by way of illustration, Sophocles' *King Oedipus* and Sophocles' *Antigone,* which Lévi-Strauss considers variants of the same myth (see Table 3.1).

Note the following about the four columns in Table 3.1: Columns 1 and 2 are contraries and so too are columns 3 and 4, although it is less apparent because the opposition appears in symbolic form. In column 4 the difficulty with walking represents the terrestrial, or autochthonous, origins of humans, while in column 3 the destruction of monsters signifies the negation of these autochthonous origins. Thus columns 1 and 2, on the one hand, and columns 3 and 4, on the other, form two contrary pairs.[4] Now if we also consider the fact that columns 1 and 2 concern the question of human origins, and columns 3 and 4 concern the question of "autochthonous" origins, then again we can see that the key term in the opposition around which the contrary relations in the left-hand pair revolve is "contrary" to the key term in the opposition around which the right-hand side contraries revolve. These myths thus use this "bridging" technique to move from an initial problem, "Is one born from one or from two?," which is the inevitable question and enigma of human reproduction, to another, derivative issue, "Is the same born out of the same or out of something which is different?"

This, then, according to Lévi-Strauss, gives us the structural law of the Oedipus myth. It confronts the impossibility of passing from

Table 3.1. Myth of Oedipus

1	2	3	4
Oedipus marries his mother, Jocasta.	Oedipus kills his father, Laius.	Oedipus immolates the sphinx.	"Labdacos" means lame.
			"Laius" means left.
Antigone buries her brother, Polynices, in defiance of the law.	Eteocles kills his brother, Polynices.		"Oedipus" means swollen foot.
Blood ties are overrated.	Blood ties are underrated.	The destruction of monsters	Difficulties in walking properly
Contraries		Contraries	
Human origins		Autochthonous origins	
Contraries			

belief in the autochthonous origins of humans to the recognition of birth from two parents. A myth is a kind of logical instrument for resolving contradictions such as these. It typically fails to resolve the contradictions, since the contradictions it confronts are nevertheless real ones. However, for Lévi-Strauss, the mere fact that the motivation for myth is to resolve a contradiction means that mythical reasoning and scientific reasoning are no different in kind; mythical reasoning is not a "primitive" form of thought that scientific reasoning has superseded.

Concerning Freud's Oedipus complex, note that Lévi-Strauss's analysis is somewhat double-edged as far as psychoanalysis is concerned. On the one hand, it claims that the Oedipus complex is universal and that it can be found in widely different cultures that have had no contact with one another. Yet this discovery, which in appearance psychoanalysis can claim to have made turns out to be a sign that psychoanalysis' epistemological pretensions are unjustified, for Freud's Oedipus complex turns out to be just another version of this myth, alongside all the others. In Lévi-Strauss's analysis of the Oedipus myth, with all of its variants, the Freudian version becomes so much grist to the anthropologist's mill: psychoanalysis cannot claim to have revealed "the truth," the true meaning, of the myth; rather, the psychoanalytic version becomes merely a modern version of the myth, indistinguishable from all the others in being just one more variant. In Freud's version, the question of autochthony disappears, it is true, but the other theme, how is one born from two?, remains. For Lévi-Strauss, this merely shows the continuing importance and relevance of the Oedipus myth across different cultural and social contexts.

Lacan takes a different view from Lévi-Strauss about the relationship between science and myth, and also about the place of the Freudian Oedipus complex. He agrees that at the heart of myth there is a point of impossibility, a "contradiction." Lacan's name for this impossibility is the real, and in the Oedipus complex this "bit of real" is the impossibility of any sexual relationship between man and woman. However, where he differs from Lévi-Strauss is in thinking that myth covers over this bit of impossibility by giving it a sense, a "bit of meaning," in the form of a fiction. The myth is, thus, a fictional story woven around this point of impossibility, or the real, which is why Lacan says that there is indeed truth in myth, but that it is truth that has the structure of fiction.

Lacan thinks that science does the opposite to this activity of myth of covering over points of impossibility. Whereas myth is something that generates sense and meaning, which is its function, the tendency of science is to reduce meaning and sense to the point of eliminating them. Science pares them away to the point where it can demonstrate an impossibility. Lacan also claims that writing is essential to this process and that there is no science, and he includes mathematics in this, without writing. It is therefore significant that myth, on the other hand, proceeds by way of speech, which is crucial to the way in which myth expresses the truth. Myth, for Lacan, accomplishes this "bridging" mentioned by Lévi-Strauss by producing something that is a mixture of the imaginary and the symbolic, and it is in actual fact a way of papering over the impossible, real kernel around which the myth is constructed and for which it was originally formulated. Science cannot write the impossible, any more than myth can *say* it; here they are on common ground. However, science differs from myth in that it can, and does, use symbolic means to demonstrate and expose this impossibility, whereas myth constantly revolves around the impossibility in recurrent attempts at resolving questions that have no answers.

For Lacan, then, Lévi-Strauss's analysis of myth actually makes myth much closer to fantasy than to science. At least it does so if we think of fantasy in the way Lacan does, which is as a phrase or proposition—"A child is being beaten," for instance—that takes the place of a point of impossibility, a "contradiction," such as the sexual relationship between man and woman, which both indicates the place of the impossibility and at the same time occludes it by a fantasmatic profusion of meaning.

We need then to distinguish four domains: myth, fantasy, science, and psychoanalysis. The difference between science, on the one hand, and fantasy and myth, on the other, comes down to the response each makes to the real. Lacan's insight was to see that this was the point at which psychoanalysis was on common ground with science, and his ambition was to make psychoanalysis more scientific at this point.

A dream is not a myth, however, and if Lacan is right in thinking that the Oedipus complex was "Freud's dream," then the Oedipus complex is not a myth either. If it is a dream, then it will have been formed according to different laws. As we know from Freud, the dream is a product, a "formation," of the unconscious. The dream work distorts and disguises the latent content of the dream in the service of unconscious desire according to the two processes by which the latent material is encoded: condensation and displacement, which are equivalent to the linguistic operations of metaphor and metonymy. These unconscious processes are both unknown to myth. This is why Lacan was able to point out the limitation of Lévi-Strauss's analysis with great precision. In "Radiophonie," a radio broadcast of 1970 prepared over the course of *Seminar XVII*, Lacan says, "Myths, in their elaboration by Lévi-Strauss, refuse everything that I have promoted in the instance of the letter in the unconscious. They perform no metaphor, nor even any metonymy. They do not condense; they explain. They do not dislodge; they lodge, even to the point of changing the order of the texts."[5]

The mechanisms of dream formation are what make it the case that dreams are specific to the language (or, as sometimes happens, languages) in which they are dreamed. Dreams rely upon the features of a language, its polysemies, ambiguities, and so on, that constitute the language as llanguage, *lalangue*, in one word. This language-specific character of dreams contrasts with the universality of the Oedipus myth. Lacan continues the aforementioned passage by adding that the myth is "untranslatable." This seems an odd thing to say, given that the one and same myth can be found in different linguistic communities with very little variation, that myth has something universal about it, and therefore that myths do indeed "translate" from one linguistic community to another. However, what Lacan has in mind is that a myth is not rooted in any given language. A myth is neither embedded in nor an expression of a particular language.

While it was only in 1970 that Lacan became fully aware of the distance separating psychoanalysis from anthropology, with hindsight it is possible to see that the crucial development in Lacan's move away from Lévi-Strauss's views occurs in 1958 with the development of the theory of the paternal metaphor, where the metaphoric process of substitution of the Name-of-the-Father for the Mother's desire places us squarely within the field of formation of the unconscious. By 1970, Lacan is aware of the significance of metaphor and metonymy and how they differ from the operations at play in the construction of myths; we can get an idea of the time it took for Lacan to understand by the degree of lag between, on the one hand, the elaboration of a theory of metaphor and metonymy and the Lévi-Straussian analysis of Little Hans in *Seminar IV* and, on the other, the critique of Lévi-Strauss in 1970.

CASTRATION AND THE OEDIPUS COMPLEX

A dream disguises; the dream work is a work of distortion. According to Lacan, then, the place given to the father in Freud's work covers up and papers over its underlying structure, presenting it in disguised form. Nevertheless, the father does not occupy just one place in Freud's work but varies from one version of the Oedipus complex to the next, from *The Interpretation of Dreams*, through *Totem and Taboo* and *Civilization and Its Discontents*, and down to Freud's final work, *Moses and Monotheism*. Nevertheless, all versions of the myth consistently paper over the same form of the real as impossible: the sexual relationship between man and woman. There is a further element that for Freud is part of the father's role and is essential to and recurrent in Freud's account of the Oedipus complex, present in all versions but absent from the original myth of Oedipus. This is the castration complex, to which I now turn.

Psychoanalysts since Freud have had difficulty knowing what to do with or how to understand the castration complex and have proposed a number of candidates as the source of the threat or fear of castration. The most popular of these is that the trauma of castration originates in the registration of the anatomical difference between the sexes, the ensuing recognition of a "lack," and the child's aggression towards the father, which comes to be turned back around upon him or (less persuasively) her in the form of the threat of castration.[6] By the same token, however, there is no real reason to specifically invoke castration in the case of the primal horde father. Why should the threat from the primal father be the threat of castration? And in the Oedipal myth, in either Freud's version or Sophocles' version, there is, strictly speaking, no particularly prominent place given to castration.

Indeed, there is no inherent link between castration and its mythical, Oedipal settings. Given this fact, it might be fruitful to acknowledge the point and begin to treat them as separate and distinct. This is what Lacan undertakes in *Seminar XVII*. Thus, on the one hand, Lacan explores the question of the castration complex independently of the Oedipal context in which it is embedded. It is this line of approach that eventually leads him to the formulas of sexuation we are familiar with from *Seminar XX, Encore*. On the other hand, we can inquire into the reasons Freud holds so strongly to the Oedipus complex itself. If we follow Lacan well enough, we may be able to see why he thinks the Oedipus complex in Freud is designed to "save the father."

For Lacan, castration is not a fantasy, and, a fortiori, is not a fantasy about a castrating father or any supposed encounter with the opposite sex. These are at best precipitating causes for what is a real operation, which is brought about by language itself. For Freud, in the case of the little girl the castration complex acts as a trigger for her to pass into the Oedipus complex, whereas the little boy exits the Oedipus complex as a result of his encounter with castration. For Lacan, castration is an operation that is brought about by language and determined by the master signifier, S_1, and arises from a confrontation between the signifier and enjoyment.

Lacan's four discourses in *The Other Side of Psychoanalysis* are an attempt to formalize the structure of this relationship between signifier, in the form of semblant, and enjoyment. All four discourses, but particularly the master's discourse, share a common aim with the myth of the primal horde in Freud's *Totem and Taboo*, in that Freud's work is as much an attempt to give an account of the social bond that binds people together, along with an account of what segregates them, as it is an account of the origin of religion.

All of this in Freud is constructed on the basis of the father's murder. There is of course no question of the father's murder describing an actual historical event, even though Freud believed it had to be true, and even though this was the work in which he took perhaps greatest pride. The primal horde tale takes precisely the place of a myth, describing as it does an ahistorical event that, as Lévi-Strauss puts it, "evokes an abolished past" that is projected into all eternity, and a fortiori into the present. If we reject the thesis that the father's murder has any role to play as a historical event, if we consider that its status is that of a myth, and, further, if we also consider castration a real operation of language, stemming from the symbolic, then the question arises of what role the father's murder plays in Freud's work.

Lacan, who raises this question in *Seminar XVII*, gives as his response the thesis that the father's murder is set in place as a myth in order to cover up the castration that institutes *both* the law *and* fantasy, which is a consequence of the law. There is a fundamental fantasy at issue here, which is that of the father who enjoys—and, in particular, who enjoys all of the women. This fantasy of the father who enjoys is of course an impossibility—as Lacan comments, a man generally finds it hard enough to satisfy just one woman, and even then he must not boast about it. The fantasy is also a retrospective effect of the institution of the prohibition of jouissance, which I am inclined to think is the sense of a difficult remark Lacan makes when he gives the myth of the father's murder the status of a "statement [*énoncé*] of the impossible."[7] The father who is retroactively created as the father who enjoys is what Lacan calls the real father; this is the real father of *Totem and Taboo*.

Lacan does not, however, completely abandon all reference to the Oedipus complex, at least not to the father of the primal horde. This might seem a little bit surprising, given that the entire thrust of his thought in *Seminar XVII* has been first to remove the link between the castration complex and the Oedipus complex and then to dismiss the family romance of the Oedipus complex itself. Yet while Lacan does separate the castration complex from the dead father, he nevertheless retains the function that the dead father has in myth, specifically the *Totem and Taboo* myth, which is the function of both enjoyer (that is, the one who enjoys) and also prohibitor of jouissance. If castration is a function of language, in the form of the master, then why does he retain this vestige of a father, this residual father, to whom he refers, somewhat obscurely, as a statement of the impossible?

The following reasoning has been suggested by Geneviève Morel.[8] If we assume that castration is a universal function of language that comes into play for any subject who both speaks and enjoys, then we have no way of explaining the fact that this function sometimes works and sometimes not, and that sometimes it works better than others. I have in mind the clinic of psychoanalysis, which includes the discovery of the foreclosure of phallic signification in psychosis and the implications this has for the way the psychotic enjoys, on the one hand, and all the possible vicissitudes of neurotic sexuation and psychopathology, on the other. Yet if castration is automatic and a mere fact of language, then why is its effect not the same in all cases? There must be individual factors, contingent elements, alongside the automatic operation of language. In other contexts, such as his discussion of *tyche* and *automaton* in *Seminar XI, The Four Fundamental Concepts of Psychoanalysis*, Lacan is very aware both of how important it is that there be a place for the contingent and of the inclination in psychoanalysis to a type of immanentism. What Lacan calls the real father is invoked as the agent necessary to explain the contingency of the encounter with castration; the real father is a contingent agent of a universal operation, which explains why there is no identity across cases, why there is contingency in the universality of language.

Lacan makes the further claim that it is impossible for any subject to know this real father; even though the real father is specific to each subject, the subject does not have access to him. There is something that does not enter into the universal operation of castration but will remain an operator unknown to the subject.

Lacan refers to this real father as master-agent and guardian of enjoyment.[9] Although impossible to analyze, he says in *Television*, it is quite possible to imagine the real father.[10] And what the subject has access to in analysis is figures of the imaginary father in his multiple representations: castrating father, tyrannical, weak, absent, lacking, too powerful, and so on.

SAVING THE FATHER

I mentioned earlier that there was a second issue to explore in this seminar, which was why Freud holds so tenaciously to the Oedipus complex itself. We now need to explore why Lacan claims it has to do with Freud wanting to "save the father."

The first thing to note is that there are some important and indeed puzzling differences between the two forms of the myth of the father in Freud—that is, the Oedipus complex and the myth of the primal horde—of which the most striking is the inversion in the relationship between desire and the law. The Oedipus complex is meant to explain how desire and jouissance are regulated by the law. Both the Oedipus myth, "borrowed from Sophocles," and the primal horde myth involve the murder of the father, but the consequences of this murder are exactly opposite in the two cases, and the reason for this is the different place occupied by the law in each. Both deal with what Lacan had previously been calling the Name-of-the-Father, which as signifier is closely bound up with jouissance and its regulation by the law, but, oddly enough, the relationship between the law and jouissance that unfolds in each ends up inverted. In Freud's Oedipal myth, the law is there from the outset; it is an inexorable law, demanding punishment even when the transgression has been committed unwittingly or unconsciously, and it exists for the subject as an unconscious sense of guilt. The law precedes enjoyment, and enjoyment henceforth takes the form of a transgression. The relationship is the inverse of this in *Totem and Taboo*, where it is enjoyment that is present at the outset, and the law comes afterwards.

The contrast between the two forms of Oedipus leads Lacan to say that there is "*une schize,* a split, separating the myth of Oedipus from *Totem and Taboo*,"[11] and raises the question of the reason for the two versions. Why does Freud initially introduce the Oedipus complex and then subsequently insist upon the primal horde father whose relationship to jouissance is so different? One suggestion is that we should see them as responses, respectively, to the clinical experience of hysteria and obsessional neurosis. On this view the Oedipus complex would be the myth that Freud creates in response to the clinic of hysteria; the myth of the primal horde father of *Totem and Taboo* is his response to the clinic of obsessional neurosis. I think this is, in rough terms, Lacan's view in *Seminar XVII*.

Lacan's thesis in *Seminar XVII* is that the Oedipus complex is something Freud produces in response to his encounter with hysteria. It is not that the Oedipus complex is invented or introduced by the hysteric; the Oedipus complex is Freud's response to hysteria, and a response, moreover, designed to protect the place of the father. Let me explain, with reference to the case of Dora.

Right from the outset, whenever Lacan discussed Dora he was always critical of Freud's treatment. He criticized Freud for missing the fact that the object of Dora's desire was a woman, Frau K., whereas Freud had relentlessly pursued the case as if her real object was a man, Herr K. From Freud's point of view, Dora's problem was that, as a hysteric, she was unable to acknowledge her desire for this man, whereas everything would have had a good chance of being brought to a successful resolution if only she could be brought to this realization. Throughout the entire analysis Freud persists in hammering away at this fact: You refuse to acknowledge that it is Herr K. that you desire. However, as Freud came to realize many years later, in assuming that Dora's object was a heterosexual one he had missed the crucial fact that the object of Dora's desire was a woman, Frau K.

As it happens, Freud's confusion in the face of hysteria did not stop there, for what he had also failed to grasp was the place and significance of the structure of desire in hysteria and in particular the role played in it by a desire for an unsatisfied desire. His failure to realize this meant that in his treatment of hysteria Freud would invariably look for some particular object or other as the object of the hysteric's desire. It is true that this object is, for Freud, typically a man, and that Freud thus misses the significance of the woman for the hysteric. But the point I am making is the slightly different one that by failing to recognize that what the hysteric desires is a desire that is unsatisfied, his search for an object of the hysteric's desire always ends up coming up with something that is forced and in one way or another rejected or resisted by his patient. And this is apparent at every turn in the case of Dora.

We owe to Freud the first real insight into the crucial, even essential, role that lack plays in female sexuality. But his conclusion from this was that a woman can never be fully satisfied until she has filled this lack by receiving the phallus and, moreover, by receiving it from the father. Freud's solution to the woman's lack was motherhood, and this solution keeps insisting in his treatment of hysteria. He thinks that the hysteric will not be properly "cured" until she has this desire to receive the phallus from the father, or rather, since Freud is in no doubt that she does indeed have this desire, until she acknowledges it. This is why we see Freud relentlessly pursuing his efforts at getting Dora to acknowledge her desire for the father's substitute, Herr K., even to the point where this eventually brings about the early and abrupt termination of the treatment. This much is clear and can be demonstrated in Freud's case history.[12]

And so what is Dora's attitude towards this father of hers? Lacan emphasizes the importance of the role that the impotence of Dora's father plays. His impotence has for her the signification of his castration vis-à-vis the woman. Now Lacan takes this to indicate that seeing her father as deficient in this way is to measure him against some symbolic, ideal function of the father. The father is not merely who he is or what he is, but he is also someone who carries a title or fills an office. He is, as he puts it, an *ancien géniteur*, a former begetter, which, Lacan says, is a bit like the title of what in French is called the *ancien combatant*, former or ex-soldier, that is, a veteran, or a returned soldier, as we say in Australia. He carries this title of *ancien géniteur* with him. And even when he is "out of action," he maintains this position in relation to the woman. Using resources of English not available to the French, we could sum up this emphasis upon the father as he who begets or engenders by appeal to the pleonasm, "The father fathers." And, as a matter of fact, one might suggest a new French verb, *perrier*, which would mean to father. Not only would this recycle a word already in existence, but it would have other advantages as well. "The father fathers" would then come out as *Le père perrie*.[13] In any case, Lacan calls this fathering father, the father who begets or engenders, "the idealized father," and he is at the core of the hysteric's relation to the father.

On the one hand, then, there is the figure of the idealized father; on the other, the hysteric's desire for an unsatisfied desire. The introduction of the Oedipal myth of psychoanalysis short-circuits the question of the hysteric's desire by guiding the hysteric's desire in the direction of the father. It is in this sense that Lacan says that the Oedipus complex gives consistency to the figure of the idealized father, and that it does so in the clinical setting.

Lacan's conclusion is that the introduction of the Oedipal myth was "dictated to Freud by the hysteric's insatisfaction" and also by what he calls "her theatre."[14] The Oedipus complex, which derives from the myth whose dynamics revolve around the father and his death, merely gives consistency to the figure of the idealized father. The complex undoubtedly has explanatory value, but this merely redoubles the hysteric's wish to produce knowledge that can lay claim to being the truth. For the hysteric, the Name-of-the-Father comes to fill the place of the master signifier S_1 where it acts as a point of blockage for this discourse that determines it.

I suggested earlier that there is a link between obsessional neurosis and the myth of the primal horde. We can begin with Lacan's comment that *Totem and Taboo* is a "neurotic product." I take this to mean that the work is a product of Freud's neurosis, and that the "something unanalyzed" in Freud crops up again in his encounter with obsessional neurosis. If this is so, then *Totem and Taboo* comes out of this encounter; it is Freud's response to the clinic of obsessional neurosis, just as the Oedipus complex is the product of his encounter with hysteria. And again, as with the Oedipus complex, it needs to be interpreted.

I return to the significant differences between the myth of the primal horde and the Oedipus complex. The first difference, which I outlined previously, is that in *Totem and Taboo* the relationship between the law and enjoyment is inverted in comparison to the Oedipus complex, since here the primal father's enjoyment of all the women *precedes* his murder at the hands of his sons and the establishment of the law. His enjoyment is in a sense the condition for the establishment of the law; in the Oedipus complex, on the other hand, the law precedes transgression.

Note a second difference, related to but different from the first, between the father of the Oedipus complex and the primal father. Of course, whereas the father of the Oedipus complex is himself subject to the law he transmits to his children, with the figure of the primal father we have an exception to this very law. The father of the primal horde is the *père sévère* ($\exists x \, \Phi x$), who is egotistical and jealous, a sexual glutton, a father who enjoys, who is not limited by any submission to the law of an order transcendent to him. His death moreover is no liberation for the sons, for his power to prohibit is only increased by his disappearance. Through his death the sons are even more strongly bound to the law of prohibition that returns in the form of his son's identification with him.

Note, and this is the third point, the striking development from the Oedipus complex to the myth of the father of *Totem and Taboo* and later of *Moses and Monotheism*. At the outset the father's function is clearly to pacify, regulate, and sublimate the omnipotence of the figure of the mother, called by Freud "the obscure power of the feminine sex." But by the end the father himself has assumed the power, obscurity, and cruelty of the omnipotence that his function was supposed to dissipate in the first place.

It is in the context of this critique of the Oedipus complex that Lacan introduces the four discourses. And central to the four discourses is the master's discourse, or, more specifically, the concept of the master itself. The interest of the four discourses, then, is that Lacan would like to dispense with the Oedipus complex—Freud's dream, he calls it—and the primal horde myth and replace them with a reference to the discourses. "A father," says Lacan, "has with the master only the most distant of relationships." And, he continues, "What Freud retains in fact, if not in intention, is very precisely what he designates as being the most essential in religion, namely, the idea of an all-loving father."[15]

There is one further consideration about Freud's *Totem and Taboo* that should be mentioned. The reference in this passage to the son's identification with the father, in relation to the ideal of acquiring his father's position, suggests that an answer to the question how in this myth the incest taboo arises should be sought in terms of an identification with the father and not merely in terms of a vaguely sociological theory of a social contract between equals. In the primal horde myth Freud attributes a crucial role in the establishment of prohibitions to the son's love for the primal father: "[The primal father] forced [the sons] into abstinence and *consequently* into the emotional ties with him and with one another, which could arise out of those of their impulsions that were inhibited in their sexual aim."[16] Now, there should be identification with the renounced object, whereas the actual vehicle of the frustration draws the subject's hatred and aggression upon himself. However, here, "forced abstinence" produces an emotional tie with the agent, in a way that runs counter to what we should expect on the theory.

There is a hiatus in Freud's views on identification, which I have discussed elsewhere; it is a hiatus concerning the identification with the father at the very moment at which he is also the agent who deprives the subject of his erotic satisfactions. The importance of this for the Oedipus complex should be obvious. As Lacan says:

> Love . . . relates to the father by virtue of the father's being the vehicle of castration. This is what Freud proposes in *Totem and Taboo*. It is insofar as the sons are deprived of women that they love the father—a bewildering remark that is sanctioned by the insight of a Freud.[17]

This brings us back to the relationship between the myth of the primal horde and obsessional neurosis, for if it is a product of an encounter with obsessional neurosis, then so too is the idea of an all-loving father. Yet this father-love combines with the father-who-enjoys to form the obsessional's master, the object of his *hainamoration*.

The consequences for the sons of murdering the father of the primal horde are not the ones expected by the sons—principally, access to a jouissance without limit—since no one accedes to the omnipotence of the vacated position. The prohibitions prior to the murder continue just as strongly afterwards because the sons agree upon them amongst themselves so that total and mutual destruction does not ensue. As Freud writes in *Moses and Monotheism*, "Each individual renounced his ideal of acquiring his father's position for himself and of possessing his mother and sisters. Thus the *taboo on incest* and the injunction to *exogamy* came about."[18]

Lacan's conclusion is that the Oedipus complex is "strictly unusable" in the clinical setting, so by implication it is unusable with respect to all hysteria. And he adds, "It is odd that this did not become clearer more quickly."[19] This is a remark that, given Lacan's long and detailed treatment of the Oedipus complex over many years, he is most likely directing at himself in the first instance. What takes the place of the Oedipus complex are the new reference points unfolding in this seminar: the introduction of a new concept of knowledge, S_2, the split between it and truth, and, importantly, the concept of master, which has "only the most distant of relationships" to the concept of father. These developments enable the Oedipus complex to play the role of knowledge claiming to be truth, which is to say that in the figure of the analyst's discourse, knowledge is located in the site of truth.

$$\frac{a}{S_2} \quad \rightarrow \quad \frac{\$}{S_1}$$

Analyst's discourse

The Oedipus complex does not regulate the hysteric's desire; the hysteric's discourse is, rather, the result, the product—in the form of knowledge claiming to be truth—of the discourse by which it is determined, and which Lacan writes in the following way:

$$\frac{\$}{a} \quad \rightarrow \quad \frac{S_1}{S_2}$$

Hysteric's discourse

The hysteric presents as a subject divided by his or her symptoms ($); he or she produces knowledge (S_2) and solicits the master signifier in the other (S_1).

> She doesn't give up her knowledge. She unmasks ... the master's function with which she remains united, ... [and] which she evades in her capacity as object of his desire. This is the ... function ... of idealized father.[20]

She wants the other to be a master, she wants him to know many things, but all the same not that he know enough not to believe that she is the supreme price of all his knowledge. In other words, as Lacan puts it, she wants a master over whom she can reign; that she should reign, and that he not govern.

Chapter 4

Signifier and Object in the Transference

The dualism in Lacanian psychoanalysis, often evoked by Jacques-Alain Miller, of signifier and object is prominent in the transference.

Freud variously describes the transference as suggestion, repetition, resistance, love, and even as a combination of all of these. He rejected the term *suggestion* quite early on, preferring to speak of "transference," and he did so for two reasons: First, whatever the force behind hypnosis, Freud wanted to distinguish it from the forces at work in psychoanalysis; second, and more importantly, the catchall phrase, "suggestion," appealed to as an explanation of all phenomena of influence, including not just psychoanalysis but hypnosis as well, was far too vague a term and served no real explanatory power—a point well made by David Sach's response to Adolf Grünbaum.[1]

The term *transference*, *Übertragung*, appears for the first time in *The Interpretation of Dreams*, where for some reason it is translated as "transcript." Freud describes how dreams are constructed out of the day's residues, that is, the insignificant and trivial memories that remain from the day preceding the dream itself. The dream strips these memories of their original meaning and reinvests them with new meaning. This "transference" of meaning operates in accordance with unconscious desires that thus disguise themselves in otherwise innocent representations. Desires express themselves through the medium of representations acceptable by virtue of their very banality; they seize upon forms that have little value in themselves and function in dreams separated from their initial meaning. These dream elements, which have little value in themselves and function in dreams as separated from their initial meaning, are best seen as signifiers.

The first appearance of the transference in Freud is therefore bound up with the general process of formations of the unconscious—dreams, slips of the tongue and pen, the forgetting of names, and bungled actions, as well as symptoms.

Freud later gave "transference" a more narrow meaning, applying it to a phenomenon that arises only within the analytic discourse,
where desire becomes attached to something quite specific—namely,
the person of the analyst. But the connection to the early use is not
merely verbal, for desire attaches less to the person than to the signifier of the analyst. The signifier of the analyst is a place or a position
within the analytic discourse. It is occupied by the analyst as person,
but the analyst should neither be identified nor, as we shall see, identify himself with this position.

There is a further reason for drawing a distinction between the
analyst as a person in flesh and blood and the analyst as a signifier,
a place within the transference relation. It concerns the quasi-automatic
manner in which the transference arises. If, as Freud says, the transference bears all of the hallmarks of being in love, then we need to ask
why it occurs more or less automatically, when falling in love requires
such specific conditions. Lacan put it this way in his first seminar,
which was on Freud's papers on technique:

> How can a transference be so easily generated in neurotics,
> when they are so fettered when it comes to love? The produc-
> tion of a transference has an absolutely universal character,
> truly automatic, whereas the demands of love are, on the con-
> trary, as everyone knows, so specific.[2]

Thus the transference is the point at which the analyst as signifier becomes the object of the analysand's desire. This calls for two observations.

The first, which I take from Jacques-Alain Miller, is that the
analyst is not external to the unconscious but internal to it.[3] This is
an observation that we ultimately need to appeal to anyway, to explain a number of readily observable phenomena. It explains both
the fact that analysands often dream *for* their analyst, as well as the
fact that, as Freud observed, "symptoms join in the conversation."
The analyst's implication in the unconscious means that there is no
vantage point outside the transference that would be accessible to
the analyst, from which the analyst can observe the analysand; the
analyst is called into question as much as the analysand. As in most
of these things, Freud gives the clearest illustration of this in his own
case studies, from which we learn as much about Freud as from *The
Interpretation of Dreams*.

What these observations on the transference suggest is that there
is a place in the subject's "inner world" that the analyst comes to
occupy. Most and probably all psychoanalytic theories recognize this,

for in acknowledging that the transference is the driving force of an analysis, there is an implicit recognition that the analyst's position is a formation of the unconscious. Differences tend to be over what this place is that the analyst comes, or should come, to occupy.

The second point is that Freud had discovered that formations of the unconscious could be deciphered and that symptoms could sometimes be lifted by this deciphering. But the transference came as a surprise, and an uncomfortable one at that. Freud did not expect to discover that the analyst would come to hold a special interest for the analysand, to occupy his thoughts, and perhaps even become his love object. In its early days the psychoanalytic method could have been regarded as applied hermeneutics, since symptoms were shown to have a hidden meaning that when deciphered and conveyed to the subject would cause a symptom to disappear. This was the truly golden age of psychoanalysis, when an afternoon strolling through the streets of Leyden with Professor Freud could cure a man of his sexual impotence and, as he was also a composer, bring him to understand why the most noble passages of his compositions would be spoiled by the intrusion of some commonplace ditty.[4]

The age soon passed, as we know, and Freud was led to the analysis of resistances, or analysands' refusal to admit the hidden meaning of their symptoms. This difficulty in getting an analysand to acknowledge the meaning, sometimes even the existence, of symptoms led to the belief that a force must be overcome before the symptoms could be removed. It was as if the unconscious had made itself less accessible to analysis, to the point where the various modifications in technique Freud introduced became necessary as a result of the evolution in the nature of the unconscious itself.

There is something charmingly innocent nowadays in many of the symptoms described in the early *Studies on Hysteria* and a guilelessness in Freud's interpretation of them—for instance, the hysteric's shortness of breath as a symptom associated with overhearing the mounting excitement of a couple making love. Following up Freud's discovery that because the transference, far from making the analysand a willing collaborator in the task of deciphering his own text, is actually a form of resistance, many post-Freudians concluded that analysis was to be regarded as an interpersonal relationship, an intersubjectivity that was only contingently mediated by language. This is a fundamental point shared by those techniques that aim at analyzing the resistance, the development of empathy, or the countertransference. Lacan is widely regarded as holding the opposite view, namely, that language is paramount in analysis. One can see why Lacan has been read as promoting the function of the signifier in psychoanalysis—not least because for a long time Lacan himself emphasized this very aspect. However, Lacan emphasizes the object equally strongly, even more strongly in his later work. And we need to discuss both signifier and object.

To return to an earlier point, which was that Freud introduced modifications in technique because of an evolution in the nature of the unconscious, it can be argued that both the unconscious and symptoms have a history. This is difficult to reconcile with the claim that the unconscious is an instinctual reservoir but quite simple to understand if it is essentially linguistic in nature.

Further, it can be argued that the unconscious is essentially a discourse, not merely structured like a language, and that with changes in the nature of this discourse, the nature of interpretation itself has also been forced to undergo modification.

Now, symptoms undergo not only historical change, but when an analysand enters analysis, their symptoms will all take on a new meaning. Freud observed this phenomenon under the name of transference meaning *Übertragungsbedeutung*. However, if it is true that symptoms take on a new meaning in analysis, then it follows that they are not fixed and frozen but change according to the person to whom they are addressed. Lacan has expressed this by saying that the symptom is addressed to the Other. The Other is not so much a person as a place, a "locus," required by the structure of discourse.

We can now give an indication of the analyst's position in analysis by saying that he is situated in the place of the Other, the place to which the message is addressed, and thus becomes its receiver. As Lacan states in "Psychoanalysis and Its Teaching," "It is only owing to the place of the Other that the analyst can receive the investiture of the transference that qualifies him to play his legitimate role in the subject's unconscious."[5]

Freud saw that the locus of the Other is also capable of provoking love—real love—in the analysand, and the erotic component of this love is often unmistakable. His remarks in "Observations on Transference-Love" on the obligation of the analyst in such a context are worth noting. Professional ethics requires that the analyst refrain from entering any sort of liaison in the circumstances; but, he says, more fundamentally, to form a liaison would run counter to the intention of the analytic treatment. The reason for this is that the transference is a repetition of unconscious desires mainly formed in childhood; in the transference these desires are transferred onto the analyst, making him their object. This is how the woman came to fall in love with Freud. But the aim of analysis is to get the analysand to remember and thereby to bring unconscious desires within the range of things over which the subject has the ability to make a choice. But the aim of remembering can only be achieved where the analyst refuses to allow the repetition actually to take place, since remembering can only occur in place of repetition. And so to form a liaison would be to allow the patient's unconscious the desired repetition, which thereby frustrates the capacity to remember and the aim of the treatment.

Although Freud suggests that transference love differs from real love by its intensity, he is more impressed by their similarities—both transference love and real love are repetitions of behavior stereotyped by conditions registered within the subject, ready to emerge under favorable external circumstances.

Lacan introduced a new concept for the place in analysis to which the analysand's message is addressed, *le sujet supposé savoir,* as a way of unifying the diverse forms under which the transference expresses itself in Freud's work, where it appears as resistance, repetition, love, and suggestion. It is not that the transference is one of these things and not the others, but rather that all are forms in which the transference can appear. As Jacques-Alain Miller has observed, the supposed subject of knowledge is the underlying constitutive principle of the transference, from which these various forms of the transference follow.

The supposed subject of knowledge is purely the consequence of this quite unusual type of discourse, the analytic discourse, in which the transference emerges as a direct consequence of following the "fundamental rule" of analysis that requires the subject to say whatever occurs to him or her, without being prevented by considerations of decency, displeasure, or irrelevance.

The key role the analyst plays in this context in which the analysand is invited to recount whatever occurs to him or her is to act as a guarantor; his presence guarantees that the result of speaking without any apparent purpose or intention will actually have a meaning, even if neither analyst nor analysand knows *what* it means. It is this very special and delicate arrangement that Lacan sees as the foundation of the phenomena that produce the transference in analysis.

The analyst's position of listener is not a purely passive one. Although the analysand is the active partner, Lacan repeatedly insisted that the listener's response, uptake, or interpretation decides not just the meaning of what is said but also the speaking subject's identity. It is true of all communication that an interlocutor has the power to decide the meaning of a speaker's words, and outside of analysis this power is shared, since one occupies both locutory and interlocutory positions. However, in psychoanalysis, the very structure of the relation is asymmetric, since one of the subjects delivers the material while the other listens. As the recipient of the material, the analyst also has the task of evaluating and, sometimes, interpreting it.

Analysis raises the question of the truth about oneself, and one undertakes to follow the fundamental rule as part of a commitment to it. However, an analysand does not seek this truth within himself or herself but looks to the analyst, in his role as Other, as the fundamental listener who decides on the meaning of the subject's discourse. This is why silence is so important, since it must leave enough space for truth to unfold within speech.

Otto Fenichel once observed that while a person may enter analysis with a demand for help in coping with this symptom or that neurotic condition, during analysis this demand will be transformed. It will eventually become the question: What is my desire? But also what does he (the analyst, the Other) want from me? Lacan argues that the analyst's silence is important here, too, and that he should not hasten to reply to this demand.

While the supposed subject of knowledge is a necessary requirement for psychoanalytic treatment, its emergence also constitutes a risk and a temptation. Michel Silvestre wrote that only with the emergence of the supposed subject of knowledge is it possible to avoid an imaginary, dual relationship and deflate the effects of the imaginary; at the same time, such a leverage point confers a degree of authority on the analyst, who is able to lend considerable weight to these same imaginary effects.

We find here, according to Silvestre, a reason to be circumspect regarding the technique of interpreting the transference. By means of the transference, repetition will implicate the analyst, who is thereby invited to interpret and expose the "false connections" made with his person. However, the subject's resolution of the transference is not a primary but a secondary effect of its interpretation. After all, the analysand knows all along that the analyst only reminds him of his father, or that he or she is merely repeating, with the analyst, aspects of his or her attitude towards his or her mother. However, Silvestre argues, if one merely detaches the signifier from the analyst through interpreting the transference, one will only manage to enhance its power over the analysand. The effect of separating the signifier from its imaginary accompaniments in the transference may well end up having the effect of purifying and thereby solidifying the subject's submission to the signifiers of his destiny. While the identification of the signifier with the analyst is thus avoided, it is at the cost of consolidating the analysand's subjection to the major signifiers (or "master signifier") of his history.[6]

I have said that there is a need to distinguish the person of the analyst from the analyst as a place or locus within the unconscious, that is, as subject supposed to know, a symbolic position that arises from the fundamental rule of analysis. I should like now to explore further why in Freud's view the analyst should never personally assume this position of the supposed subject of knowledge within analysis.

At his 1969–1970 seminar, *The Other Side of Psychoanalysis,* Lacan introduced the four discourses and spent much of the year elaborating on them: the master's discourse, the university discourse, the hysteric's discourse, and the analyst's discourse. As he points out, there is a close connection between the master's and the analyst's discourses, owing to the fact that the position of Other is a position of mastery. And over the short history of analysis there has been, despite Freud's explicit warnings, a temptation for analysts to fill this position and to exploit it in the interests of the patient.

This tendency sees analysis as a process of re-education that is to be brought about by virtue of the fact that the analyst is located as the analysand's superego. Note that the theory underlying this approach also amounts to assigning a position to the analyst in the unconscious. It holds that the analyst must occupy the place of the superego, and that the cure is the process of the analysand's identification with the analyst as superego. The belief here is that the analyst, from his position of superego, will be able to inject positive values into the subject's ego.

On this approach an analysis appears above all as a strategy for educating, or better, re-educating the analysand by suggestion, and the analyst offers himself as the measure of reality who will, by virtue of his authority, lead the subject to a superior conception of reality and a better adaptation to it. The most obvious and immediate difficulty with this approach, as Lacan was quick to point out, is that the judge of the superiority of conceptions of reality and of what is best for the analysand can ultimately only be the analyst himself.

It is then difficult to see how psychoanalytic treatment can be anything other than yet another enterprise of indoctrination, thereby becoming an attempt to crush a fundamentally uneducable desire. One can comprehend that the analysand becomes engaged in a constantly repeated struggle against the analyst's effort of indoctrination, against the analyst as a person who is full, as surely we all are, of his own prejudices.

In a paper that has been one of the most influential pieces on the question of the analyst's role in the treatment, in large measure setting the terms of subsequent debate, James Strachey argues explicitly for the view that the analyst should operate from the position of superego:

> Thus there are two convergent lines of argument which point
> to the patient's superego as occupying a key position in ana-
> lytic therapy: it is a part of the patient's mind in which a
> favorable alteration would be likely to lead to general im-
> provement, and it is a part of the patient's mind which is
> especially subject to the analyst's influence.[7]

Strachey indicates that he draws this conclusion about the suitability
of the superego to psychoanalytic intervention from Chapter 8 of *Group
Psychology and the Analysis of the Ego*. But in the passage Strachey draws
on, Freud is attempting to give an account of the power of "suggestion" in hypnosis. Freud's reason for doing this, in this uncannily
prophetic work on group psychology written in 1921, was to grasp
how it is that the members of a group can all come to identify with the
group's leader, and how their egos and behavior become "standard-
ized." Yet this particular type of ego identification with a leader is
what Strachey appeals to as the source of the analyst's power in analysis! A theory developed to account for hypnosis and for the power of
a leader over the group is being used to give an explanation of the
power of psychoanalysis itself. It is odd, to say the least, that Strachey
should use precisely this part of Freud dealing with a group's identification with a leader to attempt to articulate in his own way that the
analyst is located in the place of the Other.

However, the most serious difficulty with Strachey's view lies
elsewhere; it bears upon his conclusion that the analyst must put himself in the place of the analysand's superego so that the analysand will
identify with the analyst. Here we have a clear illustration of why
Lacan believed it necessary to " return to Freud," the original sense of
Freud's discovery having come to be distorted and lost.

While the superego may preserve a form of "adaptation to reality" for the subject, it is an adaptation completely unadapted to the
current situation, for in no way is the agency of the superego in contact with *present* reality. While the Freudian superego is a legal code,
it is an archaic one, one that carries out its function automatically and
blindly—this is the reason Freud links it to the compulsion to repeat
and the death drive. Its demands are incoherent. It is a law, an injunction, that it is impossible for the subject to obey. Lacan refers to what
he calls the "obscene and ferocious figure of the superego."[8] Insatiable
and insistent, it lies beyond the pleasure principle, which subsides
once satisfaction is achieved.

All of this is already in Freud. One can refer to any number of
passages, but there is one in particular where, in an inversion of Kant's

wonder and awe at the starry skies above and the moral law within, he describes the insatiability of the superego.

> Conscience (or, more correctly, the anxiety which later becomes conscience) is indeed the cause of drive renunciation to begin with, but . . . later the relationship is reversed. Every renunciation of drive now becomes a dynamic source of conscience and every fresh renunciation increases the latter's severity and intolerance.[9]

A third issue calls for comment with respect to Strachey's views on the position of the analyst. It concerns the shift towards the ego. Underlying Strachey's appeal to the power of the superego, and determining the entire orientation of his approach, is a view, dominant in analysis since Freud, that involves a deep and significant shift in the orientation of the entire framework of psychoanalysis. It is, again, against this shift that in the 1950s Lacan was arguing, in his appeal to a "return to Freud."

Actually this shift started to take place in Freud's own lifetime, the 1930s, which became for him a period of increasing doctrinal isolation. Support for his views on sexuality and the Oedipus complex, the death drive, and the splitting of the ego declined in the psychoanalytic movement, and the shift towards the ego is already part of this shift.

What orients Strachey's view that the analyst should use the position of superego in the interests of the analysand's re-education is that therapeutic progress is to be assessed from the perspective of the ego—in other words, that the modification of the ego is the measure of therapeutic success. Ernest Jones was quite right in saying, in the wonderfully titled "The Concept of a Normal Mind," that if we view an analytic cure from the perspective of ego modification, then the therapeutic aim has to be conceived in one of two general forms: either leading to a better adaptation of the ego, person, or personality to reality, both internal and external, or producing an increase in the ego's capacity for attaining happiness or well-being.[10]

Various views about the means of achieving these ends essentially come down to increasing the freedom of the ego, whether by reinforcing it, by making the unconscious conscious, or by replacing the unconscious superego with a harmonious conscience: (1) The ego has expanded at the expense of the id and superego. (2) The energy of the id is discharged towards the outer world via the ego and not independently of it. All these statements are merely different ways of saying the same thing.

Not only does Freud's "Copernican Revolution," however, signal a radical move away from the perspective of the ego but also the whole ethic of psychoanalysis runs counter to the view that treatment in analysis consists in the subject's identifying himself or herself with the analyst. Treatment is premised on what Lacan calls the "original pact" of analysis, on the free consent and liberty of the patient. As the recent biography of Sidonie Csillag, Freud's young homosexual woman, makes clear, the difficulties encountered in her analysis with Freud were insurmountable because her family forced her into analysis against her own wishes; the necessary pact between analyst and analysand was never a possibility under these conditions. And to conceptualize analysis as a further alienation of the subject through an identification with the analyst completely contradicts the requirement of the analysand's consent.

The discussion of the transference has so far been couched in terms such as "subject," "Other," "signifier," all of which are terms of the symbolic order. What of the old objection that this is to ignore affect, the most crucial part of the transference? Affect is also an expression of transference love, and transference love is all important in the treatment. This is because affect results from the analyst's presence as something other than a signifier; from the presence of the analyst as object in the treatment. It is now time to turn to a discussion of the object.

It is not true that for Lacan everything in the transference operates at the level of the signifier. It is true, however, that as formations of the unconscious, symptoms are fully analyzable; they are, as Freud saw, nothing but symbolic structures. What, then, lies *beyond* the signifier?

Freud grasps that there is something *beyond* the signifier at work in both symptoms and the transference with the concept of the drive, both in the form of libido and in the death drive. But there are some other remarks to which I should like to draw your attention. There is, first of all, Freud's admittedly rather enigmatic remark in "The Dynamics of Transference" in reference to the transference that nothing is destroyed *in absentia* or *in effigie*.[11] Yet if the symptom is *just* a *symbolic* structure, then it ought to be fully displaceable from object to object, and there should thus be no reason to consider the analyst as other than a mere substitute, a place marker, in an endless play of signifiers circulating from one person to another. That is, transference would be mere repetition, and the view that the transference is just a form of repetition is consistent with the idea that the transference is symbolic. If the symptom is purely a formation of the unconscious and therefore a function of the signifier, then it would appear to be par excellence that which *can* be destroyed *in effigie*.

The second indication that Freud is looking beyond the signifier is, therefore, that the transference is not *just* repetition, for which an explanation in terms of a pure signifying chain could be exhaustively given—repetition as a function of the signifying chain is precisely the sort of explanation Lacan was formulating in the seminars of the 1950s. Interpretation limited to the play of signifiers is just the basis on which Serge Leclaire's analysis of the "licorne" dream proceeds.[12] But in recognizing that the transference is also love, we are obliged to acknowledge the sometimes massive, sometimes subtle presence of the analyst qua object as something other than pure symbolic place marker.

Let me briefly elaborate on this function of the object by first referring to some of the developments in Lacan's own work on the question of desire.

Desire was, for Lacan, initially modeled on intersubjectivity. At the outset he characterized desire as the desire for recognition and the end of analysis as the recognition of desire.[13] There are, however, two difficulties with this view that soon became apparent. First, there is, as Freud points out at the end of *The Interpretation of Dreams*, the indestructibility of desire. How is it possible that desire is indestructible if desire is desire for recognition? Second, if desire is desire for recognition, then why does it express itself in such obscure terms? To be sure, these are not insurmountable difficulties, but overcoming them became irrelevant once Lacan had developed the theory of metaphor and metonymy as fundamental structures of the signifier. This development led to the articulation of a second position, which ascribes the cause of desire to the signifier. This is the view, put forward, though not unambiguously, in "The Instance of the Letter in the Unconscious or Reason since Freud," concerning the metonymy of desire: The object of desire is always a metonymy for the cause of desire; desire is always desire for something else, related metonymically to the cause of desire.[14] Whereas the cause of desire is here regarded as symbolic, in a third phase, dating from the 1959–1960 seminar on *The Ethics of Psychoanalysis*, the cause of desire came to be regarded as the real, in the form of *objet a*. Moreover, we must regard the development of the concept of *objet a* as of no small moment, given that Lacan regularly referred to it as his most important contribution to psychoanalysis.

In order to appreciate properly this category of the object and its function in the real, we need to return to Freud who is, as always, the major source for Lacan's own conceptualization.

On certain of the sociological readings of psychoanalysis, it is thought that for psychoanalysis the only reason sexuality plays a role in the etiology of the neuroses is that there are social forces opposing its free expression. Whether or not these forces are necessary is of course another question, but the argument is that *social forces* cause sexuality to be repressed and hence traumatic.

However, this view ignores Freud's repeated contention that the *very encounter* with sexuality is itself traumatic—a contention that begins with the so-called "seduction" theory and persists to this observation in *Civilization and Its Discontents*: "Sometimes one seems to perceive that it is . . . something in the nature of the [sexual] function itself which denies us full satisfaction and urges us along other paths."[15] Is this anything different from Lacan's aphorism, "There is no sexual rapport?"[16]

The second observation, which is related to the first, is that after prevaricating for some time over Otto Rank's theory of birth trauma, according to which birth is the prototype of all later traumatic experiences, Freud came to a categorical opinion: The ultimate source of trauma is castration.

Though of course they need further discussion, these brief indications nevertheless indicate Freud's view that sexuality *itself* is traumatic; and Lacan's contribution has been to theorize how it is that trauma is related to a lack, ultimately a lack in the Other, and how it is that the *objet a* is the stopgap located in the place of this lack.

There is a second point. The *objet a* plays an important role in the formation of fantasy in the psychic life of the subject. (Consider the matheme for fantasy, $\$ \diamond a$.) Though, as I say, the theorization of *objet a* was repeatedly described by Lacan as his major contribution to psychoanalysis, it is already implicit in Freud that in fantasy there is something that lies *beyond* the symbolic.

Not until 1919, with the crucial paper "A Child Is Being Beaten," did fantasy take on a special significance in Freud's work. His interest in fantasy followed closely on a period in which a practice based exclusively on formations of the unconscious and directed towards the treatment of symptoms began to encounter real and disturbing difficulties. Lacan points out that whereas it is *obvious* that the unconscious is implicated in the treatment, because of the manner in which interpretation interacts with symptoms, there is a particularly striking "inertia" associated with fantasy—particularly surprising in comparison to the responsiveness to analysis of the symbolic formations of the unconscious. He is struck by the apparent isolation of a fundamental fantasy from any symbolic network, as is indicated, for example, by the difficulty analysands have talking about their fundamental fantasy, in associating to it, as well as in its permanence and resistance to treatment.

It seems that this attention to the nature of fantasy was one of the reasons that led Freud in the 1920s to his second theory of the psychical apparatus (ego, superego, and id) and to the new drive dualism (libido and death drive).

From the mid-1970s Lacan came to consider that conducting or directing the treatment must ultimately center on constructing the analysand's fantasy. This work of construction cannot, as I am suggesting Freud saw, be reduced solely to interpreting formations of the unconscious. The reason is that the subject's position in relation to the *objet a*, to what *causes* his or her desire, is not modified by working on symbolic identifications and other unconscious formations. The symbolic operations are valid for working upon symptoms, but fantasy is *not* subject to these laws of interpretation. Fantasy is *not* interpretable. Marie-Hélène Brousse points out that it nevertheless remains the fixed point, the hub, around which interpretation revolves because of the role that transference *love* gives to the analyst.[17] The analyst retains a quality of an enigma—"What does he want?"—through which the lack in the Other is brought to life again. (Lacan calls this the "hysterization" of the subject.) As Lacan says: "Fantasy effectively holds the key to the place that the analyst occupies for the subject, which is the place of the real."[18]

The *objet a* is for Lacan the object as such, the object "in the real." Although the *objet a* is vehiculed by language as a result or product of the signifier, it nevertheless evades expression in or capture by all signifiers and appears as what is ineffable or unsayable, as falling outside signification. The object is not specular and therefore not imaginary. It is not symbolizable and thus not a signifier. It is an object, but a lost object.

It is this lost object, caught up in the drive, that is the cause of the division of the subject. It is therefore essential to the subject's entry into analysis, where this division must be inscribed in the transference in what Lacan has called the subject's "hysterization."

Freud described psychoanalysis as the third impossible profession—alongside governing and educating. Impossible or not, the aim of analysis is neither to govern nor to educate. Freud became increasingly preoccupied toward the end of his life with the tendency to view the analyst's role as that of fulfilling the superego functions of moral educator and spiritual adviser. In the final months of his life, in "An Outline of Psychoanalysis," Freud raised the question whether the position the analyst is placed in by the analysand gives him the opportunity for a sort of after-education of his patient. But he warns against this on the grounds that it runs counter to the ethics of psychoanalysis:

> But at this point a warning must be given against misusing this new influence. However much the analyst may be tempted to become a teacher, model analyst and ideal for other people and to create men in his own image, he should not forget that that is not his task in the analytic relationship, and indeed that he will be disloyal to his task if he allows himself to be led on by his inclinations.[19]

It is this ethic that the analyst's assumption of the position of superego runs counter to.

The analyst has the function of guaranteeing the analytic experience, that is, he intervenes legitimately in his role as Other, as master, when the framework of the analytic relation has to be maintained, while within this framework it is the subject that does the work.

The end of an analysis, which is the discovery that there is no real supposed subject of knowledge, constitutes the desire of the analyst; a very singular desire that Freud placed at a certain moment in history, the analyst's desire not to identify with the Other, to respect what Freud calls the patient's individuality, not to be his ideal, model, or educator but to leave the way open to the subject's own desire. Here there is something ascetic, and Lacan believed that analysts had often worked against the analytic discourse. Through placing the analyst in the position of superego, many had taken exactly the opposite path, that of offering themselves as ideals and models.

Lacan is closer to Melanie Klein, in whose theory the end of an analysis has a depressive character that shows it must be brought into connection to object loss. Object loss, the mourning of a love object, is symbolized in analysis by the rejection or abandonment of the psychoanalyst. The psychoanalyst therefore represents the residue, the detritus of the psychoanalytic operation. And it was Lacan who developed the theory that makes the analyst the reject of the operation, but at the same time the cause that all along animated the patient's desire. The end of analysis is the rejection, the refusal of the analyst as master signifier, as master of the sense of the subject's speech. This renunciation of the master in the psychoanalyst is something quite paradoxical and enigmatic. Never before Freud has such a theory for nonmastery been developed, and Jacques-Alain Miller suggests that it is perhaps because this desire is so completely novel that some psychoanalysts have renounced it. However, for others, including Lacan, the greatness of Freud was to have committed himself to this place of reject.

It is tempting for the analyst to become his patient's therapist and act, since his integrity is not in doubt, according to the patient's best interests—evaluated, and here is the rub, according to his own lights.

I have, however, been trying to present a rather different view, one that holds not only that the superego is an agent of repression and cannot be used to undo repression, but more importantly that therapy as re-education contradicts the ethics of psychoanalysis, premised on the absence of control and direction, on what Freud calls the dignity of the person.

Chapter 5

Regulating Psychoanalysis

On Wednesday, October 8, 2003, the French National Assembly passed a bill intended to regulate, for the first time, the practice of psychotherapy in France. Moved by Bernard Accoyer, a medical doctor and member of the Union for a Popular Movement, the conservative party of which Jacques Chirac is a member, the purpose of the legislation was to restrict the practice of psychotherapy to psychiatrists and clinical psychologists; it would effectively no longer be legal for any other practitioners, including psychoanalysts, to practice in the sphere of mental health.

Although the bill was passed without debate and, apparently, without objection in the Assembly, there has been a mixed but on the whole vociferous public response since. Most notably, an action group called the "Forum des Psys," established by Jacques-Alain Miller, has brought together, in united opposition to the new legislation, the Ecole de la Cause Freudienne and various groups from the field of "Psys," as the vast therapeutic industry in France is commonly referred to.[1] There have been other offshoots as well, such as the association "Vive la Psychanalyse!" that Judith Miller founded with the aim of promoting psychoanalysis in the public domain. Catherine Clément, Roland Dumas, Bernard-Henry Lévy, and Philippe Sollers, all members of the association's council, have been vocal opponents of the new legislation, both at public forums and in the press. Bernard-Henry Lévy has described the legislation as a giant backward step that takes us back some hundred years to a scientism that one would have thought the Freudian "break" had done away with. He predicted that the legislation would be the death of psychoanalysis. Jean-Claude Milner, eminent linguist and social commentator, has referred to "a mortal alliance between scientism, managerial ideology, and unrestricted regulatory control."[2]

Despite the unremarkable passage of the bill through its first reading in the Assembly, by the time it arrived in the Senate on January 19, 2004, it had become clear that the bill would not pass unchallenged. The government was able to curtail opposition to and

69

circumvent possible failure of the legislation in the Senate by presenting a modified version of the "Accoyer Bill," as it had come to be
known, and to present it as a "Government Bill," presented by the
then minister for health, Jean-François Mattéi. The effect of presenting
the legislation in the form of a government bill was that the text would
have to be voted on without amendment. The novelty of this second
bill, now known as the "Mattéi Bill," was to propose the establishment
of a National Register of Psychotherapists maintained by the prefecture. Three categories of practitioners were exempt from the requirement: those with medical degrees, registered psychologists, and, last
but not least, psychoanalysts who are registered members of a psychoanalytic association, as indicated by the membership records of their
association. It might seem that this modification would be sufficient to
appease the psychoanalysts opposed to the legislation and to allay the
concerns it gave rise to. Indeed, one group of psychoanalytic associations, which calls itself "the Contact Group," embracing Lacanians
and non-Lacanians alike, welcomed the new legislation, citing its recognition of the "specificity" of psychoanalysis and the "irreplaceable
role it plays in the training and the qualification of its members."[3] The
response of Jacques-Alain Miller, on the other, was immediate and
categorical: This legislation is worse than the original, a view he has
been supported in by both the Ecole de la Cause Freudienne and
members of the public. I return to this issue later.

When the bill was referred back to the National Assembly for the
second reading, it was to undergo yet further modification. The bill,
now referred to as the "Dubernard Bill," opined that

> The practice of psychotherapy requires either theoretical and
> practical training in clinical psychopathology or training rec-
> ognized by a psychoanalytic association.

> Use of the title of psychotherapist is restricted to professionals
> who are registered in a national register of psychotherapists.

> Registration is recorded on a list maintained by the State in
> the department of residence.

> This list indicates the training undertaken by the professional. It is
> updated, made available to the public, and published regularly.

> Accredited medical doctors, registered psychologists, and psy-
> choanalysts who are registered members of their association

are exempt from registration. The application of the present article is fixed by decrees in the Conseil d'Etat.[4]

Finally, on July 9, 2004, the Senate's second reading of the bill took place. The Dubernard Bill, which had been adopted by the National Assembly on its second reading, was further modified and adopted as the Giraud Bill, which refocused on the use of the title of psychotherapist rather than on the practice of psychotherapy.

The details are not important because as the text of the Senate and National Assembly bills remained at variance following the second reading in both houses, a joint commission of the two houses was convoked in order to establish a form of legislation that would be acceptable to both houses.

The Joint Commission met at the end of July and adopted the final form of the legislation, which was gazetted in the *Journal Officiel* on August 11, thereby becoming law.[5] It states the same requirement, that

1. all psychotherapists must be registered on a record maintained by the government; and

2. this record must be made available to the public and published regularly.

It then restates the by now familiar exclusion clause concerning doctors, psychologists, and psychoanalysts.

Medical practitioners and qualified psychologists and psychoanalysts registered as members in the records of their association have a legal entitlement to register.

And it adds a final clause concerning the decree that will be all-important to its implementation.

A decree in the Conseil d'Etat specifies the manner of application of the present article and the conditions for the theoretical and practical training in clinical psychopathology that must be fulfilled by persons referred to in the second and third paragraphs.

Now that the legislation has become law in France, the question is what to make of it. As mentioned earlier, Jacques-Alain Miller was even more vigorously opposed to the amended version of the original that was endorsed on the first reading in the Senate. To see why, and to consider whether these concerns still apply to the final form of the legislation, one needs to understand the place of decrees in French law, where the difference between statute law (adopted by the Parliament) and regulation by decree is fundamentally important. The manner in which a law is applied can be determined by decrees drafted by the executive branch rather than by the legislature; these are administrative actions, and, as such, though sometimes they require approval by the Conseil d'État, they are obviously not drafted as openly and are not subject to as much debate, as is parliamentary legislation. There are different sorts of decrees in France, but the basic principle remains the same: the government establishes, through its bureaucracy, the means by which the statute is to be implemented. In the present case, the wording of the legislation combines with the behavior of the government over this issue to lead one to fear the worst: boards responsible for making the decisions sympathetic to the position of the Minister of Health and acting from a perspective that favors a medicalization of psychotherapeutic practices and the ascendancy of cognitivist currents in psychology.

Note that the final legislation no longer gives medical practitioners the right to automatically register as a psychotherapist, irrespective of their training. Mr. Giraud maintains that registration of medical practitioners will be restricted to those who have specialist training, but while it was difficult to see how the Giraud Bill could be interpreted to support this assertion, it has been inscribed in the gazetted law.

Nevertheless, there are other difficulties with the legislation. There is, for instance, the somewhat arbitrary distinction between psychoanalyst and psychotherapist, the grounds for which have not been well argued. Furthermore, to suggest, as did Bernard Accoyer when he initially proposed the legislation, that it was motivated by a desire to protect the public from charlatanism and all the snake oil merchants (my words, not his) of this world who prey on an unsuspecting public would appear to be an idle claim if the legislation leaves it open to any group of psychotherapists to unite as a group of "psychoanalysts" and register under that category.

The strategy of some analytic groups in France has been to accept the legislation as guaranteeing their presence on the list of categories of professionals authorized to practice psychotherapy. This has been the position of the "Contact Group," for instance, which has simply noted that the Senate recognizes the "specificity" of psychoanalysis and the irreplaceable role that associations play in the qualification and training of their members.

Philippe Douste-Blazy, the new health minister since April 2004, has indicated that while he has not had the time to meet representatives of all the professions involved, as the person responsible for drafting the future decree regarding the training required for registered psychotherapists, he "undertook to allow an extensive debate, a wide-ranging gathering of information and reflection that would produce a consensus amongst the professionals."[6]

The expansion of administrative control over the lives and practices of members of the public and professions is a feature of contemporary society and, although it may appear innocuous, there are grounds for thinking the movement insidious. Whatever the reassurances of the minister concerning seeking consultation and achieving consensus, increased regulation, with its needless time wasting and costly compliance process, now appears inevitable. Perhaps this is nothing more than a nuisance, and if it produces a higher standard of professional practice, then the price may be worth paying. But the fear is that the temptation to further increase regulation and control is one that bureaucracy finds difficult to resist. Once the door of accountability is opened—and it is always opened with the best of intentions—control and compliance requirements expand. Who can be confident that the decrees will not, with time, impose increasingly arbitrary and irrelevant restrictions on the requirements that must be met for practitioners to practice and expanded measures for exclusion? What information will be gathered and what databases will be set up, and how will the information be used?

The legislation will have the effect of introducing a de facto distinction between psychoanalysts who are qualified medical practitioners or registered psychologists, on the one hand, and the rest, which in France have been dubbed "the ni-ni" or the "neither-nors." While the legislation gives de jure recognition to doctors, clinical psychologists, *and* psychoanalysts, the consequences are different in each case, owing to the differences between medical registration via the Ordre des Médecins, which has statutory recognition in France, the registration of psychologists on the basis of academic qualifications, and the registration of psychoanalysts on the basis of their membership in a psychoanalytic association. It is foreseeable that registration of psychoanalysts will significantly modify the status of a psychoanalytic association, which will henceforth have a legal reporting status, given that it will be required to maintain a register of members with legal status.

Moreover, some associations currently have nonpracticing members. This includes the Ecole de la Cause Freudienne, whose directory speaks of "members who practice psychoanalysis," implying that practicing is not a requirement of membership, and adds that practicing members come under two categories: those who, admitted as members of the school by the School's Council, have declared that they practice psychoanalysis and are registered as practicing analysts, and those the ad hoc Committee of the Guarantee has guaranteed as having met the training that the school provides, on whom the title "Analyst Member of the School" is conferred.[7] The number of nonanalyst members of the Ecole de la Cause Freudienne may be small, but the principle is nevertheless a venerable one, having its origins in the Ecole Freudienne de Paris.

A moment's reflection is enough to make one realize some fairly specific and detailed criteria for the registration of psychoanalysts will have to come out of the administrative decree to be presented by the minister of health. In the absence of such measures, the legislation alone, absurdly, might allow for any two people to found an organization that they could call an association of psychoanalysis, have it registered at the prefecture, and subsequently declare oneself a member of this psychoanalytic association. This even suggests a sort of guerilla response in the form of bureaucratic sabotage, with a series of spurious organizations, all with one or two members.

Something like the category of Analyst Member of the School may well be destined to become all-pervasive under the new law, since this is the one category that will really matter from the point of view of legislation. One can expect that the basis upon which the title is to be conferred by the school will be compelled to comply with whatever the requirements of the decree are. Either that or a new fourth category will need to be introduced. In either case, the new legal obligations of the school will no doubt challenge the principle that Lacanian psychoanalysis is a practice with "no standards but not without principles." The category "Practicing Analyst," at least in the sense in which it was introduced by Lacan and adopted by the Ecole de la Cause Freudienne, seems destined to disappear, because the ministerial decree will establish conditions for registration that any association will effectively be required to see that its practicing analyst members satisfy.

While the new legislation speaks in terms of guaranteeing the qualification and training of psychotherapists, by framing the law in terms of membership of an association, it leads to potentially absurd situations. Some psychoanalysts have opted not to belong to any psychoanalytic organization, but their training and competence have never been at issue. Equally, the situation has arisen and could always arise again where, for different reasons, analysts resign from their association. On the basis of the new legislation, in such cases analysts will no longer be able legally to practice; and in reality, the force of the law will commit analysts to remaining throughout their professional lives members of an association.

We do not know at this stage what requirements will be imposed upon psychoanalytic associations and will not know until the content of the ministerial decree (or *décret en Conseil d'État*, as it is more strictly called) is released, however, the following are possibilities.

Legal requirements: Will associations be required to exclude members if they have been convicted of a crime? The implications of this not only for the vetting of admissions and policing of the activities of members are rather horrific, but the scenario is not unrealistic.

Ethics: Will associations be required to implement a code of ethics and a complaints procedure? These typically cover such issues as responsibilities to the "client," as it has become increasingly common to call the "consumer" of therapeutic services, matters of exploitation, matters of confidentiality, contracts, involving informed consent, responsibilities to other professionals and the wider community, and a complaints procedure. It is highly unlikely that once psychoanalytic associations come under the jurisdiction of the law they will escape the requirement to implement a code of ethics and complaints procedure, the broad shape of which can be predicted on the basis of what such codes look like in the case of other regulated professions and professional bodies, and it is likely that every psychoanalytic association will be required to address all of the aforementioned issues.

What will the implications of such measures be for psychoanalysis, if, as I think is likely, they are implemented? It is possible to be rather blasé about the whole thing and declare that nothing much will change for either the better or the worse; on the one hand, cases where issues of compliance and complaints arise are extremely rare; on the other, it is not clear that a formal code is going to solve the more egregious perversions of psychoanalytic practice. It is not clear, for instance, that the Masud Khan scandal would have been any better addressed if a code of conduct had been in existence at the time. As was stated by the president of the British Psycho-Analytical Society, Donald Campbell, "Although there were rumours of inappropriate professional behaviour by Masud Khan, a case of malpractice could not be brought on the basis of rumour. I believe that attempts were made to encourage patients and ex-patients to come forward with a complaint, but none did so."[8] It is not too cynical to think that the code of conduct functions mainly as a public relations device to reassure the public that Something Will Be Done in the case of ethical misconduct.

There is the further point that government regulation will not improve standards of clinical training and theoretical formation; in fact, there is a case to be made for thinking that it will lead to their deterioration. There are two reasons. First, the standards of training required by ministerial decree will be both minimal and quantitative: together these characteristics imply that the conditions for qualification will be purely formal, as is the case with the registration of psychologists in France and elsewhere. The duration of the training will erroneously come to be taken to be the measure of the quality of the trainee. In the Ecole de la Cause Freudienne, which prides itself on being the School of the Pass, the pass is constructed around a completely different ethics, one that is consistent with and follows from the ethics of psychoanalysis: In the procedure of the pass, analysands give testimony not only about the process of an analysis—their own—thereby addressing, most valuably, the issue of research into the analytic experience, its outcomes, and its subjective effects, but it is also expected that they will make a contribution on "crucial problems of psychoanalysis."[9]

The last remark leads to a more disturbing trend in the current tendency towards regulation, or increased regulation, of psychoanalysis. In the mind of the regulators, one suspects, there is a conception of psychotherapists and ipso facto of psychoanalysts as technicians, as technicians of the unconscious as it were, whose technique and practice are straightforward and uncontroversial, at least amongst themselves. The consequence is that regulation, stagnation, and lack of innovation can all too naturally go hand in hand. Supposing the regulated environment had been put into place in 1954 and not 2004, would Lacan have been free to innovate in the way he did and change forever the nature of psychoanalytic practice?

In making these comments I am assuming that the new legislation is just the first step in a process of increasing regulation. Certain of the further developments discussed here flow directly from the legislation enacted in August 2004; this includes the conditions that we can expect to see stipulated in the *Décret en Conseil d'État* dealing with the implementation of the new law. This will occur in the short term. If the experience elsewhere and in other domains is anything to judge by, then we can expect that farther down the track the legislative and/or administrative interference in the field of "Psys" will increase inexorably. If this is correct, then it is a curiously shortsighted approach to think that psychoanalysis is protected by the new legislation that is only a threat to psychotherapy. It was Freud who spoke of psychoanalysis as the *primus inter pares* in the field of psychotherapy. Abandoning the larger psychotherapeutic community to its own devices, as agreeable as the sense of superiority may be, its origin is the narcissism of minor differences, and the attempt to form a united front of *all* the professionals directly concerned by the initial Accoyer Bill via the Forum des Psys will be shown to have been correct. Jacques-Alain Miller is no doubt correct in his judgment that the amended Mattéi legislation was worse than what it replaced, and that there is a logic to this development that will continue to unfold to the disadvantage of psychoanalysis: The inclusion of psychoanalysis in the amended legislation may turn out to be a hollow and short-lived victory if it leads to an increasingly significant impact upon the training and development of psychoanalysts.

It is important to view the legislation of the practice of psychotherapy in France in the context of what is potentially a profound change in the mental health sphere in France. The move towards quantitative, so-called "evidence-based" forms of intervention, along with the recent Cléry-Melin "Plan of Actions for the Development of Psychiatry and the Promotion of Mental Health," which Jacques-Alain Miller has critiqued, combine to indicate a disturbing tendency in approaches to issues in mental health.

Part 2

Analyzing Philosophers: Descartes, Kant, Žižek, Badiou, and Jakobson

Chapter 6

Lacan and Badiou

Logic of the Pas-Tout

"I see nobody on the road," said Alice.

"I only wish I had such eyes," the King remarked in a fretful tone. "To be able to see Nobody! And at that distance, too! Why, it's as much as I can do to see real people, by this light!"

—Carroll, *Through the Looking-Glass*

Logically, nothing, like nobody, is a universal: "Nothing is permanent" is equivalent to "Everything is nonpermanent." Its logical behavior is different from that of a proper name or noun; it is not a noun at all but what logicians call "a quantifier."[1]

The fact that "nothing" is a universal raises the question whether there is a logic of nothing that escapes the universal and remains on the side of incompleteness. The question has an important link to psychoanalysis, since Lacan, because of its centrality to the topic of sexuality, female sexuality in particular.

The logic of the nothing that is nonuniversalizable is precisely the logic of Lacan's *"pas-tout,"* which Lacan explores principally in *Seminar XX, Encore* (1972–1973) and in "L'Étourdit" (1973) in the form of the four formulas of sexuation.[2]

$$(\exists x)\sim\Phi x \qquad\qquad \sim(\exists x)\sim\Phi x$$
$$(\forall x)\Phi x \qquad\qquad \sim(\forall x)\Phi x$$

The *pas-tout* is expressed by the formula on the lower right-hand side, $\sim(\forall x)\Phi x$, or "It is not the case that all x are Φ of x." It corresponds to the negative particular statement of Aristotelian logic, variously expressed as "Some As are non-B," "Not all As are B," or "Not

81

every A is B," all of which are logically equivalent. It also, in some way, corresponds to the formula of predicate calculus, $\sim(\forall x)(Gx \rightarrow Hx)$, or, "It is not the case that for all x, if x is G then x is H."

The difference between Lacan's formulas and the formulas of the predicate calculus

Lacan's formulas	Predicate calculus
$(\forall x)\Phi x$	$(\forall x)(Gx \rightarrow Hx)$
$(\exists x)\Phi x$	$(\exists x)(Gx \ \& \ Hx)$

is that in Lacan's formulas it is assumed that the variable, x, ranges over only those things that can be said to fall or not to fall under Φ (i.e., speaking beings and not trees, rocks, or chairs), whereas the formulas of the predicate calculus are formulated in such a way that the variables, x, y, z, and so on, range over everything. Thus whereas the first of Lacan's formula says, roughly, "All x are Φ," or, "All humans fall under the phallic function," the first of the predicate calculus formulas says, "For all x, if x is G then x is H," or, "If something is a human then it falls under the phallic function."

"PAS-TOUT" IN ENGLISH

I shall take Lacan's own approach at face value and address the *pas-tout* as a conceptual or logical category, without assuming any direct link with sexuality. While it is true that Lacan introduces *"pas-tout"* in reference to female sexuality, it is not used only with that reference in mind. The *pas-tout* is a logical category, invented by Lacan, that is best taken as a formulation of a nonuniversalizable nothing. If we do this, then we see, first, that the *pas-tout* and thus the formulas of sexuation in general have no intrinsic link to the field of sexuality but are independent of it. This is the radical novelty of the approach; the formulas tell us something about the nature of sexuality precisely because they do not attempt to say what sexuality is. This is why, and this is the second point, they can legitimately be applied to different fields. There are numerous examples of this: See, for instance, the use to which Jean-Claude Milner puts it in *L'Amour de la Langue* and *Les Penchants Criminels de l'Europe Démocratique*, where his use of the *pas-tout* is central to a study of the incompleteness of language, on the one hand, and of social organization, on the other.[3]

Given the importance of the logic of the *pas-tout*, it becomes imperative to examine this logic in and for itself, and this is what I propose to do here. This is not such an easy task, because the logic is not conventional and because, as Alain Badiou points out, it seems to be rather confused—although my contention is that the confusion is only apparent.

First, though, some comment is called for on the actual term itself, *pas-tout*, for which I retain the French because not only has it been mistranslated into English but also because there is an underlying ambiguity in the term in French that is exploited by Lacan but that cannot be retained in English. The term is sometimes translated into English as "not-all," this being the most obvious rendering, as is the case in *Television*.[4] Most of the commentaries do the same. The respected translator, Bruce Fink, in his rendition of *Seminar XX*, prefers "not-whole," while some authors alternate between the two, often without explanation. As if this were not enough confusion, there is a further complication that arises in English but not in French, namely, that a rendering that retains the Aristotelian link ought to encompass "not every," given the negative particular in Aristotelian logic that has the form of "Not every A is B."

While I agree with Fink that his choice most accurately captures Lacan's use of the term, I do not believe that he sufficiently justifies it when he says that in speaking in terms of *"quanteurs"* rather than *"quantificateurs,"* or quantifiers, Lacan is indicating that his concern is not with quantity or quantification.[5] In *The Lacanian Subject*, Fink renders *"pas-tout"* as "not the whole of" or "not all of," which he justifies on the same grounds—we are not dealing with quantifiers but with something different. I agree that Lacan *is* saying something different—and I will explain just what this is—but I also think that Lacan intends there to be a clear, unmistakable reference to quantification theory as well. And this should not be neglected.

After all, if we accepted that *"quanteurs"* are not quantifiers, and that we are therefore not dealing with quantification, then the question arises, What *are* we dealing with? Also, the link to Aristotelian logic and its treatment of quantification, which is explicitly made by Lacan, would become mysterious, as would the point that we are first and foremost dealing with a logical issue and only secondarily with one of sexuation.

It would appear then that the issue of translation cannot be solved simply by adopting "not-all," or any other single term or phrase, as the English equivalent. This is a difficulty that is further compounded by the fact that the English terms dealing with quantification—"all," "each," "some," "any," "no," and so on—behave in slightly but significantly different ways from the corresponding French terms—*"tout," "tous," "chaque," "aucun," "nul," "quelque,"* and *"quelques."*

Furthermore, I think Lacan uses the term *pas-tout* in *both* the partitive ("Not all of x is Φ") *and* distributive ("No x is Φ") senses. This has been a source of confusion for English-language readers, because while *pas-tout* can be used in both senses in French, there has never been any proper explanation of why no single term in English will do.

So much for the issues of translation. Let us now move on to a more substantive question.

BADIOU'S CRITIQUE OF THE *PAS-TOUT*

Alain Badiou is critical of Lacan's theory of the *pas-tout* on two counts.[6] He argues that Lacan is confused over his use of mathematics and logic, and he accuses him of being "pre-Cantorian" in his conception of the infinite.

The first critique arises out of his criticism of the manner in which Lacan justifies the lack of logical equivalence, affirmed by both Aristotelian logic and modern predicate calculus, between "~(∀x)Φx," roughly, "Not all x are Φ of x," and "(∃x)~Φx," roughly, "At least one x is not Φ of x." Now, as Badiou points out, since castration, Φ, is supposedly universal, there can be no x whose access to jouissance assumes that not Φx, that is, it has to be false that (∃x)~Φx. How, then, does the Lacanian ~(∀x)Φx, "Not all x are Φ of x," avoid the logical implication that (∃x)~Φx, "At least one x is not Φ of x"? Lacan's explanation of how, quoted by Badiou, is set out in this lengthy passage.

> In [Aristotelian] logic, on the basis of the fact that one can write "not-every (*pas-tout*) x is inscribed in Φx," one deduces by way of implication that there is an x that contradicts it. But that is true on one sole condition, which is that, in the whole (*tout*) or the not-whole (*pas-tout*) in question, we are dealing with the finite. Regarding that which is finite, there is not simply an implication but a strict equivalence. It is enough for there to be one that contradicts the universalizing formula for us to abolish that formula and transform it into a particular. This *pas-tout* becomes the equivalent of that which, in Aristotelian logic, is enunciated on the basis of the particular. There is an exception. But we could, on the contrary, be dealing with the infinite. Then it is no longer from the perspective of extension that we must take up the *pas-toute*. When I say that woman is *pas-toute* and that that is why I cannot say Woman, it is precisely because I raise the question (*je mets en question*) of a

jouissance that, with respect to everything that can be used in the function Φx, is in the realm of the infinite.

Now, as soon as you are dealing with an infinite set, you cannot posit that the *pas-tout* implies the existence of something that is produced on the basis of a negation or contradiction. You can, at a pinch, posit it as an indeterminate existence. But, as we know from the extension of mathematical logic which is qualified as intuitionist, to posit a "there exists," one must also be able to construct it, that is, know how to find where that existence is.[7]

Badiou's criticism of Lacan is that his solution to this problem adopts two inconsistent lines of argument that he confuses. Following the first line, Lacan argues that the underlying logic is not classical but a variant of intuitionist logic. The second appeals to Cantor's set theory and introduces what Lacan describes elsewhere as the "abyss" of the actual, or completed, infinite. The immediate and obvious objection is that he appeals both to intuitionism, which rejects the actual infinite, and to Cantor, whose work presupposes it.

I grant that Lacan is grasping, sometimes tentatively, for some way of formulating in logic something about the *pas-tout* and its essential incompleteness, and that this has to do with the infinite. But Badiou illegitimately attributes a Cantorian conception of the infinite, the *actual* infinite, to Lacan in his treatment of the logic of the *pas-tout* at this point.

Whereas Aristotle had thought that any set of infinite numbers, say the set of odd numbers, was only potentially infinite in the sense that there was no last number, Cantor embraced the notion that all such infinite sets are actual. Thus, according to Cantor, sets of numbers with infinite members exist.

The logic of the *pas-tout* has to do with the infinite; Lacan says as much. But it is unwarranted to ascribe to him the view that this infinite is actual; in fact, the whole point is that the *pas-tout* can only function with an indeterminate or incompletable series, not an actual infinite one.

Badiou points out that there is something else going on in the previous passage, however, and that this apparent "contradiction" (which is in fact not one, as I have just pointed out) can be resolved. He correctly emphasizes Lacan's point, that "$\sim(\forall x)\Phi x$" is not to be taken "in extension." What Lacan means here can be explained with the help of a mundane example. "Apples are not all red" can mean i/ not every apple is red, or ii/ no apple is completely red. The first meaning is the interpretation "in extension" and implies that some apples are not red, or $(\exists x)\sim\Phi x$. On the other hand, the second, ii/, does not imply that there are non-red apples, that $(\exists x)\sim\Phi x$, but only that no apple is entirely red, that is, that there is at least one x that does not come entirely under Φ. It is this second sense in which Lacan's "$\sim(\forall x)\Phi x$" is to be taken: No woman comes entirely under the phallic function. Badiou glosses this by saying, a little obscurely, that not all x "support" the Φ from the position of all, and that the formula thus indicates a "breaching" of the Φ function.

> The essential logical point is that henceforth one cannot deduce a negative existential affirmation from the [apparent] negation of the universal in the form of the *pas-tout*. It is not true that "$(\exists x)\sim\Phi x$" follows from "$\sim(\forall x)\Phi x$."[8]

So far so good. But Badiou is unhappy with Lacan's appeal to intuitionism. In pure logic, Badiou says, intuitionism amounts to a limitation of the powers of negation. It rejects

- the principle of the excluded middle, that is, that either a proposition or its contradictory is true, or, either p or $\sim p$;

- the equivalence between a double negation and affirmation, that is, that $\sim\sim p$ is equivalent to p; and

- that the negation of a universal, $\sim(\forall x)\Phi x$, is equivalent to the affirmation of a negative existential, $(\exists x)\sim\Phi x$. In this respect, "intuitionism coincides perfectly with Lacan's wish."[9]

Why does Badiou think it is such a crime to be an intuitionist? He considers that the fundamental reason that intuitionists reject the aforementioned principles is their Canute-like reluctance to accept one of the most magnificent achievements of modern mathematics, the actual infinite, which they consider the effect of an uncontrolled, not clearly conceptualized negation of the finite. Intuitionists also reject the reductio argument, a form of reasoning where to prove that p one assumes that $\sim p$ and then demonstrates that this leads to a contradiction, $\sim \sim p$, therefore p. Of course, refusing to accept that a double negation is equivalent to an affirmative entails the abandonment of reductio arguments, but this is not the main reason for rejecting that a double negation is equivalent to an affirmative. The main reason the intuitionist wants to reject the reductio argument is that being an indirect proof it does not offer a direct proof of p but merely proceeds by demonstrating that something else is false. This method is harmless enough where finite sets are concerned, but, or so the intuitionist believes, it allows for proofs involving infinite sets that we ought to feel uneasy about.

Badiou also argues that Lacan is otherwise unsympathetic to the intuitionist program, since elsewhere he has no objection to using a reductio argument, and, moreover, he explicitly appeals to the existence of an actual infinite, which can only be proved by techniques rejected by intuitionists. This leads him to conclude that the appeal to intuitionist logic in *Encore* is opportunistic, since Lacan is happy to appeal to it in support of his argument but is otherwise unwilling to comply with the intuitionist's austere program.

RESPONSE TO BADIOU

My response will consist of showing that Lacan can both be intuitionist about mathematics—or, rather, not so much intuitionist as "constructivist"—and dump intuitionism as too "restrictive" as concerns logic.

Badiou is a little too hasty in his rejection of intuitionism, and thus a little too hasty in his criticism of Lacan. He is a realist about mathematics and, while the extent and nature of his realism is a complex issue because he cannot be described as a straightforward Platonist about mathematical objects, his opposition to intuitionism is clear, categorical, and constant.[10] It is his realism, along with his conviction that set theory is ontology, that leads him to so strongly oppose intuitionism, designed as it is to perniciously limit one to a pre-Cantorian universe.

I would like to show why the rejection of all things intuitionist is quite possibly a mistake. First, it is possible to go intuitionist about mathematics but be quite conventional about logic, as more than one philosopher has done. Quine, for instance, claims that:

> One can practice and even preach a very considerable degree of constructivism without adopting intuitionist logic. Weyl's constructive set theory is nearly as old as Brouwer's intuitionism, and it uses orthodox logic; it goes constructivist only in its axioms of existence of sets. . . . Constructivist scruples can be reconciled with the convenience and beauty of classical logic.[11]

Why one would want to adopt this line is that there are competing constructions of set theory, but not of classical logic, and so it would be nice to be able to see set theory as a construction without the consequences of doing so filtering all the way down to logic itself. If this is indeed possible, then it is apparent that Badiou's anti-intuitionist stance is a little misplaced; it now seems that Badiou's *real* debate is actually with constructivist views of mathematics, and this is a philosophical rather than a mathematical debate. Thus both Badiou and the constructivist can agree on the existence of an actual infinite and disagree over the nature not just of the actual infinite but of *all* mathematical objects.

Note that Quine's "constructivism" is not acceptable to the intuitionist (any more than it is to Badiou, for that matter) because the intuitionist, for whom mathematics is more fundamental than logic, considers that one would be rejecting what is primary and retaining what is secondary. In any case, the consequence of cleaving off logical intuitionism from mathematical "constructivism" is of course that the logical operations Badiou refers to as being unacceptable to the intuitionist—the law of the excluded middle, and so on—need not be abandoned by the mathematical constructivist: One can be constructivist about mathematical objects, even as one adheres to classical logic. This then leaves Lacan free *both* to accept these principles *and*, on other grounds, to abandon the logical equivalence

$$\sim(\forall x)\Phi x \leftrightarrow (\exists x)\sim\Phi x.$$

The intuitionists were historically motivated by their opposition to Cantor, it is true, but there are other grounds for being anti-Platonist, or for being "constructivist," about mathematics. Crispin Wright's work on Wittgenstein's philosophy of mathematics is outstanding in this regard.[12] Michael Dummett also reasons that the realist about mathematics operates with a notion of truth and falsity for mathematical statements independent of our means for recognizing their truth value.[13] The realist view makes the intuitively compelling assumption that, say, Goldbach's conjecture, which asserts that every even number larger than two is the sum of two primes, is either true or false, and this is so whether it can be proved or not. This is what is intuitively compelling about the Platonist position: there is a fact of the matter independent of whether we have demonstrated it, and the mathematical proof is like a discovery of something that is already there. If Goldbach's conjecture is true but cannot be proved, or has not been proved, then it follows that there is a mathematical reality independent of our capacity to know it. Now Dummett claims that the assumption that what makes a mathematical proposition true is some mathematical fact or state of affairs to which it corresponds is false. As a matter of fact, it is not difficult to think of many true sentences for which there is nothing by virtue of which they are true. Consider the sentence "There will never be another Napoleon," which no fact makes true. If this is so, then there are no grounds simply to assume that what makes a mathematical statement true is a mathematical state of affairs; it would be wrong just to assume that mathematical realism is true.

What this discussion implies is that on reflection we can draw a distinction between intuitionism and constructivism, and contrast realism not with intuitionism but with constructivism. It is now more apparent that Lacan should be considered a constructivist and to maintain that when in *Encore* he appeals to intuitionism, whereas elsewhere he demonstrates a rejection of its methodological strictures, it is because he is a constructivist about mathematics and not intuitionist about logic.

Badiou quotes Lacan saying, "Mathematical formalization is our goal, our ideal,"[14] as evidence for the view that Lacan is not intuitionist; but if what I am saying is correct, then it is evidence that Lacan is constructivist—this, I think, could be the only reason for such a remark—that is, Lacan can remain constructivist about mathematics while still not embracing the "prohibitions" of intuitionism.

Moreover, I think that to consider Lacan a constructivist is right on other grounds as well. And if I insist on this distinction between intuitionism and constructivism, it is because I think Lacan is constructivist about mathematics, and for reasons that are importantly related to what he elaborates concerning the formulas of sexuation.

It is true that Lacan commits himself to the view that $\sim(\forall x)\Phi x$ does not imply that $(\exists x)\sim\Phi x$ and appeals to intuitionist logic in support; that is, he endorses one of the "prohibitions" of intuitionism. And it has to be acknowledged that in his use of the *pas-tout*, Lacan thinks intuitionism provides him with support. But this is a far cry from accepting the other strictures of intuitionism ascribed to him by Badiou.

ARISTOTLE AND THE *PAS-TOUT*

This brings us to what has been left out of the discussion so far and yet which must, somehow, be fundamental to the discussion: Aristotelian logic and predicate calculus. A careful analysis of the relationship of Lacan's *pas-tout* with Aristotelian logic reveals the correctness of the earlier interpretation of what Lacan means when he declares that $\sim(\forall x)\Phi x$ is not to be taken "in extension." I will now show why.

Aristotle distinguished between three forms of statements that affirm a predicate of a subject: the singular, the universal, and the particular.[15] Leaving the singular to one side, combining negation and affirmation with the universal, and the particular produces statements of four logically different forms: universal affirmative, "All As are B," universal negative, "All As are not B," particular affirmative, "Some As are B," and particular negative, "Some As are not B."

There is no straightforward correlation between the universal and existential quantifiers of Aristotelian formal logic and the terms that express quantification in natural languages. This fact becomes particularly relevant when language refers to nothing, as we shall see, for the behavior of natural language and the intuitions of its speakers diverge from the structure of formal languages.

This contrast between the grammar of natural language and Aristotelian logic underlies a discussion of the particular in Aristotle in a work by Jacques Brunschwig that had a significant impact on Lacan's theory of the *pas-tout*.[16] Brunschwig argues that Aristotle was initially misled by the workings of natural language, and that this led to a problem of inconsistency with his logic. Aristotle eventually devised a consistent logic, but it is one in which certain intuitions implicit in natural language have been disallowed, especially in relation to particular statements, both affirmative and negative.

The matter that caused problems for Aristotle, which Brunschwig analyzes, is one that the particular statement produces in natural language, namely, the usual meaning of the particular leads to three mutually inconsistent propositions, as can be seen in the following three intuitively obvious assumptions:

1. The particular and the universal of opposite "quality" (i.e., where one is affirmative and the other negative) are contradictory. Ordinary usage thus treats the following as axiomatic:

    All As are B $\leftrightarrow$ ~Some As are not B[17]

2. A particular statement is implied by its subalternant:

    All As are B $\rightarrow$ Some As are B

    As Brunschwig points out, ordinary usage is somewhat divided on this second proposition. If I say to you that some (a lot, many) As are B, without knowing that all are, then you could reply in either of two ways: *either* with the remark, "Actually, what you say is not wrong, because in fact all As are B," *or* with the comment, "No, no, it's not just *some* As that are B; *all* As are B." My own view is that natural language is not so equivocal on this point, since in the second scenario one could come back with the rejoinder that since all As are B, it must be the case a fortiori that *some* As are B. In any case, if one agrees with my view, then one accepts that the statement "All As are B" implies that "Some As are B."

3. The two particular statements imply one another. Ordinarily, the statement "Some As are B" would be true in circumstances in which the statement "Some As are not B" is equally true. If, for instance, I make the claim, "Some cats are black," then this would seem to imply that there are also cats that are non-black.

Some As are B $\leftrightarrow$ Some As are not B

The problem with these three formal relations is that they are mutually inconsistent, as is easily shown. From "All As are B" it follows both (by 1) that it is false that some As are not B, and (by 2 and 3) that some As are not B, which is a contradiction. The contradiction can only be avoided by rejecting one of the aforementioned natural language axioms, 1, 2, or 3.

Rejecting axiom 3, the equivalence of the two particular statements, would produce the classical Aristotelian square of oppositions. The contradiction between "All As are B" and "No A is B" (where if one is true, then the other is false) remains, as do the relations of subalternation (where if the first is true, then so is the second) between "All As are B" and "Some As are B" and between "No As are B" and "Some As are not B." The equivalence of the two particular statements "Some As are B" and "Some As are not B" becomes one of subcontraries, or compatibility, where both may be true together but not false. The particular statement "Some As are B" thus becomes interpreted as saying, "At least one A is B," where it is not excluded that all are. Brunschwig calls this interpretation of "Some As are B" and "Some As are not B" where *it is not excluded that all As are (not) B* the "minimal particular."

If, on the other hand, we reject axiom 2 and retain axioms 1 and 3, then we obtain a system in which the two particulars mutually imply one another. If one wishes to maintain as contradictories "All As are B" and "Some As are not B" and "No As are B" and "Some As are B," then one is obliged to allow, paradoxically, both that each of the particulars is contradictory with the universal of the same quality and that each is still the contradictory of the universal of the opposite quality. In effect, both universals must contradict both particulars, since the latter are equivalent. And, moreover, the two universals must be equivalent because they are contradictories of equivalent propositions.

The particular statement "Some As are B" becomes "At least and at most some As are B," and the statement "No As are B" becomes "At least and at most some As are not B." That is, if it is true that "Not all As are B," then it is false that *no* As are B and equally false that *all* As are not B; there is no universal, whether affirmative or negative, that is true of As and B. Brunschwig calls this the "maximal particular."

THE "MAXIMAL PARTICULAR" AS SOURCE OF THE *PAS-TOUT*

J.-A. Miller holds that this maximal particular is the origin of Lacan's *pas-tout*.[18] This means, then, that $\sim(\forall x)\Phi x$ implies not only that $(\forall x)\Phi x$ is false but also that $(\forall x)\sim\Phi x$ is as well. On consideration, it becomes clear that this implies that the "quanteurs" are not to be taken in extension and that the only possible way to understand the maximal reading of "$\sim(\forall x)\Phi x$" is as "Not all of x is Φ."

Miller further claims, incorrectly I believe, that Lacan's *pas-tout* differs from Aristotelian quantification in another respect, which is that the universe of discourse in Aristotelian logic is finite, with the consequence that, irrespective of whether the *pas-tout* is interpreted as maximal or minimal, it is concerned with lack and incompleteness. He adds that because the Lacanian *pas-tout* assumes an infinite universe, and because it is constructed on the intuitionist model of choice sequences, it is impossible to state the universality of the predicate. If the law by which the series "All As are B" is defined is not stated at the outset, then it will be impossible, no matter how many As have been shown to be B, even without ever having found an A that is not B, to draw a conclusion about all. The sequence is "lawless," which is an attribute of the Lacanian real.[19]

The claim that the universe of discourse of Aristotelian logic is finite while Lacan's *pas-tout* assumes an infinite universe of discourse is, I believe, incorrect because Aristotelian logic holds of finite and infinite universes equally well; it makes no difference to the *logical* relations between the statements whether they refer to a finite or an infinite number of things. It makes a difference if the universe is empty. But from all As are Bs, it follows that no As are non-B, whether there is a finite or infinite number of As.

Perhaps Miller's point can be made in a different way, one that brings us back to the intuitionism/constructivism distinction. The quantifiers "$\forall$" and "$\exists$" make it possible to refer to an infinite number of objects, and hence to a totality—but on the proviso that it is possible to characterize, by a predicate, all members of the class. For instance, "$(\forall x)[(x>1)\rightarrow(x>0)]$," that is, "If a number is greater than 1 then it is greater than zero," is true of an infinite number of cases because the class of numbers is infinite. However, if there is *no* way to define the members of an infinitely large class, then the truth of the statement cannot be established. Because the class is infinitely large, enumeration of cases cannot exhaust them all; and because there is no suitable predicate, they cannot be referred to as a totality.

Again, we can see how the question of actual infinity is irrelevant to the issue, since the issue is merely one of the impossibility of defining a *potential* infinity (and of course the impossibility of enumerating an infinite number of cases).

Badiou's criticisms of Lacan seem misplaced, then, and to my mind result from his realist views about mathematics and unnecessary reference to the concept of an actual infinite.

There is one further issue that I should signal, which unfortunately I cannot go into here. A moment's reflection is enough to see that the reference to the enumeration of cases, that is, to the impossibility of doing so in the case of $\sim(\forall x)\Phi x$, implicitly means taking the formula "in extension": not a, not b, not c. . . . In other words, there are two readings of the *pas-tout*, which, one suspects, are a real source of confusion in the glosses on Lacan. How this impacts upon the logic of the *pas-tout* is another matter.

Chapter 7

Kant and Freud

Freud's references to Kant are few and brief. As suggestive as these remarks are, they appear to indicate nothing more than a broad comparison between Kant's moral law and the superego. Lacan, however, pursues the connection at length and attaches great importance to Kant's moral philosophy for the emergence of psychoanalysis—going so far as to claim that Kantian ethics was a necessary precondition for Freud's discoveries. Lacan discusses Kant at length and in detail, with reference to quite precise points in Kant's philosophy, in "Kant with Sade" and in *Seminar VII, The Ethics of Psychoanalysis.*

Despite the brevity of Freud's references to Kant, I believe that a comparison of the two authors can throw some interesting light on the nature of *desire* and on the psychological consequences of adopting a moral standpoint, that is, of being moral agents. I will take a "psychological" or naturalistic approach to Kant's moral philosophy, as I think I can draw out some significant views about the consequences of being moral agents, which have perhaps been overlooked, by so doing. One of the claims I want to argue for is that there is a close relationship between desire and the moral law. I think it will be obvious that my argument goes against a lot of what Kant says, and so I compare it to Kant's views on how desire and the moral law are related. I conclude with some remarks on the relationship between desire and pleasure, as seen from a psychoanalytic point of view, since it is around the relation to the law that they can be distinguished.

KANT'S MORAL PHILOSOPHY

Kant places essentially two requirements on action for it to have moral worth: (1) that it be universalizable and (2) that it be done for the sake of duty. I shall discuss them in turn.

Kant formulates the universalizability requirement thus: "Act only according to a maxim through which you can at the same time will that it should become a universal law." A maxim, Kant tells us, "is a subjective principle of acting," or "the principle according to which the subject acts."[1] A maxim is not the same as an intention, since not every intention is a maxim. A maxim is the underlying intention that guides our more specific intentions—such as, for instance, the intention to increase one's wealth by every possible means or the intention to live a life of pleasure. It is the overall intention that more specific intentions are intended to follow.

A common criticism of the view that the moral law enjoins us to act only on those maxims we can will as universal law is that this "law" does not actually exclude any maxims at all. Indeed, since it contains no reference to what everybody or anybody desires and merely asserts that moral agents only need to impose a certain sort of consistency on their actions if they are to avoid doing what is wrong, it is not surprising that it has been criticized as trivial or vacuous. J. S. Mill, for example, claimed that Kant fails to show "that there would be any contradiction . . . in the adoption by all rational beings of the most outrageously immoral rules of conduct."[2]

Is this criticism justified? No, I do not believe so. I think Kant is correct in claiming that universalised maxims can be self-contradictory in either of two general ways: A universalised maxim may be conceptually inconsistent. For example, while it may be possible to adopt, as a guiding principle of one's action, the maxim of coercing others who will not comply with one's will, universal coercion is a contradiction in terms; that is, there are conceptual reasons why it cannot be *universalized*.

I think this is a more favorable case than Kant's own example of keeping a promise, incidentally. Kant claims that it is inconsistent to adopt the maxim of breaking promises when it suits one, because this would lead to the collapse of the practice that the maxim presupposes. However, as Lacan points out, Kant is a bit like the character in Jarry's play who declares, "Long live Poland, for without Poland there wouldn't be any Poles." In other words, it is only inconsistent to adopt the maxim of breaking promises if one also wills that the practice of promising continue. Without this extra requirement there is no inconsistency—no inconsistency in willing something that will eventually destroy the possibility of willing it.[3]

There is a second way in which universalized maxims can be self-contradictory. Maxims that may be quite consistent when conceived may still turn out to be inconsistent when willed. This volitional inconsistency, as it is called, can arise because willing is not just a matter of wishing that something were the case but implies a commitment to doing something to bring about the situation when the opportunity arises. This entails that even where there is no inconsistency in merely *conceiving* a given maxim as a universal law, *willing* the maxim as a universal law can lead to an inconsistency between willing the maxim and willing the means of realizing it. It can be argued that the maxim of non-beneficence is such a case of volitional inconsistency.

I should like to emphasize that on its own the universalizability requirement only tells us which maxims to *reject*; it does not tell us which maxims are morally worthy, only which are morally permissible. I stress this because it is a neglected but important implication of the universalizability requirement that it places a purely negative requirement upon action. It is essentially prohibitive; it rejects as morally *unworthy* all maxims that cannot be consistently universalized but does not directly attribute moral *worth* to any. Since the universalizability requirement confers moral worth on an action only when every other course of action is proscribed, its imperative is ultimately "Thou shalt not!" It follows that I have a positive duty to perform a certain act only where to do otherwise would be to transgress the moral law.

Take the example of that most Kantian of duties, the duty to tell the truth. Kant's argument is notorious. He claims that if a person speaks nothing but the truth, then he is not responsible for the consequences, even where these involve the probable murder of an innocent person; whereas if he tells a lie, however altruistic his motive, he at once makes himself answerable for every result of his falsehood, however unforeseen.[4] It should be clear that Kant's position must be not that we have a positive duty to tell the truth but that our duty is the essentially proscriptive one of not telling a lie.

Now even if we grant that the universalizability requirement is not vacuous, as I think we should, it is still not clear how it is to be applied in any particular instance—and this is going to present a major, indeed an insurmountable, difficulty. The difficulty can be put like this. Any act can be specified more or less broadly, in terms that, at one end of the scale, pick out only this individual act or, at the other, apply to every member of the generic class of acts. There are no limits to how specific our description is between the limits set by the individual act and the generic class of acts. As Ross says, if, for example, I tell a lie to a would-be wrongdoer, then this can be characterized as (1) a lie to a person with evil intent, (2) as a lie, (3) as a statement. Kant opts, arbitrarily, for the second of these descriptions and, since such acts are generally wrong, and are indeed always prima facie wrong, he says that the particular lie is wrong. Here is Ross's criticism.

But the man who tells the lie may well retort to Kant "Why should the test of universalizability be applied to my act regarded in this very abstract way, simply as lie? I admit that lying could not properly become a general law of human society. But why not apply the test of universalizability to my act considered more concretely, as a lie told to a would-be murderer, to prevent him from committing a murder? I am willing then to face the test of universalizability. I think that human society would be better conducted if people habitually told lies in such circumstances, than if they habitually told the truth and helped murderers to commit their murders." We seem, then, to be at an impasse. The test of universalizability applied at one level of abstractness condemns the act; applied at another level of abstractness, it justifies it. And since the principle does not indicate at what level of abstractness it is applied, it does not furnish us with a criterion of the correctness of maxims, or of the rightness of acts conforming to them.[5]

As far as I know, Kant has no reply to this. Thus even if we accept that the universalizability requirement is not vacuous, we still have to reject the claim that moral action can be determined precisely and definitely in abstraction by appeal to the purely formal categorical imperative alone without reference to ends and consequences.

Furthermore, even if we do agree that not every maxim is universalizable, and hence that the universalizability requirement is not vacuous, then we can still ask whether it is powerful enough to exclude all of the maxims that should be excluded. Consider the case of Marquis de Sade, a contemporary of Kant's, as much a figure of the enlightenment as Kant himself. Let us admit for the sake of argument that de Sade acts on a maxim that can be reasonably accurately expressed in the following form: "Consent to anyone's inflicting pain on you at will." On the face of it there seems to be no reason why de Sade cannot will that this become universal law.

To be sure, for a Kantian this maxim is impermissible because it flouts the formulation of the categorical imperative in terms of treating people as means not ends; and it flouts it every bit as much as does the corresponding maxim "Inflict pain at will." We would also expect the Kantian to argue that it cannot be universalized, on the grounds that a rational being necessarily wills the happiness of others.[6] Therefore, since there would be others for whom willing this maxim would cause unhappiness, no purely *rational* being could consistently adopt the maxim, regardless of whether or not de Sade could consistently will it to be universal law.

I should at this point mention a further requirement that I believe the categorical imperative must meet if it is to generate a satisfactory moral theory. It must do more than give us an algorithm for distinguishing between moral and immoral acts; it is not enough that it should churn out the correct results; it must also give some account of *why* these are the correct results. There are two reasons for this. First, the categorical imperative must be able to challenge our moral intuitions, and so the adequacy of the theory must not be measured solely by its fit with those same intuitions. Second, actions must be rejected for reasons that show what is wrong with them; we need an explanation of what it is about an allegedly immoral action that brings it into conflict with the requirements of the theory. This is because it is only if the categorical imperative engages us in some moral reasoning that we can claim to reject an action, or a maxim, on *moral* grounds.

If we return to the maxim "Consent to anyone's inflicting pain on you at will," I believe it illustrates very well the moral law's inability to define morally permissible action. Here is why. The moral law is directed at perfectly *rational* beings, but, as Kant is aware, we humans are at best imperfectly rational. The moral law says what a perfectly rational being can consistently will, and this includes willing the happiness of others; but what the Sadian maxim shows is that what *we* as imperfectly rational beings can will may be at odds with what *a perfectly rational being* can will.

It does not help here to argue, as Kant does, that because a rational being necessarily wills the happiness of others de Sade could not rationally will his maxim to become universal law. The reason this does not help is that the *only* grounds that Kant can offer for what a rational being necessarily wills are provided by the moral law itself. But in order to draw conclusions from the moral law that would make de Sade's maxim morally objectionable, it appears that Kant is forced to make assumptions about what rational beings necessarily will—in particular, that they will the happiness of others. As a result, Kant can only exclude de Sade's maxim by reasoning in a circle.

Kant thinks that the claim that rational beings necessarily will the happiness of others is essentially the same as the claim that everyone should attempt "as far as he can, to further the ends of others."[7] But this ignores the fact that there are some people (de Sade is one of them) who have ends that do not deserve to be furthered—indeed, that we have a definite *duty* not to further.

Now Kant would no doubt say that it is not a question of furthering people's ends *simpliciter*, but of furthering their *legitimate* or *permissible* ends. But how are we to distinguish legitimate from illegitimate ends? Kant certainly cannot make the distinction, for a relatively straightforward reason: The moral law is intended to be the fundamental moral principle from which all other moral principles, obligations, and duties derive; and since de Sade's maxim is consistent with the moral law, it should be morally permissible. But if those forms of the moral law that require us to treat others as ends and not means *also* require us to distinguish between morally permissible and impermissible ends, then the moral law cannot be the fundamental moral principle. To apply the moral law we need to know how to distinguish between permissible and impermissible ends, but this distinction could not then be derived from the moral law without circularity.

In each of these cases the problem is the same: The moral law applies to perfectly rational beings, whereas humans, being imperfectly rational, are capable of choosing objectionable ends.

Kant does not let the matter rest there but in fact attempts to ground the distinction between permissible and impermissible ends. This attempt is instructive. In the second *Critique* he points out that no empirical application of the moral law can be derived directly from the law itself. His strategy for deriving empirical applications of the moral law is to introduce an "analogue" or a "typic" of the moral law that does have empirical application. An analogue enables us to ask ourselves what would happen in the empirical world if a certain maxim were universally acted upon and to take into account what we know about the way nature works. Clearly this is a crucial move. However, when we examine Kant's conception of nature we find that it is both teleological and normative. In particular, it turns out that de Sade would be engaging in "unnatural" acts—that is, acts that do not conform to the laws of nature.[8] Kant's normative view that immoral persons are acting contrary to the laws of nature is brought out well by a remark he makes about lust: "Lust," he says, "is called *unnatural* if one is aroused to it not by a real object but by his imagining it, so that he himself creates one contrapurposively [i.e., contrary to the purpose of the desire]."[9] Now from the *psychoanalytic* point of view, this definition of unnatural lust is a pretty good definition of desire per se, aroused as it is "not by its real object but by one's imagination [read fantasy] of this object." From the psychoanalytic point of view, there is no natural desire, and there can thus be no contrast between natural and unnatural desire. I shall return to this later.

So far I have been discussing the universalizability requirement. The second requirement Kant places on action for it to have moral worth is that it be done for the sake of duty. His distinction between an action done "for the sake of duty" and an action performed merely "according to duty" entails that only actions done for the sake of duty have moral worth, and that only such actions exhibit a good will, which is the only thing that can be called good without qualification.

To do an action for the sake of duty is to do it solely out of respect for the moral law, regardless of its consequences. Kant makes it clear that even a dutiful action done out of feelings of love or sympathy, while it may be fine and even compassionate, lacks moral worth every bit as much as actions done out of mere self-interest. Kant points out that an action can be in agreement with the law without having been done for the sake of the law: It is a question of motive. Thus in those cases where duty and desire dictate the same action, it makes an important moral difference whether the action is done for the sake of duty or from inclination. As far as our *motivation* for the act of doing our duty is concerned, we ought to abstract ourselves from all incentives of inclination and act solely from duty.

It is a distinctive feature of Kant's moral philosophy to draw a sharp distinction between "inclination," or desire, and duty. For Kant, desire concerns the subject's relations to the empirical, such that desire is always the desire for the empirical object that would satisfy the desire. The satisfaction of desire is ultimately the source of well-being or happiness, so to strive for happiness is to strive for both a certain harmony between different desires and the eventual satisfaction of them all. Thus to inquire into the good life, happiness, or well-being is, fundamentally, an inquiry into desire and the conditions of its satisfaction.

For Kant, then, desire ultimately concerns the subject's well-being, and he takes this to imply that desire is invariably, either directly or indirectly, linked to one's inclinations or self-love.

However, any inquiry into the good life cannot be regarded as an inquiry into the moral life, the *morally* good life. This is because no action motivated by *desire* can ever be regarded as moral, for the only *morally* worthy actions are those that are performed, as we have seen, not for the sake of our own or another's benefit but for the sake of duty alone.

Well-being or happiness is not just a question of one's own pleasure. It also involves reference to the well-being of others. This is because of our feelings of sympathy, compassion, and concern for others—which Kant calls "pathological" (in its etymological sense) love. That is, to act for the sake of others out of a sense of sympathy for them is ultimately to base one's action on feeling, and while it may well be a fine action, it is not a moral one.

To the extent that I take into consideration either my well-being or that of others—that is, my own or others' desires—my action is not a moral one. I must, therefore, set aside any "pathos" for my action to be moral. As Kant puts it, "Virtue necessarily presupposes *apathy*."[10]

The well-being of living beings is linked to the faculty of desire. Now since experience alone is capable of telling us what satisfies desire, there can be no possible a priori determination of desire. Any action based on desire is always based on a *hypothetical* imperative.

A morally worthy action, on the other hand, is an action performed by a rational being, and is done for the sake of the moral law alone. Its imperative is not hypothetical but categorical. "Do your duty, and do it for the sake of duty." The difference is the same as that between the question: "What should I do . . . to be happy?," where the answer will vary according to individual desire, and the moral question: "What should I do?," *simpliciter*, where the answer is universal, in the sense that if it is right for me to do this, then it would be right for anyone else to do it. Thus only actions done for no other reason than that they are morally correct, that is, for no other reason than for the sake of the moral law itself, have moral worth, and it is only such actions that exhibit a good will.

Kant uses this familiar example to contrast acting on a desire and acting out of duty:

> Suppose someone asserts of his lustful inclination that, when the desired object and the opportunity are present, it is quite irresistible to him; ask him whether, if a gallows were erected in front of the house where he finds this opportunity and he would be hanged on it immediately after gratifying his lust, he would not then control his inclination. One need not conjecture very long what he would reply. But ask him whether, if his prince demanded, on pain of the same immediate execution, that he give false testimony against an honourable man whom the prince would like to destroy under a plausible pretext, he would consider it possible to overcome his love of life, however great it may be. He would perhaps not venture to assert whether he would do it or not, but he must admit without hesitation that it would be possible for him. He judges, therefore, that he can do something because he is aware that he ought to do it and cognizes freedom within him, which, without the moral law, would have remained unknown to him.[11]

Placing desire, as Kant does, on the side of the "pathological," the ultimate guiding principle of which is self-love, while its aim is happiness, entails that one will choose love of life over the gratification of desire. As Kant says, the faculty of desire is determined by the sense of agreeableness, or pleasure, that the subject expects from the object of the desire. All principles that make the supreme ground for one's choices of the seeking of pleasure and the avoidance of pain are thus without exception subsumed under the principle of self-love or of one's own happiness. All of this lies within the phenomenal world, and knowledge of it is synthetic or empirical. As an empirical being, I undergo, passively, my passions, my desires. Which desire I am ruled by depends upon its strength, and the love of life, being the strongest desire of all, will prevail over all others.

On the other hand, where it is a question of right and wrong we recognize that it *is* possible to overcome this "love of life" and thus transcend considerations of happiness and well-being. Duty can lead me to choose to act against my desires, including the most important of all, my desire to live.

Note that there is a problem with Kant's reasoning here. In the way that Kant presents this distinction it looks as if he is describing an observable, empirical fact about human subjects. However, what the example illustrates is something rather different—it is pointing to the difference between the logical structure of desiring (in Kant's sense of the term) and willing. My desiring or wanting something does not imply that I make any effort to satisfy it. It is therefore possible to say both that one desires something and that for some reason—which may possibly be prudential, but it may be other things as well—the desire shall remain unsatisfied. It would be wrong to suppose that an agent cannot be said to desire to do x in the absence of all intention to do x. There are plenty of cases where we avoid those situations in which it would be possible to satisfy a certain desire. An undeclared attraction to a friend's partner might lead to seeing less of them both. A desire for a cigarette may lead one to leave a smoke-filled room.

Kant does not really have a proper theory of desire, and what is wrong here is that desire and duty are not opposed in the way he thinks. Kant seems to think of desire as some sort of internal force that causes actions—or at least will cause an action unless we will it not to. However, a desire is not just an urge to act; there are various ways in which desire is structured. It is true that our moral beliefs influence whether, and in what way, we act upon our desires. But it is also the case that the structure of desire influences the way we act. To desire is not simply to seek pleasure and the avoidance of pain; desire is, in fact, perfectly capable of ignoring pleasure and pain, happiness and love of self, just as successfully as the moral law itself can. Like the moral law, desire, too, can overcome this "love of life."

It is no doubt true that Kant's example fits a person of a certain moral character. But, Lacan asks, is there not also the character for whom his passion is a point of honor, and who may maintain his desire in defiance of, or even out of contempt for, death? Indeed, one of the classic illustrations of this made its appearance in 1787, two years after the *Groundwork* and one year before the second *Critique*, in the form of Mozart and Da Ponte's Don Giovanni—the character who remains unrepentant, even as he faces certain annihilation. Or again, consider another of Kant's contemporaries, the aforesaid Marquis de Sade. It is wrong to regard de Sade simply as a libertine, bent on the pursuit of a life of pleasure. He is more interesting than that. For while it is true that he advocates the wanton and unimpeded satisfaction of our desires, there is, nevertheless, something oddly but unmistakably Kantian about this advocacy in that for de Sade desire must be pursued beyond the limits of pleasure and the avoidance of pain.

Or, again, consider Antigone. Antigone is one of Oedipus's four children. And in the third of the Theban plays, when, under the rule of Creon, one of her brothers is killed in a quarrel, Creon forbids his burial. Antigone, defying Creon, buries her brother; she is then arrested and condemned to death by herself being buried, alive, in a tomb. As a character she is unbending in her resolution, unconcerned by the danger she herself faces—and this is brought out all the more clearly in the play as she is contrasted to her indecisive and timid sister, Ismene. Ismene is horrified by her sister's lack of concern for her own well-being and is intimidated by the force of her desire; she is despised by her sister in turn. Sophocles thus gives us a dramatic contrast between the kind, considerate, and compassionate Ismene, ready to compromise and listen to the other's point of view, while on the other hand there is the untamed and ruthless Antigone, who goes to the brink and gives every indication of having nothing to lose. She has something uncannily inhuman about her precisely because, I would suggest, the power and insistence of her desire calls into question her own well-being, along with the well-being of her society.

As I said at the outset, Freud does not often mention Kant. But it is not surprising that when he refers to the Kantian moral law, it is with particular reference to the superego, since in Freudian theory the superego is the source and locus of our ideals and moral imperatives. However, if we look closely at what Freud says about Kant, we can see that he links the categorical imperative rather more specifically to the superego as the cruel, harsh, inexorable and, ultimately, irrational source of an implacable sense of guilt.

Freud draws a sharp distinction between a conscious and what he calls, "in spite of the apparent contradiction in terms," an unconscious sense of guilt. While he does not hesitate to regard conscious guilt feelings as no more than the result of a tension between what we would like to do and what we feel we ought to do, the unconscious sense of guilt is another matter. Insofar as unconscious guilt reveals the obscene and ferocious figure of the superego, Freud refers its origin to the internalization of aggression that is unable to find external expression: the superego inhibits the expression of aggression, which it then itself makes use of and with excessive severity turns upon the ego. This unconscious guilt does not manifest itself directly but is given a central role in the explanation of certain clinical phenomena: desire to be punished, clinging to otherwise painful symptoms, and so on—in short, a paradoxical desire for suffering.

Linking the "harsh, cruel, and inexorable" superego to Kant's moral law in this way may appear to be a misunderstanding, even a parody, of Kant's ethical theory. But it nevertheless points to a certain structure of desire and its relationship to morality.

Not only does Kant argue that the moral law and moral action are independent of any considerations of well-being, he also makes the further claim that we know, on a priori grounds, that our recognition of the moral law will have two consequences for our desires and thus our well-being. The first of these is that the moral law will have a "negative" effect, as he calls it, which we will necessarily experience as painful. This is the pain (or displeasure) that we experience through the privation and self-denial that the moral law constrains us to practice. (Note how Freud links this to depression and melancholia.) The second effect is the denigration of desire, which Kant calls "humiliation (intellectual contempt)."[12]

In other words, the faculty of reason, through the moral law, causes us to suffer the pain of renunciation as well as the humiliation of our desires—is this not what Freud called the "malaise" of civilization? This moral law is not only obeyed out of respect for the law itself, ignoring pleasure, pain, happiness, and love of self, it is a source of displeasure, just as it humbles our sensual being.

This would, perhaps, be sufficient grounds for Freud to tie the harsh and cruel superego to the Kantian moral law. We could thus conclude that the relationship between the categorical imperative and the superego comes down to Freud's claim that one always has to choose between desire and the law—the choice necessarily implying a loss, a forced choice, for if a subject chooses desire, he falls prey to guilt for having failed to comply with the law, but in opting for the law, he is left to mourn his desire.

The philosopher Bernard Baas has argued that this is not the most important point of comparison we can draw between the two, for the claim that there is a conflict between desire and the law, while true, is hardly news. Indeed, is this not precisely the claim, in Freud, referred to earlier on the subject of conscious guilt, that there is bound to be tension between the ego and superego? What has this to do with Freud's claim that there is a relationship between a cruel and harsh superego and the moral law?[13]

There is another, hidden dimension to this question of the super-ego and the moral law. Kant makes the very interesting observation that alongside this pain and humiliation brought about by the moral law that calls for the sacrifice of desire, the moral law also produces a certain positive satisfaction:

> Since [the moral] law is ... in itself positive ... it is at the same time an object of *respect* inasmuch as, in opposition to its sub-jective antagonist, namely the inclinations in us, it *weakens* self-conceit; and inasmuch as it even *strikes down* self-conceit, that is, humiliates it, it is an object of the greatest *respect* and so too the ground of a positive feeling that is not of empirical origin.[14]

This positive feeling that is not of empirical origin Kant calls "self-contentment," or *Selbstzufriedenheit.*

Is it not striking to find that in the very act of renunciation in the name of the moral law, alongside the pain and humiliation, there is also a secret, nonsensual ("not of empirical origin") source of satisfac-tion? What is of the utmost importance here is that according to Kant, beyond the well-being that appears to be the aim of all our actions, and thus beyond the pleasure produced by the satisfaction of desire, there lies a further, hidden satisfaction, "self-contentment," that arises from the sacrifice of pleasure. Without suggesting that this was in-tended by Freud, it seems to me that this strange source of satisfaction has everything to do with the superego. It is, in any case, what inter-ests Lacan in Kant's moral law: that the renunciation of pleasure, that the very act of compliance with the moral law for the sake of the moral law itself, at one and the same time renders pleasure "less re-spectable"[15] and produces a surplus of satisfaction, which as Kant recognizes is distinct from pleasure, and which Lacan calls "jouissance." In Kant, beyond the pleasure that appears to be the aim of desire, there lies a law that in demanding the sacrifice of pleasure produces the particular satisfaction of jouissance.

We can now see why Lacan refers to the obscene and ferocious figure of the superego, why he claims that the Kantian moral impera-tive conceals a cruel injunction—this voice of conscience that enjoins us to do our duty for duty's sake is both a trauma and a hidden source of insatiable jouissance, which disrupts the homeostasis of the pleasure principle. This is something beyond the pleasure principle that does not consist in some empirical, "pathological" remnant that remains behind and cleaves to the moral law but rather lies at the heart of the moral law itself. As Slavoj Žižek has argued, the obscene and ferocious face of the moral law consists in the fact that it is its *form itself* that functions as a motivating force driving us to obey its command—that is, insofar as we obey the moral law because it is law and not for any positive reason: The cruelty and harshness of the moral law is the hidden face of its formal character. While Kant's categorical imperative not only stands apart from all objects that produce pleasure, but also necessarily taints them and frustrates their satisfaction, what lies hidden is the way in which their renunciation and sacrifice themselves produce a certain satisfaction.[16]

The paradox of Kant's moral philosophy is, then, the same as that of Lacan's notion of jouissance—that is, it is precisely this self-contentment that the subject derives from his moral experience in submitting to the moral law that nevertheless makes him suffer.

Lacan's views on Kant's categorical imperative and its connections to the superego do not stem, as might seem to be the case at first sight, from any supposed *opposition* between the law and desire. They stem, rather, from two claims that Kant's moral theory makes concerning the presence within the law of what Lacan called "jouissance." The first, most obvious claim is that Kant's rational subject, by virtue of being rational, is deprived of pleasure, suffers a lack or deprivation at the level of his passions—which is the price the subject pays for being subject to the moral law.

Second, the subject nevertheless derives a hidden and paradoxical satisfaction from his recognition that he is subject to the law. This satisfaction, which lies beyond the pleasure principle ("is not of empirical origin"), is paradoxical because it is satisfaction derived from the very law by which the subject suffers.

Chapter 8

Guilt, the Law, and Transgression

Kant famously held two apparently contradictory principles: first, that all that occurs in the empirical, phenomenal world is, necessarily, determined by prior events; second, that acts of the will are done freely. The freedom "in the strictest, that is, in the transcendental, sense" that Kant ascribes to the will is, as he acknowledges, incompatible with the determinism of the empirical world.[1] The freedom must therefore lie in the noumenal world and thus outside the empirical world governed by a priori causal laws. Kant's attempt at reconciling the freedom of the will with the determinism of the empirical world is widely considered unsuccessful. Therefore, the conclusion that either every event is determined or that some events are acts of free will seems inescapable.

Why, then, did Kant ever seriously attempt to reconcile freedom and determinism in this way? Or, to put the question slightly differently, what grounds are there for countenancing even the possibility of free will? Because Kant accepts the first principle, that everything in experience occurs according to causal laws, there can be no empirical grounds for this freedom. As such, he accepts that any cognition of this freedom cannot derive from experience. Kant finds these grounds elsewhere, namely, in our recognition of the moral law, which "forces this concept [of freedom] upon us," such that, were it not for the moral law, "one would never have ventured to introduce freedom into science."[2]

Kant provides a famous example to illustrate the point:

> Suppose someone asserts of his lustful inclination that, when the desired object and the opportunity are present, it is quite irresistible to him; ask him whether, if a gallows were erected in front of the house where he finds this opportunity and he would be hanged on it immediately after gratifying his lust, he would not then control his inclination.[3]

For Kant there is no question of what the man will do. "One need not conjecture very long what he would reply," he writes, and he takes this to illustrate the nature of desire: A person's desire will always be subordinate to that most overarching desire—the desire for life. A person will therefore forego the most extreme pleasure if he is convinced that it comes at the price of death. Kant then contrasts this state of affairs with another:

> [A]sk [this same person] whether, if his prince demanded, on pain of the same immediate execution, that he give false testimony against an honorable man whom the prince would like to destroy under a plausible pretext, he would consider it possible to overcome his love of life, however great it may be. He would perhaps not venture to assert whether he would do it or not, but he must admit without hesitation that it would be possible for him. He judges, therefore, that he can do something because he is aware that he ought to do it and cognises freedom within him, which, without the moral law, would have remained unknown to him.[4]

Thus a man may still be prepared to do what he thinks is right, do what he believes in, do his duty, even though he knows that his act will result in his own death. It is from the recognition of this possibility that we derive the concept of a free act. For Kant, then, if there were no free will there could be no duty, and the contrast between acting on a desire and acting for the sake of duty would not exist; he therefore takes the example to illustrate the difference between duty and desire. Lacan disagrees with Kant's analysis of the contrast between desire and duty and makes the entirely correct observation that a person may well be prepared to act on a desire in the knowledge that it will not be for his own good and may even result in his demise. Indeed, even in Kant's example, a person is quite capable of finding that the risks and dangers posed by the neighboring gallows add to the attraction of the transgression.

As a matter of fact, Kant would not have had to go very far, even in his own time, to find an illustration of such a case—south and, either west to Paris, where Marquis de Sade was writing *Philosophy in the Boudoir*, or east to Vienna for Mozart and Da Ponte's *Don Giovanni*. Both illustrate the ambiguity of desire—an ambiguity that is present in Lacan's paper "Kant with Sade"—which will not be clarified fully until later, with the concept of jouissance. The ambiguity is that if we think of the satisfaction of desire as producing pleasure then desire will always find a limit beyond which pleasure is not produced. We can call this limit the subject's well-being, but if, on the other hand, we think of desire as jouissance then, as psychoanalysis has discovered, its very essence lies in its transgression. The point is, clearly, that jouissance and transgression form a couple: There is no jouissance without transgression. But the point becomes less clear when we ask what it is that has been transgressed. While it may seem obvious that the transgression is a transgression of the law, this does not exhaust all questions. Which law is transgressed? The moral law? The law of the land? These issues, which bear upon the question of the law and its relation to jouissance, are highly relevant to psychoanalysis.

It is significant that for Freud psychoanalysis only recognizes one law: the Oedipal law that lies at the heart of all society—a law that every subject has always already transgressed. Any subsequent transgression is always and only a substitute. Yet even here there are further issues, for it is not as if Freud's Oedipus complex is unequivocal on the relationship between the law and jouissance.

Perhaps it would be better to say that Freud has two quite separate and opposite views about the relationship between jouissance and the law, one of which is expressed in the Oedipal myth, the other in the myth of the primal horde. Both are myths of the father in Freud, but with significant differences. The most striking difference is the inversion in the relationship between desire and the law. The Oedipus complex is meant to explain how desire and jouissance are regulated by the law. Both the Oedipus myth, "borrowed from Sophocles," and the primal horde myth involve the murder of the father. The consequences of this murder are exactly opposite in the two cases because of the place the law occupies in each case. Both deal with what Lacan had previously been calling the Name-of-the-Father, a signifier intimately tied up with jouissance and its regulation by the law, yet the relationship between the law and jouissance that unfolds in each, oddly enough, ends up inverted. In the Oedipus myth, the law is there from the outset; it is an inexorable law, demanding punishment even when the transgression has been committed unwittingly. The law precedes enjoyment and enjoyment henceforth takes the form of a transgression.

In *Totem and Taboo*, on the other hand, enjoyment is there at the outset, at least in appearance, and the law comes afterwards. This leads Lacan to say that there is *"une schize*, a split, separating the myth of Oedipus from *Totem and Taboo*."[5] The reason? They are responses, respectively, to the clinical experience of hysteria, and obsessional neurosis. The Oedipus complex is the myth that Freud creates in response to the clinic of hysteria, and the myth of the primal horde father of *Totem and Taboo* is Freud's response to the clinic of obsessional neurosis.

Lacan discusses the issue of the relationship between jouissance and the law in *The Ethics of Psychoanalysis* and in "Kant with Sade" in relation to Antigone. It is not always clear what Lacan has in mind in these texts, particularly in "Kant with Sade." And there has been a tendency to conceptualize what he says in terms of a distinction between the "positive law" and some form of the Law, such as, for instance, the law of the superego. On this interpretation, it seems reasonably clear how positive law and the Law (of the superego) might differ: Antigone acts in the name of a higher law, in the recognition that Creon's law, which is the positive law, falls short of it. In her no-saying to the power of the city she can be allied with civil protesters, agitators, and—why not?—terrorists insofar as she transgresses the positive law in the name of something "higher."

I think this is not only incorrect but also trivializes the distinction, reducing it, as it does, to the recognition that the legal code and the moral code are not the same thing. For while it may be true that they are not the same thing, they are not entirely distinct either—and for good reason. Let me explain.

First, there is the case of Dostoyevsky. When Freud came to explore the relationship between guilt and transgression, he came to the view that the causal chain between them was sometimes the opposite of what we would ordinarily suppose. Common sense would have it that one feels guilty because of a transgression. But Freud speculates on cases where one transgresses because one feels guilty; and by transgressing one at least gives the guilt an object. Thus a man oppressed by an unconscious sense of guilt, and therefore unaware of its origin, commits a criminal act in order that the guilt he carries unconsciously can find a real and particular object. Melanie Klein reinforced Freud's views. Aware of the intense violence and extreme cruelty the superego displays towards the subject's unconscious desires, she recognized the unbearable situation in which this left the ego. The person's response is to externalize the guilt, which it does by committing some crime or transgression for which they will be apprehended and punished. Thus Klein gives further support to Freud's thesis in suggesting that where the motive for criminal behavior is the externalization of unconscious guilt, the external situation in some way reflects the ferocious internal attack perpetrated upon the ego by a hostile and threatening superego. As a consequence, the real, external punishment becomes less threatening than the sadism of the superego, before which the ego feels itself to be more or less entirely helpless.[6] This is a process that can be understood as coming entirely under the pleasure principle—or at least would come under the pleasure principle were it not for the fact that at the same time as the "crime" is externalized, punishment by an external agent will satisfy the ego's own desire for punishment.

Note, incidentally, that Klein's analysis of guilt and transgression makes little reference to any Oedipal dynamics but relies very heavily upon an aggressiveness that is internal and innate. And in point of fact it is not quite accurate to say that Freud puts the guilt before the transgression, for the unconscious guilt in question has its own origin in Oedipal desires and wishes concerning the murder of the (primal) father.

Of course, none of what Freud says about guilt and transgression will work unless the transgression is not only a legal transgression but a moral one as well. The transgression had better be a moral one, and moreover one that is symbolically linked to the original, unconscious, Oedipal crime.

There is a second point about criminal transgression that I would like to mention: the case of wartime atrocities. There are three very common, though perhaps not universal, features of the wartime atrocity that are particularly relevant to the point I want to make concerning the light psychoanalysis is able to throw on criminal transgression. The first is that the perpetrators of the particular type of criminal act that we call wartime atrocity are, on the whole, otherwise good, decent, and law-abiding citizens. That is, they generally have no previous history of criminal transgression and generally no subsequent history of violent crime either, a fact that in itself is quite remarkable. There is plenty of postwar trauma and mental illness, of course, but actual crime is much less frequent. The second fairly common characteristic is that such actions are generally condoned, or at the very least excused, by the people on whose side and on whose behalf those who commit the atrocities are fighting. Their readiness to fight and, if necessary, sacrifice their own lives is arguably a significant factor in this response by their people to their actions.

The third feature, and the one I want to emphasize, is that wartime atrocities are rarely random events but generally display a symbolic, strictly Oedipal structure. We can see this most clearly when they take a ritualized form: the raping of women in the presence of a helpless, impotent, intimidated father or father figure; or, again, the specific forms that bodily mutilation takes. In this case, the atrocity, in its transgressive function, reflects the very form of the social fabric, and not only the social fabric of the victims but also of the perpetrators themselves. In other words, the transgression is an expression of the symbolic laws, and not just as they pertain to the victims but also as they pertain to the perpetrators' group as well.

Moreover, the symbolic link is what makes criminal behavior part of the subject's psychopathology. That is, criminal behavior is never in itself psychopathological. What makes criminal behavior psychopathological is the features it has in common with other, non-criminal, forms of psychopathology: typically, compulsive behavior, repetition, and exaggerated remorse. There will also be a symbolic link to the history of the subject.[7]

The comparison between criminal behavior and psychopathology is similar to the case of the superego in relation to moral behavior, particularly the superego of the obsessional neurotic. As we know, obsessionals are particularly moral individuals. But what reveals the presence of the pathological superego in their moral rectitude is that indignation at the immorality of others is combined with a sadistic and inhumane adherence to the moral law. Or, again, obsessionals sometimes manifest a readiness to devote themselves to the well-being of others by a general love of humanity and warm devotion to everyone, but with the exception—and here is the rub—of those they love the most.

Thus the psychopathological aspect to the behavior of the criminal manifests itself the same way it does in the behavior of the obsessional or any other neurotic. The psychopathology is not expressed by the act, criminal or otherwise, but in the form or general structure of the behavior in question, and so what is common to the behavior of the criminal act and psychopathology is the symbolic content. But in this respect whatever psychopathology might appear in criminal behavior is no different from psychopathology in other circumstances. Things are no different here than they are with respect to the differences between neurosis and psychosis. The themes are the same, the content of the symptoms and so forth are the same; where they differ is in the structure of the two conditions where one results from the process of repression, the other from foreclosure. However, Lacan also indicates that the fact that the psychotic's discourse is just as interpretable as neurotic phenomena, such as dreams, leaves the two disorders at the same level and fails to account for the major, qualitative differences between them. Therefore, if psychoanalysis is to account for the distinction between the two, then it cannot do so on the basis of meaning alone. It can only do so on the basis of the "structure," and the structures it recognizes are those familiar to us in psychopathology: neurosis, psychosis, and perversion.

Where transgression is an expression of guilt it is essential that the transgression result in loss and punishment. But it does not necessarily have to be a criminal offense. A good, nasty marriage breakup where one loses the partner, kids, and family home will do the trick just as well. We know the power of unconscious guilt in analysis, where it is not uncommon for unconscious guilt to become active, and the risk of major acting out of this kind can be quite a serious consideration. To sum up this point, it is not merely a question of transgressing the law; the transgression has not just a legal dimension but a moral one as well. This point raises a new question about the relationship between law and morality. In our societies, the movement over the past, say 150–200 years, has been to separate the law and morality, both philosophically—concerning in particular the justification of punishment—and in actual practice. Philosophically, ever since the emergence of the secular state and ever since the time of Jeremy Bentham's Panopticon, the "progressive" approach to punishment has been the utilitarian one of justifying it by its consequences, that is, punishment deters potential criminals and rehabilitates actual criminals—or it should at least aim at so doing.[8] Completely foreign to this are issues around retribution, reparation, and expiation. In my view, the notion of the therapeutic treatment of crime forms part of a general repressive approach to crime and transgression that began in the nineteenth century and that is best symbolized by the image of Bentham's Panopticon. The thesis is, of course, Foucault's, according to which the policy of reforming the individual offender emerged as the new form of social control to replace the former regime of punishment. The early interest by psychoanalysts in forensic issues led to the view that treating offenders was to be preferred over punishing them— better the couch than the cell. However, to this extent, psychoanalysis can be seen as contributing to a new view of punishment in our society, one that reinforces the repressive function of the law.

Now psychoanalytic approaches to crime since Freud have generally fit into this progressive approach, particularly in the hope that psychoanalysis may be able to contribute to crime prevention. A number of psychoanalysts, most with a background in psychiatry, became forensic specialists in the belief that psychoanalysis had something to offer law enforcement, crime prevention, and punishment. The British psychoanalyst Edward Glover contributed not only to debates on the investigation and treatment of crime over a long period from the 1920s to the 1960s, but he was also involved in the founding of both the Institute for the Study and Treatment of Delinquency and an institution called the Psychopathic Clinic, the world's first-ever psychiatric clinic concerned with delinquent study and therapy.[9] Then, in Berlin, in the late 1920s, Franz Alexander and lawyer Hugo Staub published *The Criminal, the Judge, and the Public*, which produced much interest at the time of its publication.[10] Their work includes a number of case studies of criminal offenders, including one by Marie Bonaparte. The general tenor of these contributions can be described as "progressive."

There is an appeal for a more compassionate understanding of the factors that lead to criminal behavior, and this combines with an enlightened, nonretributive approach to punishment, including the recommendation that treatment replace punishment. I do not know if any psychoanalysts have argued this, but some philosophers have appealed to psychoanalysis to argue that psychoanalytic theories of compulsive behavior and unconscious determinism imply that it is a mistake to blame offenders for their transgressions, since their behavior is beyond their conscious control. Humans never really act freely and hence cannot be held accountable for their actions. This is not, however, Freud's lesson which is that one is responsible for one's actions, even—particularly—those one does not know one is doing. Be that as it may, to view punishment as justified solely by its value as deterrent misses something of symbolic importance in any positive legal code. The point is that the law must in some way carry "moral weight," that is, it must be seen both to serve the interests of justice and to arise out of serious moral considerations. It is this connection to morality that makes for the difference in gravity between a serious crime such as murder and a lesser one such as civil disobedience. And the connection between morality and the law can get out of kilter, as when the punishment for civil disobedience exceeds the gravity of the transgression.

Renata Salecl relies upon this point, if I read her correctly, when in *The Spoils of Freedom* she refers to the "lawlessness" of socialism. She describes a situation in which the law under socialism—the law, that is, that defines what is legal, what is prohibited, what is constitutional, and what is not constitutional—was subordinate to the goal of constructing communism; the law thus became a purely utilitarian law in which the means were subordinate to the final "good." Salecl adds that under socialism the law was constantly transgressing itself, that the Party was constantly inventing new laws, constantly rewriting the constitution.

The upshot of all this, however, was that there ended up no longer being any identification with the system as such; people only obeyed the law because they were compelled to, because they were afraid of the consequences if they did not.[11] Implied here, then, is the fact that simply being afraid of the consequences is not enough. That is, the subject needs to accept the moral legitimacy of the law for the legal sanction to have the value of punishment. In the absence of this link to morality, punishment is transformed into something else: for instance, repression or revenge or, as in the case Salecl describes, mere social control, where the subjects obey the law not because they agree with the law but because they are compelled to.

Now I believe Salecl's comments do not apply uniquely to the former socialist states but apply, perhaps in a slightly modified way, to capitalist societies as well. What she describes is a legal system based on a utilitarian approach to punishment devoid of any notion that the penalty must match the crime—a utilitarian rationale that appeals uniquely to the consequences of punishment. For socialism, there was one ultimate consequence: the conditions for the establishment of communism. Under capitalism, the rationale is that punishment deters, quarantines, and rehabilitates: punishment deters potential criminals; incarceration quarantines actual criminals from society; and, perhaps less convincingly, punishment leads to the offender's rehabilitation. Unless we understand the law in this way and not just as a "positive legal code," we will not properly understand the relationship between law and its transgression.

I have discussed three ways in which transgression and the law can be related and three corresponding "types": The first is that described by Freud, where transgression externalizes guilt that is of unconscious origins and relates to the Oedipal situation. The second is that described by Kant, embodied by Antigone, where transgression is carried out in the name of the moral law. The third, described by Lacan, is the figure for whom transgression is itself a source of jouissance. This is a figure, moreover, for whom the risk of loss and punishment compounds the jouissance. I end by adding a fourth, which brings us back to Freud, the jouissance of the ascetic, of the saint—the jouissance of instinctual renunciation. As Freud puts it:

> Conscience . . . is indeed the cause of instinctual renunciation to begin with, but later the relationship is reversed. Every renunciation of instinct now becomes a dynamic source of conscience, and every fresh renunciation increases the latter's severity and intolerance.[12]

Thus we too have tended to reduce punishment to a utilitarian function, albeit a correctional one; as a consequence, the retributive function and the converse expiatory function of punishment is so far removed from our modern sentiments that retributive justice is typically associated with the vengeful God of the Bible and the Talion Law. Yet we have not given up totally on the retributive idea that the punishment must match the crime; the utilitarian approach has not so totally replaced the retributive philosophy that we think it is just to dissuade criminality by punishing the innocent where this would work.

For example, the reason we consider it unjust to destroy the house of the family of those accused of crimes against the state, when the family members have not been implicated in the crimes themselves, is that however dissuasive the actions may be, it is still wrong to punish the innocent for the crimes committed by and in the name of another. And this brings us back to the start, where the idea emerged that psychoanalysis could contribute to advances in criminology by advocating treatment over punishment, for this is part of a mental health approach to crime and punishment. It seems logical to think that if the criminal can be shown to have committed his or her crime as a kind of *passage à l'acte* that is perpetrated in the name of a punitive and sadistic superego, then the offender needs help, not hanging. However, an unintended consequence of the approach that takes the blame out of crime seems to be that it compounds the malaise in civilization.

Slavoj Žižek is sensitive to this point when discussing Kant's concept of "*Achtung*," respect for another person, who should never be treated solely as a means but always as an end. "How," Žižek asks, "do we show respect" to a "criminal who cruelly and intentionally killed another person; how do we show proper respect for him?" Žižek replies, with characteristic hyperbole, "by condemning him and shooting him, since this is the way we treat him as a free, reasonable person; whereas all the talk about the impact of social circumstances treats him 'disrespectfully'—that is, not as a free, responsible agent, but as a plaything of social mechanisms."[13] Žižek is hyperbolical to the point of being misleading, because retribution need not entail cruel and excessive punishment but simply respect for human dignity. This entails that criminals be punished for their crimes, and only for their crimes, since this is the meaning of treating a person as an ends and not as a means, just as it entails that the law must have moral legitimacy.

Chapter 9

Absolute Freedom and Radical Change

On Žižek

The importance of Slavoj Žižek's work was obvious from the first of his books in English, *The Sublime Object of Ideology*. One of the remarkable features of this outstanding work, as I see it, is the way it captures and conveys some of the sense of what made Lacan's work so exciting to a generation or two that had come under his influence in France from the early fifties through the eighties. It captured the novelty of Lacan's thinking about language and the unconscious and, indeed, the radical nature of the unconscious itself, just as it conveyed the sense of what might otherwise look like empty rhetoric, namely, that psychoanalysis is a radical and subversive doctrine whose practice calls into question dominant discourses of autonomy and subjective self-determination. Žižek's work added to this the element, present everywhere in Lacan's work but sometimes lacking from his commentators, of an intensely stimulating dialogue with an extensive psychoanalytic, philosophical, and literary tradition. In this respect, it is a significant fact that Žižek never came to Lacan directly—he is too young to have sat through the seminars whose power we can now judge only in written form—but through the seminars and teaching of Jacques-Alain Miller.

The emphasis of Žižek's later work has moved away from the sort of exposition of the work of Lacan via various fields that, if it were possible to use the term purely descriptively rather than as a proper name, might be called "cultural studies." The genre of the "everything you want to know about Lacan explained by other means" that marked his early books has given way to a more programmatic analysis of philosophy, religion, and politics and society that, while grounded in the Lacanian framework, has nevertheless other aims

119

more overtly philosophical and political. In retrospect, these aims have always been present, and his more recent work indicates not so much a shift as a shift of emphasis. The emphasis on political and social dimensions in particular is not such a common thing in psychoanalysis, for while it is true that there has been no shortage of political engagement, this has typically taken the form of an add-on to the clinical practice of psychoanalysis itself. From the other side, critical theorists, social theorists, and cultural theorists have looked to psychoanalysis for what it can contribute to an already more or less clearly defined and well articulated position. This has tended to make for an optimistic reading of psychoanalysis which, though by no means universal, argues for a reinterpretation in progressive terms of what are standardly seen as the conservative implications of psychoanalytic theory.

Žižek's political analysis arises directly from psychoanalysis of a Lacanian orientation. His is, to be sure, just one approach that could be taken, fundamentally marked as it is by a Hegelianism acquired at an earlier stage. But in my view this Hegelianism is pre-Oedipal in the true Lacanian sense; it leaves a trace that has been reconfigured *nachträglichkeit*, and the essential aspect of Žižek's work is clearly Lacanian.

While this approach in which political considerations are filtered through the lens of psychoanalysis is not the least interesting aspect of Žižek's work, it also raises some real questions. Žižek has not shied away from these, and indeed he has taken up the challenge to recent criticisms that have claimed that psychoanalysis has something inherently conservative about it. In the context of this important debate about the political implications of psychoanalysis, and of the Lacanian orientation in particular, a question arises with respect to Žižek's account of both individual action and political change. This question concerns what Žižek calls acts of "total" or "absolute" freedom. The concept of an act of absolute freedom, as I shall call it, plays a key role in his work because it is central to his account of how individuals or groups can intervene to bring about significant political or social change. I will discuss first Žižek's account, then the role it plays for him, and finally some reservations I have about it.

According to Žižek an act of absolute freedom can be performed either by individuals or groups—the structure or "logic" is the same in either case. Essentially, for Žižek, absolute freedom addresses the issue of whether everything that happens or that one can do is determined in advance by a kind of monolithic big Other. On Žižek's view, not only is it the case that what practices are authorized is determined by the Other, but also all so-called "subversive" practices that challenge and supposedly undermine the dominant code in actual fact themselves turn out to be determined and in a sense even authorized by the code and thus fail in their subversive aim. For an act to be truly subversive it must break with the code in a more radical or fundamental, or even an absolute, way, and Žižek's concept of an *act* of absolute freedom, which he says derives from the concept of act in Lacan's work, is intended to capture this idea of an absolute break.

In *Enjoy Your Symptom!* Žižek takes the "irresolution" of the ending of Rossellini's film *Stromboli* as an opportunity to discuss this notion of an act of absolute freedom—or at least the subjective dimension of such an act.[1] The film ends with Karin, having fled her husband and the suffocating life of the small village where for a number of years she made her home, reaching the region of the island's volcanic crater, where she is overcome by fumes. As she begins to lose consciousness, she negates—says "no" to—her adoptive community, but then, for a brief moment, she awakens to some sort of epiphanic experience in which the dour grimness of the island life has been transformed in her own appreciation of its eerie beauty. As Žižek stresses, the ending of the film leaves fundamentally indeterminate the subsequent step that Karin will take: return to or flight from the village. At least this is how things unfold in its Italian version, for by the artifice of a voice-over the American version leaves us in no doubt that Karin finds reconciliation with life in the village. Žižek clearly considers the American version a mistake because, he says, it is extremely important that, and this is a point made by Rossellini, Karin's *act* of renunciation should not be confused with any *action* she might subsequently carry out.

> By this very irresolution of its ending, *Stromboli* marks the proper dimension of the act: it ends at the precise point at which the *act* is already accomplished, although no *action* is yet performed. The act done (or more appropriately: endured) by Karin is that of *symbolic suicide*: an act of "losing all," of withdrawing from symbolic reality, that enables us to begin anew from the "zero point," from that point of absolute freedom called by Hegel "abstract negativity."[2]

For Žižek the subjective dimension of this act of absolute freedom portrayed in the film is that what had once been experienced as a loss or renunciation becomes transformed into the "loss of a loss itself," or the renunciation of a renunciation: that is, what "a moment ago, [Karin] was afraid to lose" in fact comes to be totally lacking in value and significance for her, and she thus becomes aware that, despite what her fears may once have been, she can lose nothing.[3] This act, which is an "*act* in the Lacanian sense," is an act of "withdrawal by means of which we *renounce renunciation itself*, [and become] aware of the fact that we have nothing to lose in a loss."[4]

This renunciation of renunciation is what distinguishes Karin's "symbolic suicide," as Žižek calls it, from "actual suicide." In actual suicide the act "remains caught within the network of symbolic communication: by killing himself the subject attempts to send a message to the Other, i.e., it is an act that functions as [for instance] an acknowledgment of guilt, a sobering warning, a pathetic appeal."[5] In contrast, an act of symbolic suicide "aims to exclude the subject from the very intersubjective circuit."[6]

This redoubled renunciation, "renunciation of renunciation" or "loss of loss," is then a defining characteristic of an act of radical freedom. A second, equally important aspect is that an act "radically transforms its . . . agent": "After an act, I'm literally 'not the same as before.' "[7] The subject is "annihilated and subsequently reborn"; "the act involves a kind of . . . *aphanisis* of the subject."[8] This aphanisis occurs because of the cut with all prior symbolic moorings by means of which the subject has acquired all previous identity. A *new* symbolic network entails the "death" of the old and the "birth" of a new subject.

Note at this point that these two features of "an act"—the rebirth of the subject and the realization that henceforth there is nothing to fear, that nothing can harm one—are ways in which religious conversion and faith have been described and give a corresponding religious tone to Žižek's notion of an act. While I wonder whether this is accidental, or incidental, this is an impression created by the fact that we have so far considered merely the subjective dimension of the issue.

We should also note that notions of radical transformation of the subject are notoriously vague as to their political or practical consequences. We know that in religious metaphors of rebirth or in more epistemological functions as in, for instance, Cartesian subjective enlightenment, while the subject is in some sense totally reborn—nothing is the same, everything is changed—this rebirth may well be achieved with no immediate or obvious or even any real change of any practical kind. This has been noted by numerous commentators a propos of Cartesian *askesis* in the *Meditations*, just as it has been noted concerning meditative experiences properly so-called. In purely subjective transformation, there is no implication that there will ever be real practical consequences for the lives of the people involved; an act of absolute freedom need not result in any practical change. It can, in an important sense, leave everything as it is. Yet while it *may* leave everything as it is, it may not either. The very example Lacan initially chose to introduce the quilting point, which is the high priest's "fear of God" in Racine's *Athaliah*, indicates the subject's anchorage in a symbolic system that not only sustains his resolve in the face of mortal danger but also converts the irresolute Abner to the cause.

To see the political dimension of the act, in which the status quo ante is irremediably destroyed, we need to consider its objective effects, which include, on the one hand, the act's consequences specifically for the agent, and, on the other, the act's consequences in a broader sense.

In both cases the consequences of an act are radically under-determined. Thus the subjective rebirth of which Žižek speaks goes along with the fact that an act is "radically unaccountable," and that one can never fully *foresee its consequences*, in particular, "the way it will transform the existing symbolic space."[9] In an act one is risking everything and putting everything at stake, oneself and one's symbolic identity included. It is a "rupture after which 'nothing remains the same.' "[10] And this is, moreover, invoked to explain why we can never foresee the way in which history will unfold in advance but can only explain its course retrospectively.

Furthermore, "the act is . . . always a 'crime,' " or a "'transgression' . . . of the limit of the symbolic community" to which one belongs.[11] Though this is not stated in as many words, the reason for this would appear to be that from the standpoint of the current symbolic Other, the act is essentially both destructive and gratuitous. Thus Žižek states that an act is always *negative*, an act is always "an act of annihilation, of wiping out—we not only don't know what will come of it, its final outcome is ultimately even insignificant, strictly secondary in relation to the NO! of the pure act."[12] It is fairly easy to see then that an act achieves what subversive practices cannot, namely, a rupture with the big Other.

Finally, Žižek considers that it is no accident that the paradigmatic example of an act, which he takes to be Antigone's "No!" to Creon, is the act of a woman. And he wonders whether the genuine act is "feminine," in contrast to the masculine performative that is the founding gesture of a new order. From this point of view, the

> difference masculine/feminine no longer coincides with that of active/passive, spiritual/sensual, culture/nature, etc. The very masculine *activity* is already an escape from the abysmal dimension of the feminine *act*. The "break with nature" is on the side of woman, and man's compulsive activity is ultimately

nothing but a desperate attempt to repair the traumatic incision of this rupture.[13]

In a further development that appears later in *Enjoy Your Symptom!* Žižek equates the genuine act to the authentic ethical act, as this is understood by Lacan. Such an act "presents the only moment when we are effectively 'free': Antigone is 'free' after she has been excommunicated from the community."[14] And Žižek suggests that acts similar to Antigone's today are typically dubbed "terrorist," "like the gesture of Gudrun Ensslin, leader of the 'Red Army Faction,' a Maoist 'terrorist' organisation, who killed herself in the maximum security prison in 1978," where what was "really disturbing . . . was not the bombs but the refusal of the forced choice, of the fundamental social pact."[15] Insisting upon this radical nature of Antigone's act, Žižek adds that "today, when Antigone is as a rule 'domesticated,' made into a pathetic guardian of the community against tyrannical state power, it is all the more necessary to insist upon the scandalous character of her 'No!' to Creon: those who do not want to talk about the 'terrorist' Gudrun, should also keep quiet about Antigone."[16] Thus, far from reproaching the Red Army Faction (RAF) for going too far when they suspended even elementary ethical principles, we should acknowledge that their "suspension of the ethical" is the refusal of the subject's alienation in a universal symbolic pact.[17]

It is important for Žižek's purposes that Antigone's act not just lie outside the law but that it be a complete rupture with the law. Yet the comparison to Enslinn is surely pushed too far. In both cases, to be sure, there is a no-saying to the state power, just as there is a similarity in their suicidal act. And it is also true that Antigone is no "guardian of the community," since her act is blind to the consequences it may have for those amongst whom she lives and presumably, though there is little evidence of this in the play, for whom she cares. But it does not follow that what was "really disturbing about the [Red Army Faction] 'terrorism' was not the bombs but the refusal of the forced choice, of the fundamental social pact."[18] On the contrary, it is precisely the campaign of terror that distinguishes the Red Army Faction from Antigone, who is no terrorist but a person who refuses to comply with a command she thinks is wrong—and who does so, moreover, in the name of a higher law.

Indeed, I think that Žižek is too quick to lump together cases that are actually different in important ways. Not only are Antigone and Enslinn different cases but so too are Antigone and Sygne de Coûfontaine, whom Žižek also compares to one another. I argue later that Antigone's act is *not* an act of absolute freedom in the required sense. It is arguable that Sygne de Coûfontaine's act is, but not Antigone's. And the reason Antigone's is not is that she is acting, and sacrificing herself, blindly, in the name of the law—even if it is the fractured law of Oedipus.

Žižek's notion of an act has an important role to play in his response in *The Ticklish Subject* to a criticism Judith Butler makes of psychoanalysis. This response occurs in the context of a defense of Lacan against the criticism that his views allow no possibility of resistance to the existing power structure because, as Butler argues in *The Psychic Life of Power*, all resistance "presumes the continuation of the law" and thus "contributes to its status quo."[19] If this is so, then all "resistance appears doomed to perpetual defeat."[20]

Žižek's response is to claim that Butler has gotten Lacan wrong. Indeed, for Lacan, "radical rearticulation of the predominant symbolic Order is altogether possible—this is what his *point de capiton* . . . is about: when a new *point de capiton* emerges, the socio-symbolic field is not only displaced, its very structuring principle changes."[21] Thus "Lacan leaves open the possibility of a radical rearticulation of the entire symbolic field by means of an *act* proper, a passage through 'symbolic death.' "[22] And this, he claims, is the whole point of Lacan's reading of *Antigone*:

> Antigone . . . risks her entire social existence, defying the socio-symbolic power of the City embodied in . . . Creon. . . . For Lacan, there is no ethical act proper without taking the risk of such a "momentary suspension of the big Other"; an authentic act occurs only when the subject risks a gesture that is no longer "covered up" by the big Other.[23]

Butler's point that, for psychoanalysis, opposition to the law is merely its acknowledgment and preservation by other means mirrors an old one made within psychoanalysis itself, dating back to Freud, whose account of the primal horde captures what is at issue: The brothers' revolt against the father merely reinforces their own subjugation to his law. And do we not all know, from Lacan's public pronouncements, that he endorses this view himself? His contemporary criticism of the French student revolution, in which he referred to the *mois*, egos/ months, of May, and his accusation that they were in search of a master whom, moreover, they would no doubt find, is a prima facie indication that all revolt acts within and confirms the law whose chains it thinks it is breaking. The point is—is it not?—that revolt is structural, for while structures do not march in the streets, they determine who will: how, then, can resistance lead to radical change?

Žižek is in general agreement that real social change is no easy matter. He says, on the one hand, that there can be "imaginary" resistance to the symbolic order, which is a "misrecognition of the symbolic network that determines us," and, on the other, that Butler is both too optimistic and too pessimistic from a Lacanian point of view.[24] Her optimism stems from her overestimation of "the subversive potential of disturbing the functioning of the big Other through the practice of performative reconfiguration [and] displacement"—optimism because such practices "ultimately support what they intend to subvert, since the very field of such 'transgressions' is already taken into account . . . by the . . . big Other," which includes both "symbolic norms *and* their codified transgressions."[25] On the other hand, her pessimism does not allow for the radically subversive "act" that is capable of producing a "thorough restructuring of the hegemonic symbolic order in its totality."[26] Whereas Butler insists that any "protest" imitates the law it claims to overthrow, and that the hegemonic symbolic order can only be subverted by marginal gestures of displacement, Žižek counterclaims that the *act*, which defies and says "No!" to the big Other, is the sole event capable of producing a complete reconfiguration of the symbolic order itself.

Thus we can see that the *act* of which Žižek speaks assumes, and indeed must assume, considerable importance for him in the context of change. The constraining effects of the prevailing social order are manifest not just in subjective compliance with its imperatives but also in the "subversive" acts that transgress its norms. Yet from the point of view of political change, there would also appear to be a very disturbing implication of this view of an act: its radical indeterminacy, which implies that *all* political action is gratuitous and gratuitous in an absolute sense—not just from the point of the present order but gratuitous per se. To see this, let me turn to Žižek's, and Lacan's, treatment of what is something of a paradigm case, which is *Antigone*.

For Žižek's purposes, it is important that Antigone's act lie outside the law. But is this really so? While I can agree that Antigone's refusal, her "No!" to Creon, is fundamentally indeterminate, and that such is the nature of the *point de capiton* in general, her action is not a lawless one, nor is it beyond the symbolic world. Thus while the cases of Antigone and Ensslin have some obvious parallels, there are also fundamental differences: It is an extremely important feature of Antigone's act that it be nothing other than a no-saying. Her opposition is mute and stubborn, she may well be indifferent to the consequences of her act for her city, she does not attempt to overthrow or subvert Creon's law, and no actual attempt is made to destroy his city, which is also her city, for she knows that there is a "higher law" in the name of which she acts. In this respect she is more like Luther who, with his "Here I stand and can do no other," is resolute in the knowledge that he is doing God's will. Furthermore, the reason she is more like Luther is that her motivation comes from her obedience to the law of the father.

It is true that Antigone makes a choice: She chooses death and, as Lacan observes, in choosing death she is choosing to be the guardian of the being of the criminal as such. Is this choice one of radical freedom? Or shall we say, at least assuming for a moment that she is not a character in a play, that her choice is a neurotic choice and, moreover, that she is seriously neurotic? If we are prepared to look at Antigone from this point of view, then it seems to me that the "clinical case" of Antigone was demonstrated by Freud in his *Studies on Hysteria* with Anna O., a young woman devoted to the ideals of the father and to sacrificing herself, her own desires, to the perpetuation of the Oedipus complex. Just as Antigone does.

There is a difference though. While the character in the play acts entirely on her own and neither seeks nor requires assistance of any kind, Anna O., the neurotic, has her symptoms. She complains about them, and they lead her to seek help. This is part of what is meant by hysteria: In their symptoms, men and women will refuse a sacrifice they have made in the name of the father—a point easier to consider in light of Lacan's subsequent clarification of his position on the name of the father, when, in *Seminar 17*, he situates the aim of analysis beyond the Oedipus complex. Since in the case of Antigone we are not dealing with a clinical situation organized in order to give analytic form to symptoms, we cannot really treat it in the way we would treat a case. But we have known since Freud that it is very common for hysterics, despite their complaints, to manifest a desire to sustain the father's desire more than their own. This is something that can extend a long way. As we know, for example, from the clinic of anorexics, it can extend to the point of death.

If we consider Antigone in this way, then, if we compare her to a case, we might say that at the initial point at which she refuses Creon she best resembles a hysterical young woman. For she is a woman who when dreadful contingencies in her life catch her in a situation in which she is forced to make a decision decides somewhat blindly. If I am right in this, then the important question to ask is in what sense Antigone is acting on her desire and, consequently, whether her "act" can be described in the way Žižek sees it.

If it is true that Antigone is "acting on her desire," then we have to consider what this means. The first thing to notice is that while throughout the play she is, apparently, acting upon her desire, it is her *conscious* desire that is at stake. At no point is there any reflection upon, wonder about, doubt or rumination over, or analysis of what her desire is. She is always and constantly acting upon her desire and is oblivious to what drives her. The second thing to notice is that if there is any moment at which she can be said not to have given ground over her desire, as Lacan puts it in *Seminar VII*, then it comes when she has passed beyond the point of acceptance of her death sentence.[27] Now if she has not given ground with respect to her desire, then this is far from being a moment at which she has gone beyond the Other in an act of absolute freedom; it is, rather, a moment in which she recognizes what she has been for the Other, and she has accepted it.

Moreover, the pathos of the tragedy of *Antigone* draws our attention to a particular type of relation to desire that tends, owing to its inherent and structural unsatisfaction—a desire for an unsatisfied desire—to go beyond the limits of everything, but especially, here, beyond the limits of the person's own ideals. This is hysterical desire. And if psychoanalysis can speak of "hysterical desire," then it is because one can distinguish between the hysteric's and the obsessional's desire. This is why Hamlet appears as an example of the depressive obsessional, whereas Antigone presents as the epitome of manic hysterical behavior; whereas Hamlet has become the prisoner of the figure of an ideal father, Antigone has become a hero of, a martyr to, the father's desire.

This is why for Lacan the turning point in *Antigone* is the point at which Antigone becomes aware of and is moved by the loss she has experienced. It is not the point when she decides, "I will bury my brother" and says "No!" to Creon. At this point, whatever she may believe her desire to be, it is in fact a conscious decision that is an expression of her symptom, which is her tendency to sacrifice and to act in conformity with her family destiny. This means that of her desire Antigone might say something like: "I have been the eyes of my blind father. I have been his most beloved treasure and as dear to him as his own gaze—this gaze which represents his crime. Moreover, I have been this crime myself."

This at least is how things stand at the outset, on the occurrence of her initial no-saying to Creon. Note, however, that there is a subsequent crucial moment in the play. It plays the role of a certain *capitonnage*, quilting, that retroactively determines the meaning of Antigone's initial act. It is only *after* she has come to accept what her written destiny has been and what the signifiers of this destiny are that she can also accept some loss in her identification—hence, her lamentation. It is only at the time of this lament, when she is "between two deaths" and *still* chooses to do it because she knows that it *is* her fate and that she has accepted it after all, that we can say she has abandoned the ideals of her life and that she can be considered as belonging to a field beyond the pleasure principle.

Initially the situation is constructed in such a way that she is forced to choose between two alternatives—either bury her brother or give ground over her desire. The loss of ideals that is described at the second moment, the renunciation and abandonment of her feminine ideals especially, allows her to transform what had been a symptomatic position into a new relationship to her womanhood. She moves from a position in which she *incarnated* the Oedipal object to a point at which she consents to be an object in a different way—someone, at least in principle, capable of loving and being loved and, at least in principle, capable of having a child. Thus at this point she sees herself not only as a daughter—and I think this explains the puzzling point about the loss of a brother and the loss of a husband—but as a virtual bride and a virtual mother. At this moment she formulates, for the first time, an idea of what her accomplishments as a woman might have been. Even as she realizes what she has lost—this is very important and is emphasized by Lacan—in spite of this acceptance she still decides to realize and enact her destiny in all of its consequences.

In summary, then, the general point I would like to make about Antigone's "act" is that far from creating the absolute freedom to which Žižek refers, her initial "No!" to Creon is entirely consistent with, and binds her to, her family destiny and paternal law. Her "No," which is an act of both defiance and sacrifice, is initially quite ambiguous in its status; she defies the law of her city in the name of her (Oedipal) law—a law to which, by the very same act, she defiantly sacrifices herself. Indeed, this ambiguity *is* resolved, but only in the second moment when she renounces her ideals and seals her fate. But this second moment *also* entails the recognition and acknowledgment of those ideals. To my mind there is no "loss of loss" but a late *acknowledgment* of her loss, even as she *renounces* her ideals.

There is a similarity here with the aim of a psychoanalysis, which is to arrive at the point where one discovers what the law of one's destiny has been. This is a point that in *Seminar VII* Lacan makes in the following way: "This law is in the first place always the acceptance of something that began to be articulated before him in previous generations, and which is strictly speaking *Atè*."[28] Thus Lacan makes the claim, and it is one that applies to Antigone, *both* that the subject is the result of the Other's desire *and* that there is an acceptance of this on the part of the subject. In psychoanalytic treatment we are not dealing with something completely automatic. There is choice required by the subject. This choice always involves the *acceptance* of what Lacan describes as an *Atè*. Even if this *Atè* "does not always reach the tragic level of Antigone's *Atè*," it is nevertheless "closely related to misfortune."[29]

In the case of Antigone, as elsewhere, we should distinguish between a desire for death and the death drive. In this case, and in others too, they may well correspond. This is not in dispute. But Lacan is more interested in showing how the death drive can enter someone's life than he is in any pure desire for death. But we can also say that a pure desire will always be a pure desire for death. In fact, in Lacan's subsequent work—in the final pages of *Seminar XI*, specifically—we find the claim that there is no such thing as a pure desire that is not a desire for death.[30]

I mention this point because I believe that Žižek has a somewhat idealized view of desire. And I think that to properly consider Lacan's position on Antigone's desire and on her sacrifice, which means not idealizing the whimsical and gratuitous aspect of either, we should draw upon these last pages of Lacan's 1964 *Seminar XI*, which cast a different light on the case of Antigone discussed in 1960 in *Seminar VII*. Lacan makes some comments in support of the view that the exaltation of desire and its occasional confusion with whimsical behavior a propos of the case of Antigone can mislead us seriously about the ethics of psychoanalysis. Lacan puts it thus: "The offering to obscure gods of an object of sacrifice is something to which few subjects can resist succumbing, as if under some monstrous spell. . . . There are certainly few who do not succumb to the fascination of the sacrifice in itself."[31] Alongside Antigone we can place Kant as a philosopher who has the idea of a pure desire. And, as in the case of Antigone, Kant's ethics entails a secret jouissance of sacrifice—a point well made by Žižek in fact.

There is a further indication relevant to Lacan's thoughts about this "pure desire" in these last pages of *Seminar XI* when he also warns us that desire in its pure state culminates in the sacrifice, strictly speaking, of everything that is the object of love in one's human tenderness. Not only the rejection of the pathological object, in Kant's sense of "pathological," but also its sacrifice and its murder. So from this point of view in which we take Lacan's views of four years later into account, I think that the sum of Lacan's considerations about Antigone, about her desire, about how far she is beyond everyone and does not give ground over her desire, is not to be seen as an endorsement or exaltation of this "pure desire."

To summarize Žižek's position, as I see it, central to his analysis of political action is the concept of an act of absolute freedom. And the key to this concept is the notion of a rupture with the big Other: Any practice that does not rupture with the big Other will be condemned to repeat one or another of the practices made possible by the Other itself, which remains unaltered and unthreatened as a result. Thus the only practice that can rupture with the big Other is one that has the characteristics of an act, as outlined earlier.

Now the question that this raises is how radical this rupture needs to be to ensure a transformation of the big Other. And here it strikes me that Žižek is faced with an undesirable dilemma. On the one hand, the act needs to be grounded in a radical no-saying that is inexplicable not just in terms of a given big Other but in terms of *any other Other whatsoever*. This is because the act of absolute freedom, as Žižek understands it, derives its essential features (its freedom, its gratuitousness, its criminality, its unaccountability and unpredictability) from the fact that it lies outside all possible symbolic dimensions. It strikes me that not only does Antigone not conform to this requirement but also that it makes an act indistinguishable from mere whimsicality. There is no objective criterion, and there can clearly be no appeal to any subjective features to distinguish an act of absolute freedom from a gratuitous act. On the other hand, an act of absolute freedom may be free relative to a given symbolic order. This of course makes freedom relative rather than absolute—relative to a particular form, or determination, of the Other. It will be free from *its* strictures, gratuitous from *its* point of view, criminal in *its* eyes, and perhaps unaccountable and unpredictable within *its* framework. But it is unclear whether it is capable of doing the work that Žižek wants it to do, namely, to provide the means of rupture with a given framework.

Finally, I think that Žižek is inclined to overestimate how radical Antigone's act actually is, at least in terms of it being an absolute no-saying or refusal. I think it is improbable that her act is an act of absolute freedom in the required sense because, as discussed earlier, her no-saying reveals an allegiance to the autochthonous law of the father that is the source of her motivation. I see little ground for "absolute freedom" in this act.

Chapter 10

Descartes and the Subject of Science

Science was an ideal for Freud, one that included psychoanalysis, with its slow but careful advances and limited but important successes. Freud believed that psychoanalysis, like scientific inquiry, was on the side of *logos* and thus, with its "submission to the truth," it entailed the renunciation of pleasure through the "rejection of illusions."[1] "Science," including psychoanalysis, "is . . . the most complete renunciation of the pleasure principle of which our mental activity is capable."[2]

Lacan does not share Freud's idealism about science, nor does he deny the importance of science for psychoanalysis. He speaks on numerous occasions about science and its connection to psychoanalysis, and the indications are that there is a theory of science in Lacan's work.

Psychoanalysis, he says, would not have been possible without modern science—a general claim that we can break down into at least the two following theses:

1. The subject on which we operate in psychoanalysis is also the subject of science.

2. This subject of science is the Cartesian cogito.

In this chapter I develop this connection between psychoanalysis and science, specifically via this question of the subject.

FROM EPISTĒMĒ TO THEORIA

To see the importance Lacan attributes to the concept "subject of science," consider the following reasoning concerning the relationship of science to the four discourses discussed in *Seminar XVII, The Other Side of Psychoanalysis,* in particular, the relationship between science

133

and the discourse of the master. Lacan is discussing Plato's *Meno* in connection with what he calls the two faces of knowledge, of "*savoir.*" The French use two words, *savoir* and *connaissance,* whereas English makes do with one, "knowledge." "Savoir" is "knowing that," that is, it is propositional, whereas "connaissance" is, to use Bertrand Russell's term, knowledge by acquaintance. The two faces of *savoir,* then, are, first, its so-called articulated aspect as theoretical knowledge and, second, what Lacan calls "*savoir-faire,*" know-how.

He considers the familiar example in which Socrates demonstrates that if one asks the right questions, one can extract from the slave knowledge that the slave does not know he has—in the example he chooses, knowledge of how to draw a square that is double the area of a square with sides two feet long. The slave of course first makes the mistake of doubling the length of the sides but is then led by a series of questions to the correct answer, which involves use of the square root of two. While Socrates takes this to be proof of his theory of anamnesis, recollection, and, therefore, proof of prior incarnation, Lacan draws a different lesson from the example. He argues that it illustrates the implication of philosophy in the ultimate appropriation of the slave's knowledge, his know-how, and its incorporation into the discourse of the master:

> The entire function of the *episteme* insofar as it is specified as transmissible knowledge . . . is always borrowed from the techniques of craftsmen, that is to say of serfs. It is a matter of extracting the essence of this knowledge in order for it to become the master's knowledge.[3]

In the example the slave is made to appear rather ridiculous, a kind of fall guy, a figure of derision, but what is surreptitiously acknowledged in this derisory fashion is the expropriation of the slave's knowledge; it is being converted into the master's knowledge. Thus Lacan claims that philosophy acts in the service of the discourse of the master and here reveals "its historical function" of "betrayal" of the slave's knowledge and its transmutation into the master's knowledge.[4] Interesting though it would be to pursue this issue about the place of philosophy, I want to look at what conclusions we can draw about the place of science.

It could be argued that this science that dominates us is the fruit of this transmutation, to use Lacan's phrase, of the slave's know-how into the master's *savoir.* It is easy to see why one might think that this transformation is at least a necessary condition for science. The reasoning might go something like this: The artisan's practical know-how resides with each individual artisan, who will have most likely served a period of apprenticeship in order to learn the craft and acquire the required practical knowledge. The training will have been essentially individual and the knowledge of the craft typically transmitted on a one-by-one basis. Moreover, the social structures required do not need to be of any great complexity. To be sure, the artisan's tools and equipment may be crafted by others, which requires a division of labor and a system of exchange, and there may be guilds or societies that guarantee standards and/or protect the interests of members. But there probably does not need to be much more.

Now consider the case of modern scientific knowledge. It can no longer be said to reside with the individual. It is fragmented, being distributed throughout usually very complex social institutions of one kind or another in such a way that there is no one person who can be said to be the repository of scientific knowledge in its modern form. No one person, in a modern scientific context, possesses all the knowledge required to carry out his or her own piece of scientific research—the necessary knowledge is shared with colleagues, laboratory technicians, manufacturing industry, and so forth. The consequence of this is that the knowledge of modern science requires a network of complicated and highly structured social institutions—universities, laboratories, manufacturing plants, industrial complexes—in which this knowledge is lodged. The knowledge is simply too complex for a single person to hold. Moreover, complex social structures—universities, technical colleges, schools, professional colleges—are necessary for its transmission. In point of fact, we could say that the modern scientific knowledge is embodied in and distributed throughout the material world we inhabit, in the very machines and instruments the scientist requires for his or her work, and in the computers, power tools, and all of the other forms of energy-using machinery surrounding us.

This point was well made by the scientist Peter Medawar, who some twenty years ago (i.e., before the advent of personal computers) took the example of the television set to illustrate this point:

> A television set (perhaps the most complicated science-based contraption in everyday use) is not within the effective comprehension of any one mind, for there is no one person who knows the electronics and the glass and vacuum technology and has the know-how of plastic molding to such a degree of proficiency that if some holocaust were to obliterate science and technology so that we had to begin again, this one

knowledgeable human being could reinstruct and redirect the activities of those who would in due time reconstruct a television set. Clearly it was a committee or consortium of engineers and technologists, not any one man, that had the theoretical understanding and practical know-how to build a TV set. It was a great cooperative enterprise that brought TV sets into being, unlikely though it may at one time have seemed.[5]

The suggestion might then be made that Plato's *Meno* illustrates this expropriation of the slave's or artisan's knowledge and spoliation by the master, as the first stage in a long process that ultimately culminated in modern science. The question, then, is whether the transmutation of the slave's/artisan's knowledge into the master's knowledge can in and of itself produce anything like the point of emergence of science. Lacan's position is that while Plato's example has everything to do with the construction of the master's discourse, it has nothing, or at least very little, to do specifically with the emergence of science.[6] At best, it produces *theoria*—in Plato's case, knowledge of virtue and of other eternal, a priori, truths, but not science.

THE EMERGENCE OF SCIENCE

The emergence of scientific knowledge required something else; it required the emergence of the Cartesian subject. Science was born, Lacan claims, with Descartes, who "extracted the function of the subject from the strict relationship between S_1 and S_2."[7] One must distinguish, he adds, between this passage of knowledge from the slave to the master and "a certain way of raising . . . all possible functions of the statement (*énoncé*) insofar as the articulation of the signifier alone supports it."[8]

That is, modern science required a particular historical event: the emergence of the modern form of the subject, and this emerges with Descartes' cogito. Lacan's article "Science and Truth," in which he makes this claim, was the first session of his seminar for the period 1965–1966 on *The Object of Psychoanalysis*.[9] There is further discussion suggesting that Lacan's position on science in the later texts differs from the claims made in "Science and Truth."[10] Whether this is so, and if so how radically his later views depart, is an issue I cannot elaborate on here, nor will I discuss those authors who have commented on this.[11]

It is easy to forget how unusual is this claim that modern science required the emergence of the Cartesian cogito. To be sure, there is no disputing the fact that Descartes is the first modern philosopher, and this in many ways; but his scientific views are typically seen as confined to the metaphysics of *res extensa*. Koyré, for instance, distinguishes between the "Cartesian spirit" that refuses to inscribe the mind in the "cosmos of the Gods" and the cogito whose very constitution implies the existence of God.[12] Indeed, Lacan may well have been echoing these remarks of Koyré's when he declared that "Descartes inaugurates the initial bases of a science in which God has no part."[13] But in Lacan's view, what was decisive for the emergence of science was not *just* the constitution of a new object in the form of mathematized nature but *also* the emergence of the Cartesian cogito as the subject of science.

The standard view of Cartesian philosophy has it that it was by packing that which is not quantifiable, namely, thought and sensation, into the inner world of the cogito that Descartes was able to establish a fully mathematizable metaphysics of the physical world. Now while it is not quite a complete reversal of the standard view to claim, as Lacan does, that the cogito is also the subject of science, it is nevertheless a radical departure from it. But in fact it may be more accurate to speak of the Cartesian cogito as "the *correlate* of science," to employ Lacan's expression.[14] This would mean that Lacan's thesis is not a complete revision of the philosophy of science of his mentors, Koyré and Kojève, but rather an attempt to fill out what Lacan thinks it lacks.

EPISTEMOLOGY OF SCIENCE

In any case, in pursuing this question of the subject of science, I will focus on "Science and Truth."

The importance Lacan attaches to the *subject* of science leads him to criticize epistemological approaches for having failed in their attempts to define the object of individual sciences. In general terms, epistemology has, he says, ignored what he considers an essential precondition for the constitution of the object of all (modern) science, which is the emergence of the Cartesian cogito; epistemology has therefore not been able fully to explain this "decisive mutation" that, in the first instance, founded modern science by way of the new physics of Galileo:

> A certain reduction that . . . constitutes its object . . . is necessary [and] is . . . always decisive in the birth of a science. Epistemology proposes to define this in each and every case, without having proven itself . . . equal to the task.[15]

It is not clear quite whom Lacan has in his sights, but it is true that epistemological approaches to science have a long lineage, particularly in the empiricist tradition, and can be traced back at least as far as David Hume, with his "attempt to introduce the experimental method of reasoning into moral subjects," as the subtitle of his *A Treatise of Human Nature*[16] would have it, and perhaps even back to Bacon. But the epistemological approach finds arguably its best, and certainly its best known, exponent in Karl Popper, attempting as he does to define a demarcation between science and non-science by means of the essentially epistemological criterion of falsifiability: be bold in making hypotheses and fearless in attempting to show them false. The *locus classicus* is where Popper defines the problem of demarcation as that "of finding a criterion which would enable us to distinguish between the empirical sciences on the one hand, and mathematics and logic as well as 'metaphysical' systems, on the other."[17]

Lacan also speaks of a "demarcation" between science and the rest. But unlike Popper's, Lacan's demarcation will not draw a line between "empirical" science, on the one hand, and logic or mathematics, on the other. And while mathematical physics is Popper's model for scientific inquiry at its best, his criterion gives mathematics no particularly privileged place in science, apart from the fact that through its precision it has the merit of increasing the falsifiability of the hypothesized laws and theories expressed in mathematical terms.

The Subject

"Science and Truth" interweaves two separate issues concerning the subject and science. First, as suggested in the preceding discussion, the subject of science is the subject that makes science possible as the mathematical study of nature. As it turns out, for Lacan, this specifically modern form of subjectivity and science are imbricated in two ways: First, the modification in the "modality" of the subject in the form of the emergence of the Cartesian subject plays an inaugural role in science. Second, science has since its inception proceeded to reinforce this position of the subject ever further. As Lacan puts it, "What seems radical to me is the modification in our subject position, in both senses of the term, for it is inaugural therein and science continues to strengthen it ever further."[18] On Lacan's account, this "reinforcement" of the subject of science is essentially the product of the exponential expansion of technology, which Lacan describes as "the galloping form of the inmixing [of science] in our world" in the form of "chain reactions that characterize what can be called the expansions of its energetics."[19] This second point, concerning the technological dimension of science, with its impact upon subjectivity, is an important issue in the context of this discussion of the subject of science. By regarding knowledge, S_2, as able to be embodied in material objects, gadgets, machines, and industry, all of technology is seen as an embodiment of the formulas of science. As Lacan puts it, "The Lunar Landing Module . . . is Newton's formula realized in the form of an apparatus."[20]

The second issue concerning the subject arises around the claim that the subject of science is not, as Descartes thought, what is *excluded* from science; it is itself, in ways to be discussed, also amenable to scientific study. If to this we add the further observation that the subject of science *is also* the subject of the unconscious, then the interest psychoanalysis has in the question of science becomes immediately apparent.

As I stated at the outset, there is a theory of science in Lacan, one that in crucial respects differs from the views of Freud—and in Freud's case, one can really only speak of "views," not of a theory—on the matter. Lacan's more complex, less idealizing attitude relies upon close attention to the historical understanding of modern science and its origins, and upon considerable theoretical reflection and elaboration. As an illustration of this, consider the following commentary that Lacan makes on Freud. It is instructive both for the approach Lacan takes and for the conclusions he reaches.

Freud refers to the three "major blows" to the "naïve self-love" of humankind of which psychoanalysis, by showing that the ego is not master in its own house, was the third.[21] The first such blow was the "Copernican revolution," which destroyed the belief that humans regarded themselves as at the center of the cosmos, "when they learnt that our earth was not the centre of the universe but only a tiny fragment of a cosmic system of scarcely imaginable vastness." Freud adds that "this is associated in our minds with the name of Copernicus, though something similar had already been asserted by Alexandrian science."[22]

Lacan comments, first, that it is Kepler, not Copernicus, who should be credited with the crucial step in the scientific revolution; and, second, the crucial step was not relinquishing a geocentric view in favor of a heliocentric view of the universe but rather giving up circular for elliptical motion of heavenly bodies.[23] It sounds a bit fastidious, to be sure, but the point here involves more than a mere question of historical accuracy. The popular view in the history of science has it that Copernicus's theories were a victory for science over the prejudices of the mediaeval church. But what, Lacan asks, is so "revolutionary" (*sic*) in recentering our solar system on the sun? The really radical step, according to Lacan, was to replace circular with elliptical motion. For a start, this meant breaking with imaginary notions such as the circle as "perfect form," replacing it with an elliptical orbit with two foci, one of which was empty. But also, and more importantly, Kepler's laws of planetary motion paved the way for Galileo's great discovery of the law of inertia, which provided an explanation of Kepler's laws. This in turn made possible Newton's discovery of the law of gravitation, which brought under the one law both the motion of planetary bodies ("it turns") and the motion of ordinary mundane objects ("it falls"). Thus for Lacan the development from Kepler's original laws of planetary motion to Newton's universal law of gravitation that governs both heavenly and mundane bodies indicates a progressive overcoming of the imaginary by virtue of a mathematical mapping of the cosmos.[24] In other words, Lacan places particular emphasis on the subversive weight of Newton's formula, over and above the challenge to the imaginary privileging of the circle as a "perfect form."

We can add to this Freud's thesis that the origins of science are to be found in theories of sexuality, and that as science emerges it progressively "delibidinizes," desexualizes, the reality of which it speaks. This is an old thesis in Freud, of course, and finds many echoes in Lacan, such as when he states, "At the limit, primitive science would be . . . a sort of sexual technique."[25] And it then follows, by direct implication, that it is *because of* the mathematization of nature that, in the words of Jacques-Alain Miller, "the scientific approach assumes a desexualisation of the view of the world, . . . a desexualisation of being in the world."[26]

But even this is not the main point; the most important step, in Lacan's view, occurred when Newton introduced the notion of action at a distance by means of a mathematical formula, "which at each point submits the element of mass to the attraction of others for as far as this world extends, without anything playing the role of a medium to transmit this force."[27] One can also compare this to the following remark by Lacan:

What is crucial, as some people have noticed, is not Copernicus, but more specifically Kepler, due to the fact that in his work it does not turn in the same way—it turns in an ellipse, and that already throws into question the function of the centre. That toward which it falls in Kepler's work is a point of the ellipse that is called a focus, and in the symmetrical point there is nothing. That is assuredly a corrective to the image of the centre. But "it falls" only takes on the weight of subversion when it leads to what? To this and nothing more: $F = g.mm'/d^2$.[28]

I am stressing the particular emphasis Lacan places on the subversive weight of Newton's formula, over and above the challenge to the imaginary privileging of the circle as a "perfect form." The discovery was momentous because, first, the law of gravitation, $F = g.mm'/d^2$, was a purely mathematical formula introduced to explain natural phenomena; second, the natural phenomena were explained by *nothing but* the mathematical law. Newton's notion of action at a distance hypothesized no intervening mechanism—*hypotheses non fingo*—and the controversy that this notion produced in Newton's own day, its rejection by Huygens and Leibniz, is testimony to the upheaval wrought by a change in view that was able to produce an explanation in purely mathematical terms without recourse to hypothesized mechanical causes.

Newton's remark, "*Hypotheses non fingo*," was made in the context of the controversy over gravity and action at a distance. It refers to his cleaving solely to a mathematical formulation of the law of gravity. Leibniz regarded Newtonian gravity as an "occult quality" that could never be understood, even by God.[29]

As Lacan sees it, the revolution consists less in destroying the prejudices of our narcissism—pace Freud—than in the mathematization of the empirical world. And, again, I reiterate the point made earlier: It is this mathematization of the universe that reduces and eliminates the imaginary from science and knowledge.

Many details of Lacan's account derive from Koyré's work on the emergence of modern science. A central thesis of Koyré's is that the "transmutation" (a term he takes from Bachelard) that led to the emergence of modern science was brought about by the "geometrization of space," that is, the disappearance of the "concrete space" of pre-Galilean physics and its replacement by the "abstract space of Euclidean geometry."[30] This was, he says, a necessary change for the discovery of the law of inertia. What Lacan emphasizes is the metaphysical transformation induced by this mathematization.

And of course Cartesian metaphysics played a key role in this metaphysical transformation of the material world. Descartes reduces the properties of the material world to extension and movement, thereby guaranteeing its mathematization and contributing to modern cosmology.

As it happens, the mathematizability of the physical world is about the *only* thing that is modern about the Cartesian world. There is no vacuum, no empty space; there is just one single, homogeneous, infinitely extended thing which, while it is objective and measurable, bears little resemblance to subsequent scientific theories about matter.

Conversely, the distinction between secondary ("how things seem to us") properties and primary ("how things really are") properties attributes all that escapes scientific study to the realm of the mental. The secondary properties may well be ascribable to entities—minds—that are part of the furniture of the universe; they are not, however, susceptible to scientific study.

However, Lacan reads the cogito differently, and the frequent returns he makes to this issue indicate both its importance to him and the lengthy working through that theorizing the cogito entails. Some indication of the ground covered can be seen by comparing Lacan's 1949 remark that the experience of psychoanalysis "sets us at odds with any philosophy directly stemming form the *cogito*,"[31] and his claim that in 1964 he took as his guiding principle, "a certain moment of the subject that I consider to be an essential correlate of science, a historically defined moment, the strict repeatability in experience of which perhaps remains to be determined: the moment Descartes inaugurates that goes by the name of *cogito*."[32]

DESCARTES

In his *Meditations*, Descartes sets out to establish truth that is "stable and liable to last."[33] To this end he employs the method of hyperbolic doubt, which consists of doubting whatever one can find the slightest grounds for doubting, in order to determine whether anything absolutely certain and thus immune to this radical doubt remains. The doubt is arrested in the Second Meditation by the emergence of the absolute certainty of the cogito; from the mere fact of my thinking (doubting, wondering, etc.), it follows that I exist.

> [It is possible that] there is a deceiver of supreme power and cunning who is deliberately and constantly deceiving me and let him deceive me as much as he can, he will never bring it about that I am nothing so long as I think that I am something. So after considering everything very thoroughly, I must finally conclude that this proposition, *I am, I exist,* is necessarily true whenever it is put forward by me or conceived in my mind.[34]

As far as I know, Lacan always refers to the alternative and better-known formulation *"Cogito ergo sum,"* "I am thinking, therefore I am," which does not appear in the *Meditations* but in other works—

in the *Regulae* and, in French, in the *Discours de la Méthode*. However, the way in which Lacan interprets the cogito, and the fact that he writes "*Cogito, 'ergo sum,'* " "I am thinking, 'Therefore I am,' " makes it clear, as do his commentaries, that it is the *act of utterance* that gives the cogito its certainty. Nor should one forget the formulation Lacan expresses in bastardized French: "*Je suis pensant.*" In this respect, the *Meditations* formulation, which refers to the *act of enunciation* ("whenever it is put forward by me or conceived in my mind"), better reflects Lacan's intuition that the *necessity* of "I exist" lies entirely in the act by which it is formulated. I take this to be Lacan's point when he says, "Descartes apprehends his *I think* in the enunciation of the *I doubt*, not in its statement, which still bears all of this knowledge to be put in doubt."[35]

Now if the certainty of the "I am" derives purely from the *act* of utterance, then this certainty is "point-like," momentary, evanescent, and episodic; if there is a certainty, it is a certainty that lasts no longer than the time of the utterance, "I am thinking." Guéroult uses the term *assertoric* truth to express this,[36] and a similar point is also made by Hintikka.[37] However, Descartes wishes to establish truth that is *stable and liable to last*. But this assertoric truth of the cogito neither gives nor grounds the required stability and permanence. It therefore cannot lay to rest the skeptical challenge; indeed, the cogito might even be seen as the ultimate ironic victory of skepticism by reducing the subject to a repetition of the gesture of endlessly grounding its own certainty through a reiteration of, "I am, I exist; I am, I exist."

It is true that Descartes immediately concludes that he is a thinking thing, a *res cogitans*. As he says, "But what then am I? A thing that thinks. What is that? A thing that doubts, understands, affirms, denies, is willing, is unwilling, and also imagines and has sensory perceptions."[38] But, as Lacan points out, this is a hasty and unwarranted leap that Descartes makes from the *assertoric* certainty of "I am thinking" to the conclusion that the I that is thinking is a substance, a *res cogitans*. As Lacan puts it:

> Certainty, for Descartes, is not a moment that one may regard as acquired, once it has been crossed. Each time and by each person it has to be repeated. . . .
>
> When Descartes introduces the concept of a certainty that holds entirely in the *I think* of cogitation, . . . one might say that his mistake is to believe that this is knowledge, to say that he knows something of this certainty, and not to make of the *I think* a mere point of fading.[39]

Bertrand Russell makes the objection against Descartes' cogito that if one is prepared to grant the premise "I am thinking," then the rest follows.[40] However, he says, the premise concedes too much; the most one is authorized to say is not "I am thinking" but "There is thinking going on." Lacan's thesis is the diametrical opposite: He grants that there is a subject but concludes that it is a substanceless subject. Of course, to be able to arrive at this conclusion one has to stop at the evanescent and point-like cogito of the Second Meditation, at the point at which the Cartesian meditator says, " 'I am, I exist' is necessarily true whenever I say it or conceive it in my mind," thus reducing the cogito to its pure utterance.

THE SUBJECT OF SCIENCE

This, then, is the Cartesian subject as Lacan reads it. It may or may not be an accurate reading of the Cartesian cogito, but it is certainly a defensible one. The question remains though, in what way does it qualify as "scientific"?

Jean-Claude Milner answers this question in the following terms. Just as classical mathematical physics eliminates all qualities from objects, so a theory of the subject corresponding to this physics will also have to be stripped of all qualities.

> No appropriate qualitative marks of empirical individuality, whether psychical or somatic, will suit it [the subject]; the qualitative properties of a soul will not suit it any better; it is neither mortal nor immortal, neither pure nor impure, neither just nor unjust, neither sinner nor saint, neither damned nor saved; it will not be suited by the formal properties that for a long time were thought of as constitutive of subjectivity as such: it has neither self nor reflexivity nor consciousness.[41]

According to Milner, then, the Cartesian subject, itself dissociated from all qualities, whose thought is itself, strictly speaking, undifferentiated and "without quality," or, as he says, *La pensée même par quoi on définit [le sujet cartésien] est strictement quelconque.*[42] This subject is not only appropriate for modern science, it is also, as Lacan purportedly demonstrates, necessary for the foundation of the Freudian unconscious.

This is an ingenious suggestion, but I do not think it will do. In thinking that the subject of modern science is the reflection of modern science itself, one encounters a difficulty that has traditionally confronted modern philosophers from Descartes onward—the attempt to characterize subjectivity in terms of the epistemological requirements of modern science. To take an example, the Kantian subject, or what Kant calls the transcendental unity of apperception, is described in terms of what a subjectivity has to be in order for science (as he understands it) to be possible. The result of this in the case of Kant is a very complicated and probably incoherent theory of the subject.[43]

I am not disputing the properties, or lack thereof, that Milner attributes to the subject of science. Indeed, Milner's view is not off the mark; what he says about this "subject without qualities" is entirely consistent with an important thesis of Lacan's in "Science and Truth," one that is a further implication of "the subject of science." Rather, my concerns are over the reasoning that the same ascesis has to be carried out on the cogito as on *res extensa* if the cogito is to be raised to the dignity of the object of science. That is, the problem with Milner's view is that he assumes that the subject in question must be understood in the following terms: Given that we have science, what must the subject be like that makes it possible?

What I think Milner's explanation misses here, at least on this point, is that the subject in question, the subject of science, is not *only* the subject that makes science possible but *also* the subject that science excludes—to use Lacan's term, the subject that science "sutures." This combination of what makes science possible and of what science excludes is what is distinctive about the Lacanian subject of science. This is why *science* cannot articulate this subject. I return to this later.

The thesis that mathematical physics, indeed modern science in general, is made possible by the inauguration of the cogito gives rise to an interesting issue that bring us back to the "demarcation" between science and non-science. As Lacan puts it, "To say that the subject upon which we operate in psychoanalysis can only be the subject of science may seem paradoxical. It is nevertheless here that a demarcation must be made, failing which everything gets mixed up and a type of dishonesty sets in that is elsewhere called objective."[44] When physics is taken as the paradigm of modern science, attempts at establishing a science of the subject have tended to build upon observation—think of Hume's "experimental reasoning" into "moral subjects." Modern so-called scientific psychology and the social sciences have this lineage. Or else they have tried to insist upon a deep methodological distinction between the "hermeneutic" and the "natural" sciences. The structuralism by which Lacan was influenced, particularly that of Lévi-Strauss and Jakobson, had the merit of cutting across such dichotomies.

Now, when in "Science and Truth" Lacan refers to the expression "human sciences," his rejection of the term is based on the notion of the subject of science. Hence, the subject of science serves in the first instance as a "guiding principle" for drawing a new line of demarcation between science and non-science, one that includes both physical and nonphysical sciences—sciences of the subject, shall we say—on the side of science. But it also thereby provides both a criterion and a justification for distinguishing between bona fide "sciences of the subject" and mere pretenders to the title. It is this criterion of demarcation that serves to exclude as *non*-scientific the work of Jung, with a subject composed of an archetypal relationship to knowledge; Levy-Bruhl and the notion of a prelogical, primitive mentality; Piaget and the child-subject's so-called "egocentric" discourse; and, finally, closer to home, the ever-present temptation in psychoanalysis to "infantilize" the subject. What links all of these is that they are, or they imply as their counterpoint, a "full" subject. Thus the mentality of the "primitive," or of the child, is measured by comparison with an ideal of the subject. All presuppose a "full" subject, a "human" subject, a subject endowed with psychological properties of one kind or another—a logical, ratiocinative subject; a knowing, archetypal subject; an infantilized, yet-to-be-developed subject.

Lacan is quite explicit on this point. In every case where the subject has been endowed with physical, psychological, or indeed any other properties, where the subject has been fleshed out in any way that "attempts to incarnate the subject further," there is invariably produced the "archaic illusion, . . . 'psychologization of the subject.'" This "temptation" is as present in psychoanalysis as elsewhere.[45]

On the other hand, Lacan places on the side of science the subject such as it is incorporated into: games theory, with "the thoroughly calculable character of a subject strictly reduced to the formula for a matrix of signifying combinations"; linguistics, where "one can construct a poetics that owes no more to references to the mind of the poet than to its incarnation";[46] and logic, the subject of which is, as mentioned earlier, "the correlate of science."[47] The case of logic is particularly interesting; I return to it later.

The matter of demarcation here raises the question of how well the proposed criterion does the job: To what extent is it possible to unify fields as diverse as psychoanalysis, set theory, and mathematical physics by means of the notion of the subject of science? What do they have in common? Or, alternatively, how unified a notion of the subject can there be across these diverse fields?

THE SUBJECT OF THE UNCONSCIOUS

The subject on which we operate in psychoanalysis can only be the subject of science. Or, as Lacan expresses it, "To be distinguished from the question of knowing whether psychoanalysis is a science (that is, whether its field is scientific) [is] the fact that its praxis implies no other subject than that of science."[48] Far from being immune to the temptation to introduce a "psychological" subject, the history of psychoanalysis is marked by theories that do just that—though this is a failing of post-Freudian theories rather than of Freud himself.

While the subject of the unconscious is the subject of science, Lacan reserves a special place for psychoanalysis in the treatment of the subject: In particular, whereas psychoanalysis promotes the division of the subject, science is an attempt, always unsuccessful, to "suture" the subject. Thus if we adopt Lacan's formulation that transference is a form of love addressed to knowledge, then this division of the subject that the psychoanalytic discourse promotes between knowledge and truth finds expression in the transference. Lacan claims that Gödel's incompleteness theorem indicates a failed attempt on the part of science to suture the division of the subject. Gödel's theorem, with its proof that some truths of mathematics are themselves unprovable, is a stark mathematical example of the unbridgeable gap between truth and knowledge. Gödel's theorem indicates the failure of the attempt by science, by making all truth knowledge, to suture the subject. But while his theorem gives a clear illustration of this failure, even in mathematical physics we can see this. Lacan takes the example of Gauss who withheld his work on non-Euclidean geometry because, in Lacan's words, "no truth can precede what it is bearable to know."[49]

PSYCHOANALYSIS AND THE IDEAL OF SCIENCE

I now return now to Freud's views on the relationship between psychoanalysis and science.

As I stated at the outset, Freud places psychoanalysis on the side of science and holds that what is true in psychoanalytic theory has been gained through the renunciation of pleasure derived from illusions of one kind or another: illusions of religion, illusions surrounding the perfectibility of humankind, illusions concerning the attainment of social ideals.

Some have taken the view that while Freud sees psychoanalysis as needing to conform with, or perhaps better aspire to, a certain scientific model or ideal, psychoanalysis does not and indeed cannot meet the requirements of the ideals of science. They have argued that Freud's belief in a scientific ideal for psychoanalysis is merely an indication of his positivism, a vestige of his training in anatomy and of his adherence to the ideals of the Brücke-Helmholtz school. No one seriously believes any more that psychoanalysis is a science, and it must have been Freud's positivism that prevented him from seeing this.

On the other hand, by referring not to Freud's "positivism" but to his "scientism," Lacan indicates a more nuanced evaluation of Freud's attitude to the relationship between psychoanalysis and science: Freud's scientism "pave[d] the way that shall forever bear his name. . . . [T]his way never shed the ideals of this scientism . . . and . . . the mark it bears of this latter is not contingent but, rather, remains essential to it."[50]

Freud aspires to a certain scientific model for psychoanalysis. It might be thought that Lacan shares this attitude with Freud, excepting that his model sciences are linguistics, mathematics, and logic (one thinks of his mathemes) in place of those Freud found in the Brücke-Helmholtz school, but in fact his attitude is very different. His position is not that science provides psychoanalysis with an ideal model of the relationship to truth and knowledge. The remark that the subject of science is the subject on which psychoanalysis operates implies that science is implicated in psychoanalysis, in that the very object upon which psychoanalysis operates, the "subject," is structured by science itself.

The thesis that the subject on which we operate in psychoanalysis can only be the subject of science is Lacanian rather than Freudian, developed through his reflection on science and his knowledge of its history. Some glimpses of this we have seen earlier, in particular through the work of Koyré and Kojève. It is this insight that makes it possible for Lacan to transform the old question of whether psychoanalysis is a science into the new one: "What is a science that includes psychoanalysis?"[51]; or, as Lacan observes, "The question of knowing whether psychoanalysis is a science" is to be distinguished from "the fact that its praxis implies no other subject than that of science."[52]

I have examined a number of issues raised by what Lacan refers to as the subject of science. I have not looked at these issues exhaustively, nor have I exhausted the issues. The general argument is as follows: Science for Freud was an ideal against which psychoanalysis was to be measured. For Lacan, it is a historical moment that transmuted subjectivity. There is a subject of science, just one; it is the Cartesian cogito. Psychoanalysis came in the wake of both science and the cogito. This was not an accident of history, since the advent of both science and cogito was a prerequisite for the invention of psycho-analysis. The implication of science in psychoanalysis gives rise to the question of what we are to make of science in light of psychoanalysis.

Chapter 11

Lacan and Jakobson

Metaphor and Metonymy

Lacan maintained that the linguistic nature of the unconscious was already recognized by Freud. The thesis that the unconscious is symbolic and thus a chain of signifiers is his, he says, "only in the sense that it conforms as closely to Freud's texts as to the experience they opened up."[1] Freud's ignorance of the discoveries that were being made in linguistics in Geneva and Petrograd in his own day makes "all the more instructive the fact that the mechanisms described by Freud as those of the primary process, by which the unconscious is governed, correspond exactly to the functions this school of linguistics believes determines the most radical axes of the effects of language, namely metaphor and metonymy."[2]

This theory of metaphor and, to a lesser extent, of metonymy does a lot of work for Lacan. Condensation, one of Freud's primary process mechanisms, he says, is a type of metaphor, as displacement is of metonymy. The subject is a metaphor; the father of the Oedipus complex is a metaphor; the symptom is a metaphor; and love, too, is a metaphor.[3]

Underlying all of this is a theory of metaphor that drives the way Lacan conceptualizes his thesis that the unconscious is structured like a language. Although on this theory "metaphor" is still recognizably linked to its usual meaning, it is nevertheless understood in a particular way, one that deviates significantly from its customary usage. Moreover, this theory does not appear to me to have been all that clearly understood, even by those authors who have written about it in detail. This applies as much to those who have attempted to give a sympathetic exposition of Lacan's views as it does to those who have found little of merit in his theory. In what follows I give a detailed and at times critical analysis of Lacan's theory of metaphor. It seems to me that Lacan's theory is best understood if it is considered in relation first to Roman Jakobson's article that inspired it and second in relation to certain attempts, none of which I suspect Lacan was familiar with, by analytic philosophers to say what metaphors are.

Underlying my analysis of both Jakobson and Lacan is the view that while the structure of metonymy is relatively straightforward, there are three main types of metaphor, each with a different structure. I shall call these substitution metaphor, extension metaphor, and appositive metaphor, for reasons that shall become clear later. The point of this distinction is that both Jakobson's and Lacan's accounts apply to only one of these three types. I shall show how a number of conflicting definitions can be reconciled within a more comprehensive theory of metaphor that takes this structural diversity into account.

JAKOBSON

Jakobson's theory of metaphor and metonymy has been widely discussed, but I do not think it has been well understood. His exposition is difficult to follow at times, and some of what he says is somewhat misleading. What follows is I think a clear and accurate characterization of Jakobson's position in the article in question, one that brings out the single most important—indeed fatal—difficulty for his theory. Jakobson has of course been subject to various criticisms over his theory of metaphor, but this criticism has often been misplaced. Later I discuss one that I believe misreads Jakobson in a fairly typical way.

Jakobson's 1956 article, "Two Aspects of Language and Two Types of Aphasic Disturbances," appeared as Part 2 of Jakobson and Halle's *Fundamentals of Language.* Approaching the question of the relation of language to speech, Jakobson argues that the syntagmatic and paradigmatic axes of language, which relate the units of a language to one another in two series of relations, known by Saussure as *in absentia* and *in praesentia,* mean that speech involves the double operation of the selection of linguistic units from a paradigmatically related series and their syntagmatic combination into units of a higher degree of complexity. It follows from this, he continues, that each side of this speech operation is in turn double. The isolation of one unit from a number of units (which involves the possibility of having been able to select another) implies that others could be substituted for it, while the combination of units into larger ones implies that each unit occurs within a context that is provided by further units. The paradigmatic and syntagmatic relations, also described as relations of similarity and contiguity, are, Jakobson says, the metaphoric and metonymic poles of language. Jakobson suggests that this has clear implications for the study of aphasia, since "every form of aphasic disturbance consists in some impairment, more or less severe, either of the faculty for selection and substitution or for combination and contexture. . . . Metaphor is alien to the similarity disorder, and metonymy to the contiguity disorder."[4]

The moral of this is that any account of organically based speech disorders cannot, if it hopes to be descriptively adequate, afford to ignore linguistic studies, given that aphasia manifests in ways that can best be understood in terms of the structure of language.

The following list sets out the relations between the aforementioned terminology[5]:

axis	paradigm	syntagma
mode	selection substitution	combination context
relation (Saussure)	in absentia	in praesentia
relation (Jakobson)	similarity	contiguity
trope	metaphor	metonymy

"The development of a discourse," Jakobson continues, "may take place along two different semantic lines: One topic may lead to another either through their similarity or through their contiguity. The METAPHORIC way would be the most appropriate term for the first case, and the METONYMIC way for the second, since they find their most condensed expression in metaphor and metonymy, respectively."[6]

However, before passing from the relations of similarity and contiguity to metaphor and metonymy, he needs to distinguish the two aspects he calls semantic and positional. This gives positional similarity and positional contiguity, and semantic similarity and semantic contiguity. Now Jakobson offers an adequate definition of positional similarity: "The capacity of two words to replace one another is an instance of positional similarity."[7] And it is easy to see that positional contiguity would then be the possibility of two words to combine with one another. However, for semantic contiguity and semantic similarity, it is not at all clear how they should be defined.

The particular examples he offers and his discussion of them show that for there to be a metaphor ("den" for "hut") or a metonym ("thatch" for "hut") in his sense, there has to be positional similarity between the two terms, underpinning semantic similarity in metaphor and semantic contiguity in metonymy. The difference between metaphor and metonymy is thus a difference between *semantic* similarity and *semantic* contiguity. So since both metaphor and metonymy rely upon positional similarity, they would both appear to be rhetorical devices that preserve syntactic structure while modulating the paradigmatic axis of selection and substitution. In this respect, the distinction between the semantic and the positional is obviously vital to Jakobson's account of metaphor and metonymy (and, perhaps, to his account of the very existence of the tropes), since it has been introduced solely for that purpose. So how should it be understood?

The distinction does not seem to me to be a clear one, but the following seems to be what Jakobson has in mind. If positional similarity is the capacity of two words to replace one another and positional contiguity the possibility of two words to combine with one another, then "whatever stirs this mortal frame" contains a metaphor, because "frame" and "body" are positionally similar and related by semantic similarity. On the other hand, "Oh had he been content to serve the crown" is a metonym, because "crown" and "king" are positionally similar and semantically contiguous.

This characterization of metaphor and metonymy is noteworthy for its attempt to relate the tropes (where by "trope" I mean, following the Oxford English Dictionary [OED] the use of a term in a sense other than what is proper to it) to the (semantic) structure of language. While it may well be feasible to describe the tropes by means of the relations between the objects to which the terms refer (part to whole, the container for the contained, the cause for the effect, etc.), Jakobson's account is valuable for attempting to show that tropes are made possible by relations internal to language, namely, semantic contiguity and semantic similarity, but he has given no clear definition of the latter. While we may have an intuitive grasp of the distinction in examples such as the above—"frame" and "body" may seem to be semantically similar, and "crown" and "king" semantically contiguous—the distinction still stands in need of explanation; particularly if, as Jakobson's analysis suggests, they are meant to be mutually exhaustive of all of the possible pairs of positionally similar signifiers. Even if these signifiers are restricted to nouns and noun phrases, it does not seem possible to make a clear distinction so that all pairs would be either semantically contiguous or semantically similar.

The notion of similarity has played an important role in theories of metaphor. From Aristotle onward, metaphor has been described as based on "similarity," "resemblance," or "analogy," and this is perhaps what Jakobson's term means to capture. Doubtless some things are perceived as more similar than others; similarity is clearly involved in what is called the "metaphoric extension" of meaning to new cases ("mouth" said of rivers, bottles, caves, volcanoes, etc.), though here our being aware of a similarity is still an effect of language, as much as of any natural resemblance between things. We shall return to the extension metaphor later. There is another type of semantic similarity, described by Lakoff and Johnson, where the perceived similarity is much more clearly structured by the signifier itself.[8] Here associatively related themes ("Argument is war," "Theories are buildings," "Language is a vehicle or conduit") facilitate certain metaphoric discourses ("His argument came under fierce attack," "That position is indefensible," "He demolished my thesis," "He gets his ideas across nicely").

However, Jakobson's notion of semantic similarity is not the similarity of the classic works, and neither similarity reduces to the other. Indeed, on comparing Jakobson's view on metaphor and metonymy to one such as that proposed by Pierre Fontanier, the following points emerge.[9] First, Fontanier, highly classificatory, distinguishes between metonymy and synecdoche on the grounds that metonymy involves a relation of "correlation" or "correspondence" in which the objects are separate "wholes," while synecdoche involves a relation of "connection" where the two objects together form a "unit" (ensemble) or a "whole." But if we call them both "metonymy"—the classification of metonymy as the substitution of (the sign of) the part, cause, container, and so on for (the sign of) the whole, effect, contained, and so on, so that "crown" appears in place of "king" or "country," and "sail" in place of "ship"—then this classification is essentially the same as Jakobson's category of metonymy. Both stress the relations between the "manifest" and "latent" terms. The difference would then be that Jakobson shows how the relation that Fontanier describes as holding between things can be accounted for in terms of the semantic relations within language. If this is right, then Jakobson's "semantic similarity" is meant to reflect the classical characterization of metaphor as involving a relation of "resemblance," "similarity," or "analogy."

But it seems more correct to say that a metaphor depends upon no particular semantic relation between signifiers. For instance, neither Emily Dickinson's description of a snake as "a narrow Fellow in the Grass," or Keat's calling autumn the "Close bosom-friend of the maturing sun," depends upon an already existing semantic relation between these signifiers in the way metonymy does; the situation is rather that a new relation (and perhaps a new meaning) is created by these metaphoric descriptions.[10]

The second point that emerges is that metaphor may or may not involve substitution. While "the twin pillars" may be substituted for "the basis" of society, and "the sifting" for the "examination" of evidence, there is also the much more common metaphor that emerges not through the substitution of signifiers but through their juxtaposition. Examples are "Silence is golden," "Love is war," or "You will be the death of me." Let us call this type of metaphor the "appositive metaphor," in contrast to the substitution metaphor. Notice that "of" in the expression "A of B" has two uses in English, namely, the appositive use (as in "a sea of blood," "a wave of nostalgia," "a heart of gold") and the genitive use (as in "the scales of justice," "the hand of God"). These two uses correspond, respectively, to appositive and substitution metaphors. "The twin pillars of law and order" is an appositive metaphor, but the same expression is used genitively, thereby producing a substitution metaphor, when Shakespeare has Mark Antony described as "the triple pillar of the world transformed into a strumpet's fool."

The appositive use says that A is B, that the sea is (made of) blood, that the heart is (made of) gold, and that the wave is (that is, consists in) nostalgia, while the genitive use can be transformed, typically with the use of the possessive, into the form "justice's scales," or "God's hand." This shows, then, that a metaphor is not necessarily the result of a substitution (compare Lacan's *L'amour est un caillou riant dans le soleil*). This contrasts markedly with metonymy, however, since a metonym can only be produced by substitution.

These two points—that there is a semantic relation that may prove characterizable in metonymy but not in metaphor, and that all metonyms, but not all metaphors, are produced by substitution—indicate a dissymmetry between metaphor and metonymy, which is already discernible in a study such as Fontanier's. Having described synecdoche and metonymy in terms of specific relations (part to whole, etc.), he then describes metaphor as the trope of resemblance, which consists in "presenting one idea under the sign of another more striking idea which, moreover, has no other link with the former than that of some form of conformity or analogy."[11]

As it stands, this definition does not tell us much; any pair of terms will fall under it, since everything resembles everything else in one aspect or another. But what it does suggest is that there are no specifiable semantic relations involved in metaphor as there are in metonymy. This dissymmetry is important, but it is disguised by Jakobson's semantic opposition of contiguity and similarity.

The third point to be made about Fontanier's theory of tropes is that there are metaphors that Jakobson fails to take into consideration—for example, the qualifying or adjectival metaphor and the verbal metaphor—produced by the juxtaposition of positionally contiguous signifiers: "smouldering rage," "downy windows" (as Christine Brooke-Rose points out, a double metaphor of substitution: "windows" for "eyes" and "downy" metaphorically qualifying "eyes"), "green thoughts," or the aforementioned "Silence is golden."[12] Examples of the verbal metaphor are "He ploughed her and she cropped," or "A crowd flowed over London Bridge," where again the relation between the metaphor terms is juxtaposition rather than substitution. There seems no obstacle to considering all parts of speech as susceptible to metaphors. We have already suggested two differences between metaphors and metonyms, and now we have a third difference: All metonyms are substantives, while metaphors extend to all parts of speech. I shall only be dealing with noun metaphors here, since they are the most important kind. All others are either appositive metaphors ("Silence is golden") or extension metaphors ("The mouth of the river"), and their most striking characteristic is that they displace their semantic effect, Lacan's "meaning effect," "*effet de sens*," onto nouns.

The differences between substitution, extension, and appositive metaphors are important, since a failure to appreciate them is the reason for the limitations of most theories of metaphor.

A number of authors have attempted to give a general account of metaphor in terms of the concept of semantic deviance. They include Paul Ziff, Hilary Putnam, perhaps Noam Chomsky, and, it would seem, J.-F. Lyotard. The idea is that a sentence may be syntactically but not semantically well formed. A metaphor is a semantically deviant sentence that requires a nonstandard, hence "metaphoric," semantic interpretation. Putnam gives the example from Dylan Thomas: "A grief ago I saw him there." These theories, which base metaphor on semantic deviance, are at their most plausible where the appositive metaphor is concerned but have trouble accommodating extension and substitution metaphors. Substitution theories have come to grief on the appositive metaphor because attempts to account for it as a case of substitution metaphor have led to trying to replace the metaphor with the literal words that have supposedly been supplanted. But this is to confuse exegesis or explication of an appositive metaphor with the eliciting of the latent term in a substitution metaphor.

The most promising account of metaphor is the "interactionist" view, proposed most notably by I. A. Richards and taken up by Max

Black.[13] According to Richards, "In the simplest formulation, when we use a metaphor we have two thoughts of different things active together and *supported by a single word, or phrase,* whose meaning is a result of their interaction."[14] The inadequacy of this view is that it fails to distinguish between the ways that differently structured metaphors achieve the "interaction" in question. I return to this later.

It may not be a serious drawback for Jakobson's account not to agree well with the traditional classifications; a better explanation of the tropes may easily lead to a theory that cuts across standard groupings. But the limitation of his account is that it disguises certain properties of both metaphor and metonymy that are crucial to an adequate account of their functioning, to an account, that is, of the syntactic means by which tropes are brought about and of the semantic effect they produce. One thing, for example, that has not been appreciated by Jakobson is precisely the different syntax and semantics, and their connection, of metaphor and metonymy. Surely the fact that metaphor displays no particular semantic relation while metonymy does is related to the fact that not all metaphors are substitutions (there are also appositive and extension metaphors), while all metonyms are substitutions.

Metonyms and substitution metaphors require that the latent term, which does not appear in the chain of signifiers, be somehow implied by what does. And a semantic connection between a manifest and a latent term (container and contained, part and whole, etc.) helps secure the latent term. In the appositive metaphor ("Silence is golden"), however, where there is no latent term, this requirement is not needed. The unusual juxtaposition of terms just is the metaphor, without any special semantic relation between the two being required.

The reason there are no appositive metonyms is simply that the semantic relation between signifiers in metonymy is not appositive but genitive. The appositive use of metonymy is excluded by the nature of the semantic relation between the two terms, while the genitive use, which *is* possible, fails to produce a trope. For example, "sail" and "glass" are, respectively, metonyms for "ship" and "wine." But used in apposition, "the sail of the ship" or "the glass of wine," no appositive reading is possible. In "the wave of nausea," the nausea is a wave, but in "the sail of the ship," the sail is not the ship. While the appositional reading is not possible in the case of metonymy, the genitive reading is, except that in this case it fails to produce a trope. The "sail of the ship" is appositive, since it can be transformed into "the ship's sail." But because of the semantic relation between "ship" and "sail," this is not a trope.

On the other hand, however, there is no impediment to the construction of appositive metaphors, because there is no special semantic relation between the metaphoric terms.

While Jakobson's analysis can be applied to metonymy, I believe it is unable to account for any form of metaphor. In the case of the substitution metaphor, specifically, an account needs to be given of the means by which the metaphor is effected, because we cannot rely on there being any special semantic relation present. Jakobson's analysis has to be supplemented by an account of the syntactic means used to do this. Lyotard points out that simply substituting one term for another does not produce a metaphor or a metonym but a new sentence.[15] He considers this a major objection to an attempt such as Jakobson's to give a purely structuralist account of tropes. Jakobson's account is certainly deficient, but not for the reasons Lyotard suggests. We have given reasons why the expression "semantic similarity" cannot account for the structural diversity of metaphor, but even if we limit ourselves to the substitution metaphor ("the triple pillar of the world") and the metonym ("this mortal frame"), for which Jakobson's account was devised, his theory will still not do. What remains to be explained is the fact that in the substitution metaphor and in the metonym the replaced word is still latently present; it is only partially obscured, and a trace of what has been eclipsed remains.

Let us take a step back for an overview of the different issues involved at this stage. The first issue concerns the substitution tropes. Here some account has to be given of how it comes about that a latent signifier remains attached to the manifest chain of signifiers in the case of the metonym and the substitution metaphor. One also has to explain the *difference* between substitution metaphor and metonymy. A second issue is to give some account of the appositive metaphor. A third issue is that of non-noun metaphors. An account is required of the metaphor where the metaphoric term is not a noun phrase. Concerning the first issue, Jakobson provides no answer. He gives no account of how a latent signifier remains attached to the manifest chain. He explains the difference between substitution metaphor and metonymy, however, in terms of semantic similarity and semantic contiguity, but he seems not at all to have considered either the appositive metaphor or metaphors not involving nouns. So Jakobson considers only one of these different issues, that is, the difference between the substitution metaphor and the metonym.

Now, we have been able to give an account of semantic contiguity, but semantic similarity has proven to be more elusive. However, there is a reason for this elusiveness, which is just that metaphor does not contain a particular semantic relation. So it is not possible to describe any kind of "similarity" or "resemblance" that would apply to all substitution metaphors. The result of this is that we can describe metonymy as a special case of substitution metaphor in which certain relations hold between two signifiers and simply dub all cases in which none of these relations hold "metaphor." We shall then have metonyms, substitution metaphors, extension metaphors, and appositive metaphors of various kinds (verbal, nominal, adverbial, etc.). What I now intend to show is that Lacan uses "metonymy" in this sense of a case of substitution metaphor in which special relations hold and "metaphor" in the sense of substitution metaphors where these relations are absent.

It is well known that Jakobson's article on aphasia found an immediate echo in Lacan's "The Instance of the Letter in the Unconscious, or Reason since Freud," stimulating Lacan's claim that metaphor and metonymy are poetic functions equivalent to the unconscious mechanisms first uncovered by Freud of condensation and displacement. Nowhere prior to 1957 does Lacan attach any particular importance to metaphor and metonymy, even though as early as 1952 the influence of Jakobson's work is apparent.[16]

It has also been remarked that Lacan and Jakobson differ in the way they compare condensation and displacement to rhetoric. Jakobson puts displacement and condensation along the paradigmatic axis of similarity. Nicolas Ruwet, the French translator of this article, writes:

> One can see that the same comparison is not made by Jacques Lacan . . . [who] respectively identifies condensation and metaphor, and displacement and metonymy. Roman Jakobson . . . thinks that the difference is to be explained by the imprecision of the concept of condensation which, in Freud, seems to cover both cases of metaphor and cases of synecdoque.[17]

Lyotard disagrees that this divergence is due to Freud's imprecision and argues that it results from two other factors: the application of linguistic concepts onto the field of the unconscious, and the wish to rediscover the operations of speech in dream work.[18] He takes this lack of agreement to undermine Lacan's claim that the unconscious is structured like a language. In my opinion, though, the difference between the two is rather the result of different views about how best to categorize metaphor and metonymy. Despite his clear, and acknowledged, debt to Jakobson, Lacan ultimately offers a different account, and if the claim that metaphor is related to condensation and metonymy to displacement is to be understood then this difference has to be appreciated.

Lacan is happy enough to consider the substitution of "sail" for "ship" a case of metonymy: "The connection between ship and sail is nowhere other than in the signifier, and . . . metonymy is based on the *word-to-word* nature of this connection."[19] The metonymic relation of semantic contiguity defined earlier makes this example, though hackneyed, a genuine case of metonymy. The passage continues: "We shall designate as metonymy the first slope of the effective field that the signifier constitutes, so that the sense [*sens*] may take place there,"[20] which is an allusion to the Saussurian syntagmatic axis, so important for Jakobson's account of metonymy. On metonymy, then, Lacan appears to be quite standardly adopting Jakobson's analysis.

Lacan gives the stanza from "Booz endormi," "His sheaf was neither miserly nor hateful," as an example of metaphor. But if, as Lacan rightly points out, "sheaf" stands in the place of "Booz," then the semantic relation should be one of contiguity (classically, "a thing for its owner"), and so the example should be one of metonymy. But the example is indeed a metaphor: Consider first Lacan's remark on the importance of the possessive: "But once *his* sheaf has thus usurped his place, Booz cannot go back to it, the slender thread of the little 'his' that attaches him to it being an additional obstacle thereto, because it binds this return with a title of ownership that would detain him in the heart of miserliness and hatred."[21] This in itself seems no reason to regard the example as a metaphor, since the semantic relation between "Booz" and "gerbe" is still one of contiguity. The key phrase, though, is the "title of ownership," for not here but in another place Lacan makes it clear that "sheaf" stands directly in place, not of Booz but of the phallus.[22]

So Booz is represented in this passage by another signifier, the phallus. Therefore, the example is a metaphor because there is no semantic relation between the sheaf and the phallus.

A remark is called for here about the phallus as a symbol, since there is an obvious natural resemblance between the "sheaf" and the imaginary phallus. However, it is important not to confuse this natural resemblance of two objects with the notion of semantic similarity. The "natural" contiguity in space and time between ship and sail no more founds metonymy than, as David Hume saw, constant conjunction founds causality. Natural contiguity has to be subtended by semantic contiguity for metonymy to be possible, and not all relations of semantic contiguity are so subtended.

Similarly, the fact that the "sheaf" and the phallus resemble one another will not establish a relation of semantic similarity between them. In fact, things that really do look alike make difficult metaphors for one another, as is recognized by the suggestion that a striking or new resemblance is what characterizes metaphors, though, it is true, novelty is generally taken more as a mark of quality than as being important to the actual making of a metaphor. Here again we need to distinguish between the extent to which things naturally resemble one another and the extent to which a metaphor has been used and banalized. The former is a fact about the world, the second about language.

Novelty in good metaphors is not just a question of use. Striking metaphors make unexpected comparisons, and it is precisely the metaphor itself that makes us notice something new. This is why it is correct to say that there is no semantic relation ("resemblance," etc.) between latent and manifest signifiers that could account for the substitution metaphor.

Lacan says, in a passage that grasps the crucial element lacking from Jakobson's account, that the occurrence of the metaphor depends upon the relations that the latent signifier maintains, not with the signifier that has replaced it, but with the other signifiers in the chain to which it is related by contiguity:

> Metaphor's creative spark does not spring forth from the juxtaposition of two images, that is, of two equally actualized signifiers. It flashes between two signifiers, one of which has replaced the other by taking the other's place in the signifying chain, the occulted signifier remaining present by virtue of its (metonymic) connection to the rest of the chain.
> *One word for another*: this is the formula for metaphor.[23]

In "His sheaf was neither miserly nor hateful," "Booz" remains present not through a relation of semantic similarity with "his sheaf" (there is none) but through its link, which Lacan calls "metonymic," with the rest of the chain. The predicate clearly applies to Booz, which illustrates how the substitution metaphor is well able to function without there being any semantic relation between the two signifiers involved.

The previously quoted passage contrasts Lacan's own view of metaphor with Breton's.[24] One of Breton's examples of a "strong image" is *"Sur le pont la rosée à tête de chatte se berçait,"* which corresponds to what I described earlier as the appositive metaphor, where there is not a substitution but a juxtaposition of terms. Although Lacan might deny that this is a metaphor, because he has only the substitution metaphor in mind, his "modern metaphor," *"L'amour est un caillou riant dans le soleil"* (Love is a pebble laughing in the sun), is no less appositive. (Its modernity is due to the semantic juxtaposition that makes it a case on the borderline of sense, since the appositive metaphor is, of course, as old as language.) Lacan says it has the same structure as "his sheaf was neither miserly nor hateful," but it is in fact much closer to the structure of an appositive metaphor such as "Silence is golden," or "Love is war."

Lacan describes metonymy as the "word-to-word connections between signifiers." Some of these connections are semantic and they make possible substitution metaphor and the metonym. The contiguously related signifiers, in referring or applying to the latent signifier rather than to the manifest signifier that has taken its place, act to produce the metaphor. In, for example, "Weepe you no more, sad fountaines," the nonmetaphoric elements (Max Black's "frame") apply to the latent "eyes" and to the manifest "fountaines," while the metaphoric effect, what Lacan calls an *"effet de signification,"* is produced by the quite special way in which latent and manifest terms are brought together—an effect that no explicit equation of eyes and fountains would accomplish. It has been suggested that metaphors, like this one, work because the manifest term (Black's "focus") and the latent term belong to a series of semantically similar terms that pick out a class of objects of which a certain predicate is true—in this case it would be the class of all things from which water issues.[25] But this cannot be right since, as "Love is a pebble laughing in the sun" shows, metaphors do not invariably pick out similarities between terms: Some metaphors depend more on "collision" than on "collusion."

So what is the "signification effect" exactly? It varies according to the type of metaphor in question. Take the extension metaphor, where the meaning of a term is extended or enlarged so that the term applies to objects to which it would not normally apply ("the mouth of the river"). This is often catachresis. The meaning effect of an extension metaphor is the creation of new meaning, which will eventually make its way into dictionary entries. The meaning of words changes, and the extension metaphor has little to do with the creative talents of the individual speaker, since it will be present potentially in the language before actually being employed and gaining currency.

The fact that mouth may have a primary meaning (OED: "The external orifice in an animal body which serves for the ingestion of food . . . ") and a secondary meaning (OED: "Applied to things resembling a mouth") has led some authors to assume that the word was at one time used only in its primary meaning and *then* extended to other objects. I do not want to deny that this extension of meaning ever takes place; no doubt it does, but the idea that this is how extended, secondary meaning actually comes about is almost certainly false.

Moreover, as Saussure pointed out, it is a fallacy to think that one can explain a term's meaning, which is a synchronic property of language, by appeal to diachronic fact. So it seems that even if it were true in a particular case that a term was once used in its primary meaning and then extended, this is no explanation of the difference between primary and secondary meaning.[26]

But what about the appositive metaphor? Black treats "the poor are the Negroes of Europe," which is an appositive metaphor, as an extension metaphor, where "in the given context the focal word 'Negroes' obtains a new meaning, which is not quite its meaning in literal uses, nor quite the meaning which any literal substitute would have."[27]

Concerning the appositive metaphor, ask what "Love is war" or "You are my sunshine" means and you will get any number of different answers. Donald Davidson is surely right in inveighing against "the idea that metaphor carries a message, that it has a content or meaning (except, of course, its literal meaning)."[28] If we take him to mean the appositive metaphor, then his suggestion that it does not say but intimates is well said. For in the appositive metaphor there is neither too much nor too little metaphoric meaning for us satisfactorily to paraphrase because there is no metaphoric meaning. We have in "Love is war" two themes that we can develop and elaborate indefinitely, without ever arriving at a completed paraphrase. The error is to confound this metaphor either with the extension metaphor, thereby suggesting that the meaning of "war" or "love," or both, is extended beyond what it ordinarily means, or with the substitution metaphor.

The substitution metaphor ("this mortal frame," for example), on the other hand, is the closest to the traditional conception. Here there is substitution of one term for another term that remains retrievable. Here the poetic interaction of signifiers takes place according to the associative series of contrasts and likenesses, oppositions and concurrences between the manifest and latent signifiers; and this is the product, a "new species in signification," as Lacan describes it, of the (substitution) metaphor.

Metonymy is structurally similar to the substitution metaphor, since both have a latent and a manifest term. The difference is that there is an established semantic link between latent and manifest terms in metonymy (cause and effect, container and contained, etc.) But this link mitigates against the meaning effect, which relies upon collision, not collusion. On the other hand, this link means that little support from the "frame," that is, the manifest chain apart from the metaphoric term, is needed to maintain the latent term in place.

Metaphors do not just operate by a semantic relation between a manifest and a latent signifier but make use of any means the language has at its disposal. In "The very dice obey him," the definite article makes the noun phrase a definite description that has, or purports to have, a precise reference. This metonymic contribution of the structure of the sentence is enough to ensure a metaphoric reading. A function similar to that of the definite article can be performed by a subordinate clause, as in "That undiscovered country from whose bourne no traveller returns," where "undiscovered country" refers to death, but with the difference that the metonymic support given to the latent signifier is more complex, since the subordinate may bear upon either the latent signifier or signifiers, the manifest signifiers, or upon both manifest and latent structure at the same time. As Lacan demonstrates with "His sheaf was neither miserly nor hateful," the possessive adjective is also capable of binding latent signifiers to the manifest chain. The effect is the same when, upon the death of Antony, Cleopatra laments, "It were for me to throw my sceptre at the injurious gods, to tell them that this world did equal theirs, till they had stol'n our jewel," where there would have been no metaphoric effect, "our jewel" for Antony, had Shakespeare employed an article. Finally, demonstrative adjectives may fulfil the same role, so that in "These quicksands, Lepidus, keep off them, for you sink," "these" refers the statement to the context of its utterance, and therefore to its role as metaphor, rather than as a literal statement.

In neither "The very dice obey him," nor "It were for me to throw my sceptre at the injurious gods, to tell them that this world did equal theirs, till they had stol'n our jewel," is there any semantic link between the latent signifiers and the metonymically related manifest terms. The only semantic link between manifest and latent terms in each case is that between the actual focal term and something unstated ("dice" and chance, "knot" and love), and this link suffices to bring about the metaphoric reading of the entire manifest chain. However, "That undiscovered country from whose bourne no traveller returns," is different. It shares a common structure with the adjectival metaphor, a structure in which the manifest adjective, adjectival, or subordinate clause may apply to the manifest term, to the latent term ("the starry floor" for the night sky), or to both.

Moreover, the existence of latent and manifest chains of signifiers allows the metaphor to be elaborated on and developed: "With as little a *web* as this I will *ensnare* as great a fly as Cassio." A conceit, a parable, or an allegory has this same structure. Some oxymorons are also metaphors where a qualifying term, typically an adjective, applies to the latent term rather than to the manifest one. For example, "Now I feed myself with most delicious poison." "With as little a *web* as this I will *ensnare* as great a fly as Cassio" is like other cases in which the qualifying terms (adjectives or clauses), rather than the focal term, establish the metaphor. The "deviance" in such cases consists only in the fact that the qualifying terms may not (but sometimes will) apply to—in the sense that they are patently false of or in the context inappropriate to—the manifest signifiers.

It is an error to regard the semantic criterion upon which the substitution metaphor is based as a relation, dimly perceived, of "resemblance" or "analogy" between manifest and latent terms, rather than as the effect of the substitution of manifest for latent term. There is a difference of degree only between metaphoric and non-metaphoric, or literal and non-literal, expression, and it results from the nature of the semantic relation between the manifest signifiers. In all cases the metonymic relations may maintain the latent signifier "underneath" the manifest chain, but the metaphoric effect, Lacan's "new signification," or "new species in signification," depends upon the (semantic) relation between the latent, "eclipsed" signifier and the manifest, metaphoric signifier. (Lacan calls the actual maintaining of the latent signifier "underneath" the manifest chain the "meaning effect.")

The metaphor is then not infra- or supra-linguistic but depends upon and is brought about by exactly the same linguistic structures as is the most prosaic language. It may be buttressed by all of the grammatical means at a language's disposal, which are themselves capable of making a metaphor with no contribution from a resemblance relation.

As was shown earlier, the substitution metaphor depends upon the metonymic support that the latent term derives from the manifest terms. This is so because the semantic link, inadequately described as "resemblance," between the latent term and the term that replaces it in the manifest chain, is generally unable to effect the metaphor unaided. But in the dead or dormant metaphor ("the mouth of the river," for example) the metonymic support can be emptied of all semantic content, to the point of lending a purely syntactic support.

The so-called "dead" metaphor ("the mouth of the river," "sifting the evidence") is typically an extension metaphor, and it need never have actually been a living one. As an extension metaphor, it tends to make its way into dictionary entries, too, where it will appear as extended meaning or secondary meaning.

Metonymy cannot be catachresis, since by definition a metonym demands two terms and catachresis only one. There are cases of "dead metonyms" ("the crown versus . . ." in Britain and Australia), however, where a metonym is generally used in place of what it stands for.

Finally, let us now turn to a subspecies of substitution metaphor, the more complicated "analogy" metaphor, such as Aristotle's "the evening of life" for old age. Aristotle sees not two but four signifiers in the form of an abbreviated comparison or analogy: Evening is to day as old age is to life, A is to B as C is to D, so that there are two latent signifiers, not one. This type of substitution metaphor, already mentioned, is very common: "the flower of the age," "the face of the water," "The riches of the ship is come ashore," "the Kingdom of God." Consider this from Shakespeare:

> The next Caeserion smite!
> Till by degrees the memory of my womb,
> Together with my brave Egyptians all,
> Lie graveless. . .

The metaphor "the memory of my womb" stands for Cleopatra's descendents. Here we find a lot of semantic support for the latent terms in the manifest chain. But the more important difference between this and the other metaphors considered so far is that here there is an effect of displacement. Though the focus is "memory," the metaphor has repercussions elsewhere, particularly upon "womb."

The true analogy metaphor is one of substitution, and Chaim Perelman, in a work that Lacan refers to, soon gets out of his depth when he takes the appositive example he finds in Berkeley, "an ocean of false learning," for a substitution metaphor and tries to analyze it as a "condensed analogy."[29] I have no debate with his claim that this is a richer and more significant metaphor than is Aristotle's, but in my opinion the reason he gives for why this is so is wrong. Treating "an ocean of false learning" as based on the analogy A is to B as C is to D, he claims that in saying A of C (and not, like Aristotle, C of B or A of D), it leaves the terms B and D to be evoked by the reader.

Aristotle produced the first matheme of metaphor. He based the metaphor "the evening of life" for old age on the analogy: Evening is to day as old age is to life. By substituting letters for terms, we get: A is to B as C is to D as the basis of the two metaphors: A of D for C ("the evening of life" for "old age") and: C of B for A ("the old age of the day" for "evening"). Or, schematically,

$$\frac{C}{A} \quad of \quad \frac{B}{(D)} \quad and \quad \frac{A}{C} \quad of \quad \frac{D.}{(B)}$$

The structure of "an ocean of false learning," says Perelman, is neither of the Aristotelian ones (A of D for C or C of B for A) but simply A of C, and this leaves it up to the reader to supply the two missing terms, B and D. In "the evening of life," the four terms of the analogy are supplied, albeit two implicitly. In "an ocean of false learning," however, the reader is required to furnish the terms B and D, so the metaphor will mean different things according to how the terms B and D are interpreted: as "a swimmer" and "a scientist," "a stream" and "the truth," or "terra firma" and "the truth." Or rather, he claims, the metaphor will mean all of these things simultaneously, and this is the source of its greater semantic richness.

But Lacan is surely right in objecting that the fact both that Perelman has to appeal to these couples and that they can be multiplied indefinitely shows that nothing of all this is implied by the metaphor itself.[30] Insofar as there is a metaphoric meaning effect in this example, it is a case where in fact it does spring from between two manifest signifiers (the terms A and C). But if this is the case, then Lacan's attempt to construe this example as structured like a substitution metaphor cannot be correct either—and his transcription of it onto the formula

$$\frac{an\ ocean}{learning} \quad of \quad \frac{false}{x} \quad \rightarrow \quad an\ ocean \left(\frac{1}{?}\right)$$

appears incorrect. The metaphor is appositive: The ocean *consists of* false learning; the false learning is an ocean, and it should therefore not be treated as a substitution metaphor.

Here, moreover, lies the difference between Lacan and Breton. The juxtaposition of two disparate images can never create a substitution metaphor unless metonymic relations maintain a latent signifier in position "underneath" the manifest chain. The substitution metaphor is not comparable to the comparison or simile, nor to the juxtaposition of images, but consists in using syntactic means to keep signifiers latently present in discourse.

Syntactically, the metaphor is quite complex. I have shown that there are at least three types of metaphors: substitution, appositive, and extension. There has been a general tendency to ignore this syntactic complexity, resulting from the attempts to find one semantic characterization common to all varieties.

Syntactically, there is only one type of metonym. It involves a particular type of semantic relation, for which Jakobson's term *semantic contiguity* seems as appropriate as any. Though Lacan suggests that all metaphors are substitution metaphors, I have shown that some of the examples that Lacan uses are best seen as appositive metaphors. The interactionist accounts of Richards and Black refer to the appositive metaphor, but they both to some extent confuse the appositive with the substitution metaphor. Their attributing metaphoric meaning to the appositive metaphor results from this confusion. Davidson is essentially correct in saying that metaphors have no metaphorical meaning, provided that we take this to apply to appositive metaphors only. Only in the case of substitution metaphor can we talk of metaphoric meaning.

Notes

CHAPTER 1

1. Jacques Damourette and Édouard Pichon, *Des mots à la pensée: essai de grammaire de la langue française*, 7 vols. (Paris: Bibliothèque du Français Moderne, 1932–1951). Pichon was also a psychoanalyst and senior colleague of Lacan's in the Société Psychanalytique de Paris. An interesting aside is that this vast work of some 4,500 pages was in part motivated by the desire to preserve the genius of the French language, which, as the "most logical and most policed of all modern languages" (vol. 1, para. 7), necessarily makes the French thinker a clearer thinker than speakers of any other language. The Maurassian implications of this thesis—Pichon was a member of the Action Française—are made explicit in their observation that certain subgroups of French speakers do not have optimal access to the language, including Jews, the poor (para. 2589), and bilingual individuals who have "a system of thought which is a compromise, halfway between two languages" (para. 74). See Jean-Marc Dewaele, "Is It the Corruption of French Thought Process that Purists Fear? A Response to Henriette Walter," *Current Issues in Language and Society* 6 (1999): 231–34.

2. Jacques Lacan, *The Seminar of Jacques Lacan, Book III, The Psychoses, 1955–1956*, trans. Russell Grigg (New York: Norton, 1993), 321.

3. See Jacques Lacan, "Ouverture de la section clinique," *Ornicar?* 9 (1977): 7–14.

4. Lacan, *Psychoses*, 85–86.

5. See Jacques Lacan, "Response to Jean Hyppolite's Commentary on Freud's 'Verneinung,' " in *Écrits*, trans. Bruce Fink (New York: Norton, 2006), 321–27; see also Jacques Lacan, *The Seminar of Jacques Lacan, Book I, Freud's Papers on Technique, 1953–1954*, trans. John Forrester (New York: Norton, 1988), which includes, along with Lacan's original discussion, Hyppolite's article, "A Spoken Commentary on Freud's *Verneinung*, by Jean Hyppolite."

6. Sigmund Freud, "From the History of an Infantile Neurosis," in *Standard Edition*, 17: 79–80, translation modified. This passage illustrates the difficulty of tracking the term through the *Standard Edition*. Freud's "*Eine Verdrängung ist etwas anderes als eine Verwerfung*" is rendered as "A repression is something very different from a condemning judgment."

7. Ibid., 84. Again, I have modified the English version, but this time by restoring Freud's punctuation.

8. Lacan, "Response to Jean Hyppolite," 324.

9. Ibid. Compare with Freud's observations on the mechanism of paranoia in the Schreber case: "It was incorrect to say that the perception which was suppressed internally is projected outwards; the truth is rather, as we now see, that what was abolished internally [*das innerlich Aufgehobene*] returns from without." Sigmund Freud, "Psycho-Analytic Notes on an Autobiographical Account of a Case of Paranoia (*Dementia Paranoides*)," in *Standard Edition*, 12: 71.

10. Lacan, *Psychoses*, 150.

11. The first use in writing of this term, which occurs in the Rome Report, published in 1956, links the symbolic father to the law: "It is in the *name of the father* that we must recognize the basis of the symbolic function which, since the dawn of historical time, has identified his person with the figure of the law." Jacques Lacan, "The Function and Field of Speech and Language in Psychoanalysis," in *Écrits*, 230.

12. Jacques Lacan, "On a Question Prior to Any Possible Treatment of Psychosis," in *Écrits*, 465.

13. Jacques Lacan, *De la psychose paranoïaque dans ses rapports avec la personnalité* (Paris: Éditions du Seuil, 1975), 207.

14. "The elementary phenomena are no more elementary than what underlies the entire construction of a delusion. They are as elementary as a leaf in relation to the plant . . . there is something common to the whole plant that is reproduced in certain of the forms that make it up. . . . A delusion . . . , too, is an elementary phenomenon. This means that here the notion of element is to be taken in no other way than as structure, differentiated structure, irreducible to anything other than itself." Lacan, *Psychoses*, 19.

15. In Schreber's verbal hallucinations we can recognize "quite other [differences] than those by which they are 'classically' classified, . . . namely, differences that stem instead from their speech structure, insofar as this structure is already in the *perceptum*." Lacan, "On a Question," 450. Lacan is following a distinction that Roman Jakobson draws between message and code in "Shifters, Verbal Categories, and the Russian Verb," in *Selected Writings*, ed. Stephen Rudy (The Hague, the Netherlands: Mouton, 1971), 2: 130–47.

16. Lacan, "On a Question," 450.

17. "What is actually involved is an effect of the signifier, insofar as its degree of certainty (second degree: signification of signification) takes on a weight proportional to the enigmatic void that first presents itself in the place of signification itself." Ibid.

18. Daniel Paul Schreber, *Memoirs of My Nervous Illness*, 2d ed., ed. and trans. Ida Macalpine and Richard A. Hunter (Cambridge, MA.: Harvard University Press, 1988), 182–83.

19. Jakobson, "Shifters," 131.

20. Lacan, *Psychoses*, 47–53; "On a Question," 457–58.

21. Lacan, "On a Question," 474.

22. Ibid., 481.

23. Ibid.

24. Ibid.

25. Lacan, *Psychoses*, 251.

26. See Maurits Katan, "Schreber's Prepsychotic Phase," *International Journal of Psycho-Analysis* 34 (1953): 43–51; "Structural Aspects of a Case of Schizophrenia," *The Psychoanalytic Study of the Child* 5 (1950): 175–211; also see Helene Deutsch, "Some Forms of Emotional Disturbance and Their Relationship to Schizophrenia," *The Psychoanalytic Quarterly* 11 (1942): 301–21.

27. Lacan, *Psychoses*, 203.

28. Lacan, "On a Question," 481.

29. Jacques Lacan, *Le séminaire de Jacques Lacan, Livre XXIII, Le sinthome, 1975–1976* (Paris: Éditions du Seuil, 2005).

30. Lacan, "On a Question," 482.

31. Ibid.

32. Ibid., 458.

33. Colette Soler, "L'expérience énigmatique du psychotique, de Schreber à Joyce," *La Cause Freudienne* 23 (1993): 50–59.

34. Lacan, *Le sinthome*, 22.

35. Jacques Lacan, "Lituraterre," *Littérature* 3 (1971): 3.

36. "By an epiphany he meant a sudden spiritual manifestation, whether in the vulgarity of speech or of gesture or in a memorable phase of the mind itself. He believed that it was for the man of letters to record these epiphanies with extreme care, seeing that they themselves are the most delicate and evanescent of moments." James Joyce, *Stephen Hero* (London: Jonathan Cape, 1956), 216.

37. Robert Scholes and Richard M. Kain, eds., *The Workshop of Daedalus: James Joyce and the Raw Materials for* A Portrait of the Artist as a Young Man (Evanston, IL: Northwestern University Press, 1965), 21.

38. This explains Lacan's 1966 comment that in paranoia jouissance is identified as located in the place of the Other as such. See Jacques Lacan, "Présentation des *Mémoires* du Président Schreber en traduction française," *Ornicar?* 38 (1986): 7. This article originally appeared in *Cahier pour l'Analyse* 5 (1966).

39. Jacques Lacan, "Psychoanalysis and Its Teaching," in *Écrits*, 371.

40. See Jacques Lacan, "The Youth of Gide, or the Letter and Desire," in *Écrits*, 639–40.

CHAPTER 2

1. Sigmund Freud, *Totem and Taboo*, in *Standard Edition*, 13: 1; *Moses and Monotheism*, in *Standard Edition*, 23: 7.

2. Sigmund Freud, *Group Psychology and the Analysis of the Ego*, in *Standard Edition*, 18: 105 ff.

3. Melanie Klein, "Early Stages of the Oedipus Complex," in *Love, Guilt, and Reparation and Other Works, 1921–1945*, ed. Roger Money-Kyrle (New York: The Free Press, 1975), 190.

4. Jacques Lacan, "Presentation on Transference," in *Écrits*, 176–85.

5. Ibid., 179.

6. Sigmund Freud, "Fragment of an Analysis of a Case of Hysteria," in *Standard Edition*, 7: 34.

7. Sigmund Freud, "Some Psychical Consequences of the Anatomical Distinction between the Sexes," in *Standard Edition*, 19: 248.

8. See Sigmund Freud, *Inhibitions, Symptoms, and Anxiety*, in *Standard Edition*, 20: 143.

9. Jacques Lacan, "The Neurotic's Individual Myth," *Psychoanalytic Quarterly*, 48 (1979): 405–25.

10. Lacan, "On a Question," 464.

11. Ibid., 464 ff.

12. Lacan, "Psychoanalysis and Its Teaching," 376.

13. Lacan, *Freud's Papers on Technique*, 184.

14. Sigmund Freud, *Civilization and Its Discontents*, Standard Edition, 21: 125–26.

15. Ibid., 129.

16. Ibid., 139.

17. Sigmund Freud, "Mourning and Melancholia," in *Standard Edition*, 14: 243–58.

18. Sigmund Freud, *The Ego and the Id*, in *Standard Edition*, 19: 28–39.

19. Freud, *Moses and Monotheism*, 82.

20. Freud, *Group Psychology*, 124, emphasis added.

21. Freud, *Civilization and Its Discontents*, 102 ff.

22. Lacan, *Le sinthome*, 150.

23. Serge Cottet, *Freud et le désir de l'analyste* (Paris: Navarin, 1982), 157–64.

24. Lacan, *Freud's Papers on Technique*, 198.

CHAPTER 3

1. Jacques Lacan, "The Function and Field of Speech and Language in Psychoanalysis," in *Écrits*, 229.

2. Jacques Lacan, *The Seminar of Jacques Lacan, Book XVII, The Other Side of Psychoanalysis, 1969–1970* (New York: Norton, 2007), 136.

3. Claude Lévi-Strauss, "The Structural Study of Myth," *Journal of American Folklore* 78 (1955): 428–44.

4. Two propositions are contraries when both cannot be true, though both can be false; contradictories are propositions that cannot be either true together or false together.

5. Reading, along with Geneviève Morel, "*textes*" for "*tentes*." Morel gives a very interesting account of the comparison between myth and dream in *Oedipe aujourd'hui* (Lille: Association de la Cause Freudienne, 1997).

6. See Russell Grigg, Dominique Hecq and Craig Smith, eds., *Female Sexuality: The Early Psychoanalytic Controversies* (New York: The Other Press, 1999).

7. Lacan, *The Other Side of Psychoanalysis*, 125.

8. Morel, *Oedipe*, 51.

9. See the discussion of "agent" in chapter 8 of Lacan, *The Other Side of Psychoanalysis*.

10. "I hold that it is out of the question to analyze the real father; far better the cloak of Noah when the Father is imaginary." Jacques Lacan, *Television: A Challenge to the Psychoanalytic Establishment* (New York: Norton, 1990), 19.

11. Jacques Lacan, *Le séminaire de Jacques Lacan, Livre XVIII, D'un discours qui ne serait pas du semblant, 1970–1971*, session of June 9, 1971 (unpublished).

12. The fact that we can do this, incidentally, indicates that what is remarkable about Freud's case histories is that even when he misses something crucial, traces of it can still be found in the text.

13. This is homophonic with *"le père périt"* (the father perishes).

14. Lacan, *D'un discours*, session of June 9, 1971.

15. Lacan, *The Other Side of Psychoanalysis*, 114.

16. Freud, *Group Psychology*, 18: 24, emphasis added.

17. Lacan, *D'un discours*, session of June 9, 1971.

18. Freud, *Moses and Monotheism*, 23: 82, emphasis in original.

19. Lacan, *The Other Side of Psychoanalysis*, 99.

20. Ibid., 94.

CHAPTER 4

1. David Sachs, "In Fairness to Freud: A Critical Notice of *The Foundations of Psychoanalysis*, by Adolf Grünbaum," in *The Cambridge Companion to Freud*, ed. Jerome Neu (Cambridge: Cambridge University Press, 1991), 309–38.

2. Lacan, *Freud's Papers on Technique*, 142.

3. See Jacques-Alain Miller, *Cinco Conferencias Caraquenas sobre Lacan* (Caracas: Editorial Ateneo de Caracas, 1980). Cf. his remark, p. 85, that the case of Dora is also the case of Freud. For this chapter I have derived much inspiration from Miller's lectures.

4. See the account of Freud's encounter with Mahler in Ernest Jones, *Sigmund Freud, Life and Work*, vol. 2 (London: The Hogarth Press, 1974), 88–89.

5. Lacan, "Psychoanalysis and Its Teaching," 379.

6. Michel Silvestre, "Le Transfert," in *Demain la Psychanalyse* (Paris: Navarin, 1987), 64–66.

7. James Strachey, "The Nature of the Therapeutic Action of Psycho-analysis," *International Journal of Psycho-Analysis* 15 (1934): 149.

8. Jacques Lacan, *The Seminar of Jacques Lacan, Book VII, The Ethics of Psychoanalysis, 1959–1960*, trans. Dennis Porter (New York: Norton, 1992), 15.

9. Freud, *Group Psychology*, 18: 128.

10. See Ernest Jones, "The Concept of a Normal Mind," *International Journal of Psycho-Analysis* 23 (1942): 1–8.

11. Sigmund Freud, "The Dynamics of Transference," in *Standard Edition*, 12: 108.

12. See Serge Leclaire and Jean Laplanche, "L'inconscient, une étude psychanalytique," in *L'inconscient*, ed. Henri Ey (Paris: Desclée de Brouwer, 1966), 95–130.

13. In particular, see Lacan, "The Function and Field."

14. Lacan, "The Instance of the Letter in the Unconscious or Reason since Freud," in *Écrits*, 412–41.

15. Freud, *Civilization and Its Discontents*, 21: 105.

16. Lacan, *On Feminine Sexuality: The Limits of Love and Knowledge* (New York: Norton, 1998), 35.

17. Marie-Hélène Brousse, "La formule du fantasme? $ <> a," in *Lacan*, ed. Gérard Miller (Paris: Bordas, 1987), 105–22.

18. Jacques Lacan, "Comptes rendus d'enseignements," notes from the seminar *Problèmes cruciaux pour la psychanalyse, Ornicar?* 29 (Summer 1984): 10.

19. *Standard Edition*, 23: 175.

CHAPTER 5

1. For much of what follows, see the Web site of the "Forum des Psys," http://www.forumpsy.org/index.html.

2. Quoted in *Agence Lacanienne de Presse, Bulletin spécial Accoyer* 5, Paris, December 1, 2003, http://www.forumpsy.org.

3. See the Web site of the Société Psychanalytique de Paris, http://www.spp.asso.fr/Main/Actualites/Items/21.htm.

4. The text of the Dubernard Bill can be found on any number of Web sites, such as the following: http://www.etatsgeneraux-psychanalyse.net/actualites/Dubernard.html.

5. For the full text, consult the Web site, http://www.legifrance.gouv.fr/.

6. See the Web site of the Senate, http://www.senat.fr/cra/s20040709/s20040709H35.html.

7. *Annuaire et textes statutaires* (Paris: École de la Cause Freudienne, 2001), 16.

8. *London Review of Books*, Letters, vol. 23, no. 6 (March 22, 2001).

9. *Annuaire*, 16.

CHAPTER 6

1. Quantifiers are those elements of language such as "all," "none," "some," "every," "more than one," and so on, that enable us to say that something is true of all, some, or none of the members of a class.

2. Lacan, *On Feminine Sexuality*; "L'Étourdit," *Scilicet* 4 (1973): 5–52. I have changed the symbols to ones easier to print; this alters nothing, since the formal relations between the expressions remain the same.

3. Jean-Claude Milner, *L'amour de la langue* (Paris: Éditions du Seuil, 1978); *Les penchants criminels de l'Europe démocratique* (Paris: Verdier, 2003).

4. Lacan, *Television*, 40.

5. Ibid., 13, 72.

6. See Alain Badiou, "Sujet et infini," in *Conditions* (Paris: Éditions du Seuil, 1992), 287–305.

7. Lacan, *On Feminine Sexuality*, 102–103, translation slightly modified.

8. Badiou, "Sujet et infini," 291.

9. Ibid.

10. He declares his Platonism in Alain Badiou, "Platonisme et ontologie mathématique," in *Court traité d'ontologie transitoire* (Paris: Éditions du Seuil, 1998), 95–109. On Badiou's anti-intuitionism and realism, see the sensitive and informed treatment by Oliver Feltham, *As Fire Burns: Of Ontology, Praxis and Functional Work*, Ph.D. diss., Deakin University, Geelong, 2000, especially pages 108–15.

11. W. V. O. Quine, *Philosophy of Logic* (Englewood Cliffs, NJ: Prentice-Hall, 1970), 88.

12. Crispin Wright, *Wittgenstein on the Foundations of Mathematics* (London: Duckworth, 1980); see also his *Frege's Conception of Numbers as Objects* (Aberdeen: Aberdeen University Press, 1983).

13. See Michael Dummett, "Wittgenstein's Philosophy of Mathematics," in *Truth and Other Enigmas* (London: Duckworth, 1978), 166–85; see also his *Elements of Intuitionism* (Oxford: Clarendon Press, 1977).

14. See Lacan, *On Feminine Sexuality*, 119, 108.

15. The substance of Aristotle's logic is found in his two works, *Prior Analytics* and *Posterior Analytics*. The first contains the analysis of argument in the form of the syllogism, Aristotle's most important contribution to logic, which is under discussion here.

16. Jacques Brunschwig, "La proposition particulière et les preuves de non-concluance chez Aristote," *Cahier pour l'Analyse* 10 (1969): 3–26.

17. Here "↔" means "if and only if," and below "→" means "if . . . then. . . ."

18. Jacques-Alain Miller, "Notice de fil en aiguille," in Lacan, *Le sinthome*, 207–208 .

19. Ibid., 208.

CHAPTER 7

1. *Groundwork of the Metaphysics of Morals*, in *Practical Philosophy*, ed. and trans. Mary J. Gregor (Cambridge: Cambridge University Press, 1996), 73 & n.

2. *Utilitarianism* (London: Fontana, 1962), 254.

3. This point was suggested to me by Liam Murphy.

4. "On a Supposed Right to Lie from Philanthropy," in *Practical Philosophy*, 612. See also J.-P. Sartre's short story, *The Wall*.

5. W. D. Ross, *Kant's Ethical Theory* (Oxford: Clarendon Press, 1954), 32–33.

6. As Kant puts it, ends that are also duties (and hence willed by any rational being) are "one's own perfection and the happiness of others." *Metaphysics of Morals*, pt. 2, in *Practical Philosophy*, 517

7. As he argues, "For, the ends of a subject who is an end in itself must as far as possible be also *my* ends, if that representation is to have its *full* effect in me." *Groundwork*, 81, emphasis in original.

8. *Metaphysics of Morals*, 549.
9. Ibid., emphasis in original.
10. *Metaphysics of Morals*, 536, emphasis in original.
11. *Critique of Practical Reason*, in *Practical Philosophy*, 162–63.
12. *Critique of Practical Reason*, 201.
13. Bernard Baas, *Le Désir Pur* (Louvaine: Peeters, 1992).
14. Kant, *Critique of Practical Reason*, 181, emphasis added.
15. "Kant with Sade," in *Écrits*, 647.
16. See Slavoj Žižek, *The Sublime Object of Ideology* (London: Verso, 1989), 81–82.

CHAPTER 8

1. Kant, *Critique of Practical Reason*, 163.
2. Ibid.
3. Ibid.
4. Ibid., 163–64.
5. See Lacan, *D'un discours*, session of June 9, 1971, available at http://gaogoa.free.fr/.
6. Melanie Klein, "Criminal Tendencies in Normal Children," in *Love, Guilt, and Reparation and Other Works, 1921–1945*, ed. Roger Money-Kyrle (London: Virago, 1975), 170–85.
7. This point is discussed in Jacques Lacan, "A Theoretical Introduction to the Functions of Psychoanalysis in Criminology," in *Écrits*, 102–22.
8. That "prisons departments" have become "corrective services" symbolizes this shift.
9. See Edward Glover, *The Roots of Crime* (London: Imago Publishing, 1960), xii.
10. Franz Alexander and Hugo Staub, *The Criminal, the Judge, and the Public: A Psychological Analysis*, trans. Gregory Zilboorg (London: Allen & Unwin, 1931).
11. Renata Salecl, *The Spoils of Freedom: Psychoanalysis and Feminism after the Fall of Socialism* (London and New York: Routledge, 1994), 99.
12. Freud, *Civilization and Its Discontents*, 21: 59–145.
13. Slavoj Žižek, "Kant with (or against) Sade," in *The Žižek Reader*, ed. Elizabeth Wright and Edmond Wright (Oxford: Blackwell, 1999), 293.

CHAPTER 9

1. Slavoj Žižek, *Enjoy Your Symptom!* (New York: Routledge, 1992).
2. Ibid., 43, emphasis in original.
3. Ibid., 22.
4. Ibid., 43.

5. Ibid., 44.

6. Ibid.

7. Ibid.

8. Ibid.

9. Ibid., 45.

10. Ibid.

11. Ibid., 44.

12. Ibid.

13. Ibid., 46, emphasis in original.

14. Ibid., 77.

15. Ibid., 76–77.

16. Ibid., 77.

17. Ibid., 78.

18. Ibid., 77–78.

19. Judith Butler, *The Psychic Life of Power* (Stanford, CA: Stanford University Press, 1997), 88.

20. Ibid.

21. Slavoj Žižek, *The Ticklish Subject: The Absent Centre of Political Ontology* (London: Verso, 1999), 262.

22. Ibid.

23. Ibid., 263–64.

24. Ibid., 262.

25. Ibid., 264, emphasis in original.

26. Ibid.

27. For Lacan's exact formulation, see *The Ethics of Psychoanalysis, 1959–1960*, 319.

28. Ibid., 300.

29. Ibid.

30. Jacques Lacan, *The Four Fundamental Concepts of Psychoanalysis*, trans. Alan Sheridan (Harmondsworth: Penguin, 1979), 275.

31. Ibid.

CHAPTER 10

1. Sigmund Freud, *New Introductory Lectures on Psycho-Analysis*, in *Standard Edition*, 22: 182.

2. Sigmund Freud, "A Special Type of Choice of Object Made by Men," in *Standard Edition*, 11: 165.

3. Lacan, *The Other Side of Psychoanalysis*, 22.

4. Ibid., 22.

5. Peter Medawar, *The Limits of Science* (Oxford: Oxford University Press, 1985), 72–73.

6. Lacan intends this to be a criticism of Hegel.

7. Lacan, *The Other Side of Psychoanalysis*, 23.

8. Ibid.

9. Jacques Lacan, "Science and Truth," in *Écrits*, 726–45.

10. Jacques Lacan, "Radiophonie," in *Autres écrits* (Paris: Editions du Seuil, 2001); *The Other Side of Psychoanalysis*; and *The Four Fundamental Concepts*.

11. Bruce Fink, "Science and Psychoanalysis," in *Reading Seminar XI*, ed. Richard Feldstein, Bruce Fink, and Maire Jaanus (Albany: State University of New York Press, 1995), 55–64; Jean-Claude Milner, *L'oeuvre claire* (Paris: Éditions du Seuil, 1995).

12. Alexandre Koyré, *Entretiens sur Descartes* (Paris: Gallimard, 1962).

13. Lacan, *The Four Fundamental Concepts*, 226.

14. Lacan, "Science and Truth," 727, emphasis added.

15. Ibid., 726.

16. David Hume, *A Treatise of Human Nature* (Oxford: Oxford University Press, 2000).

17. Karl Popper, *The Logic of Scientific Discovery*, rev. ed. (London: Hutchinson, 1968), 34.

18. Lacan, "Science and Truth," 726.

19. Ibid.

20. Lacan, "Radiophonie," 423.

21. Sigmund Freud, *Introductory Lectures on Psycho-Analysis*, in *Standard Edition*, 16: 284–85.

22. Ibid., 285.

23. See Lacan, "Radiophonie," 420–23.

24. Ibid.

25. Lacan, *The Four Fundamental Concepts*, 151.

26. Jacques-Alain Miller, "Elements of Epistemology," trans. Russell Grigg, *Analysis* 1 (1989): 29.

27. Lacan, "Radiophonie," 422.

28. Jacques Lacan, *The Seminar of Jacques Lacan, Book XX, Encore: On Feminine Sexuality: The Limits of Love and Knowledge, 1972–1973*, trans. Bruce Fink (New York: Norton, 1998), 43.

29. Alexandre Koyré, *From the Closed World to the Infinite Universe* (Baltimore. MD: Johns Hopkins University Press, 1975).

30. Alexandre Koyré, *Galileo Studies*, trans. John Mepham (Hassocks, Sussex: Harvester Press, 1978), 3.

31. Jacques Lacan, "The Mirror Stage as Formative of the I Function, as Revealed in Psychoanalytic Experience," in *Écrits*, 75.

32. Lacan, "Radiophonie," 5.

33. René Descartes, *Meditations on First Philosophy*, trans. John Cottingham (Cambridge: Cambridge University Press, 1986), 1.

34. Ibid., 17.

35. Lacan, *The Four Fundamental Concepts*, 44.

36. Martial Guéroult, *Descartes selon l'ordre des raisons* (Paris: Aubier, 1968).

37. Jaako Hintikka, "*Cogito, Ergo Sum*: Inference or Performance?" *The Philosophical Review* 71 (1962): 3–32.

38. Descartes, *Meditations*, 19.

39. Lacan, *The Four Fundamental Concepts*, 224.
40. Bertrand Russell, *History of Western Philosophy* (London: Allen & Unwin, 1961), 550.
41. Milner, *L'oeuvre claire*, 39, my translation.
42. Ibid., 40.
43. There is an excellent discussion of the relationship between the Cartesian cogito and the Kantian transcendental unity in Slavoj Žižek, *Tarrying with the Negative* (Durham, NC: Duke University Press, 1993), 12 ff.
44. Lacan, "Science and Truth," 729.
45. Ibid., 730–31.
46. Ibid.
47. Ibid., 727.
48. Ibid., 733.
49. Jacques Lacan, *Le séminaire de Jacques Lacan, Livre XII, Problèmes cruciaux pour la psychanalyse, 1964–1965* (unpublished).
50. Lacan, "Science and Truth," 728.
51. On the back cover of Jacques Lacan, *Le séminaire de Jacques Lacan, Livre XI, Les quatre concepts fondamentaux de la psychanalyse, 1964* (Paris: Éditions du Seuil, 1973).
52. Lacan, "Science and Truth," 733.

CHAPTER 11

1. Jacques Lacan, "The Subversion of the Subject and the Dialectic of Desire," in *Écrits*, 676.
2. Lacan, "Subversion," 676–77.
3. See Lacan, "The Instance of the Letter," 412–41; Jacques Lacan, "Metaphor of the Subject," in *Écrits*, 755–58; Jacques Lacan, *Le séminaire de Jacques Lacan, Livre VI, Le désir et son interpretation, 1958–1959*, session of January 15, 1958 (unpublished).
4. Roman Jakobson, "Two Aspects of Language and Two Types of Aphasic Disturbances," in Roman Jakobson and Morris Halle, *Fundamentals of Language* (The Hague, the Netherlands: Mouton, 1971), 91.
5. See Jean-François Lyotard, *Discours, figure* (Paris: Klincksieck, 1978), 252, for a slightly different list to which he adds, following Jakobson, the "genres" of poetry and prose and, on the one hand, the "schools" of romanticism and symbolism and, on the other, realism.
6. Jakobson, "Two Aspects of Language," 91.
7. Ibid., 92.
8. George Lakoff and Mark Johnson, *Metaphors We Live By* (Chicago: University of Chicago Press, 1980).
9. Pierre Fontanier, *Manuel classique pour l'étude des tropes* (1821), in *Les figures du discours* (Paris: Flammarion, 1968).
10. Compare C. Day Lewis's prescriptive characterization of "poetic truth" as "the collision rather than the collusion of images." C. Day Lewis, *The Poetic Image* (London: Jonathan Cape, 1969), 72.

11. Fontanier, *Manuel classique*, 99. Richard Whateley defines a metaphor as "a word substituted for another on account of the Resemblance or Analogy between their significations." See Richard Whateley, *Elements of Rhetoric*, 7th ed. (Ithaca, NY: J.W. Parker, 1846). Quoted by Max Black, "Metaphor," in *Models and Metaphors* (Ithaca, NY: Cornell University Press, 1962), 31.

12. Christine Brooke-Rose, *A Grammar of Metaphor* (London: Secker and Warburg, 1958).

13. I. A. Richards, *The Philosophy of Rhetoric* (Oxford: Oxford University Press, 1936); Black, "Metaphor."

14. Ibid., 93, emphasis added.

15. Lyotard, *Discours, figure*, 254–55.

16. Compare Lacan, "Function and Field," 221–22, and Roman Jakobson, "Results of a Joint Conference of Anthropologists and Linguists," in *Selected Writings*, ed. Stephen Rudy (The Hague, the Netherlands: Mouton and Company, 1971), 2: 565.

17. Roman Jakobson, *Essais de linguistique générale*, ed. and trans. Nicolas Ruwet (Paris: Minuit, 1973), p. 66, n. 1.

18. Lyotard, *Discours, figure*, 253.

19. Lacan, "The Instance of the Letter," 421, emphasis in original.

20. Ibid.

21. Ibid., 422.

22. Lacan, "Metaphor of the Subject," 758.

23. Lacan, "The Instance of the Letter," 422, emphasis in original.

24. André Breton, "Manifeste du surréalisme," in *Manifestes du surréalisme* (Paris: Gallimard, 1963), 52–53.

25. This is the approach taken by, among others, Jean Dubois et al., *Rhétorique générale* (Paris: Larousse, 1970), and Samuel Levin, *The Semantics of Metaphor* (Baltimore, MD: Johns Hopkins University Press, 1977).

26. In any case, I have never seen this thesis supported by any evidence. But any amateur can establish the following: the OED gives circa 897 for the first occurrence of the Old English "muo" in a literal context, and 1122 for the first occurrence of "muoe" for a river mouth. On the other hand, Gover, Mawer, and Stenton give the earliest occurrence of the English place-name "Axmouth" ("Axanmuoan") as purporting to be 880–885, though the actual copy of the document consulted dates from the year 1000. See John Gover, Allen Mawer, and Frank Stenton, *The Place-Names of Devon*, part 2 (Cambridge: Cambridge University Press, 1932), 636.

27. Black, "Metaphor," 38–39. This is not the same as Richards' position, although Black believes it is. For Richards, "In the simplest formulation, when we use a metaphor we have two thoughts of different things active together and *supported by a single word, or phrase*, whose meaning is a resultant of their interaction" (p. 93, emphasis added). Richards is suggesting that the metaphoric term, his "vehicle," expresses its literal meaning and another meaning that interact to express the metaphor, or the metaphoric meaning. This is confirmed by his remark that "the co-presence of the vehicle and tenor results in a meaning (to be clearly distinguished from the tenor) which is not attain-

able without their interaction" (p. 100), since vehicle and tenor are thoughts, or meaning. So Black gets it wrong in thinking "Richards says that our 'thoughts' about European poor and American Negroes are 'active together' and 'interact' to produce a meaning that is a resultant of that interaction" (p. 38). Further, the reason that Richards says that "talk about the identification or fusion that a metaphor effects is nearly always misleading and pernicious" (p. 127) is not, as Black says, that "for the metaphor to work the reader must remain aware of the extension of meaning – must attend to both the old and the new meanings together" (p. 39), but that the metaphor not only has us notice similarities between two thoughts brought into interaction but also has us bear in mind the disparities and contrasts between them.

Black's failure correctly to read Richards' position leads him into the further error of claiming that Richards has lapsed "into the older and less sophisticated analyses he is trying to supersede" (ibid.) in referring to the common characteristics between tenor and vehicle as the ground of the metaphor, "so that in its metaphorical use a word or expression must connote only a *selection* from the characteristics connoted in its literal uses" (ibid., emphasis in original), while "usually, Richards tries to show that similarity between the two terms is at best *part* of the basis for the interaction of meanings in a metaphor" (ibid., n. 20, emphasis in original). For does not Richards immediately comment on the passage to which Black refers, that "a metaphor may work admirably without our being able . . . to say . . . what is the ground of the shift" (p. 117)?

Finally, Black hints at the possible syntactic complexity of metaphor when in a suggestive passage that is unfortunately left undeveloped he concedes that his own strict definition of metaphor defines the term overnarrowly. A characterization more sensitive to common usage would probably lead to a classification of metaphors "as instances of substitution, comparison, or interaction" (p. 45). I do not think Black is correct in saying that "only the last kind are of importance in philosophy" (ibid.). But even if he were, I should still consider my general account relevant for showing how conflicting definitions of metaphor apply to different types of metaphor.

28. Donald Davidson, "What Metaphors Mean," in *Inquiries into Truth and Interpretation* (Oxford: Clarendon, 1984), 261.

29. Chaim Perelman and Lucie Olbrechts-Tyteca, *Traité de l'argumentation* (Paris: Presses Universitaires de France, 1958), 2: 497–534. Lacan refers to this work in "Metaphor of the Subject."

30. Lacan, "Metaphor of the Subject," 757.

Bibliography

NOTE

Standard Edition = *The Standard Edition of the Complete Psychological Works of Sigmund Freud*, 24 volumes, edited by James Strachey et al. London: The Hogarth Press and the Institute of Psychoanalysis, 1953–1974.

Agence Lacanienne de Presse, Bulletin spécial Accoyer 5 December 1, 2003, http://www.forumpsy.org.

Alexander, Franz, and Hugo Staub. *The Criminal, the Judge, and the Public: A Psychological Analysis*. Translated by Gregory Zilboorg. London: Allen & Unwin, 1931.

Annuaire et textes statutaires. Paris: École de la Cause Freudienne, 2001.

Baas, Bernard. *Le désir pur*. Louvaine: Peeters, 1992.

Badiou, Alain. "Platonisme et ontologie mathématique." In *Court traité d'ontologie transitoire*, 95–109. Paris: Éditions du Seuil, 1998.

———. "Sujet et infini." In *Conditions*, 287–305. Paris: Éditions du Seuil, 1992.

Black, Max. "Metaphor." In *Models and Metaphors*, 25–47. Ithaca, NY: Cornell University Press, 1962.

Breton, André. "Manifeste du surréalisme." In *Manifestes du surréalisme*, 1–47. Paris: Gallimard, 1963.

Brooke-Rose, Christine. *A Grammar of Metaphor*. London: Secker and Warburg, 1958.

Brousse, Marie-Hélène, "La formule du fantasme? $ <> a." In *Lacan*, edited by Gérard Miller, 105–22. Paris: Bordas, 1987.

Brunschwig, Jacques. "La proposition particulière et les preuves de non-concluance chez Aristote." *Cahier pour l'analyse* 10 (1969): 3–26.

Butler, Judith. *The Psychic Life of Power*. Stanford, CA: Stanford University Press, 1997.

Carroll, Lewis. *Through the Looking-Glass*. New York: Exeter Books, 1986.

Cottet, Serge. *Freud et le désir de l'analyste*. Paris: Navarin, 1982.

Damourette, Jacques, and Édouard Pichon. *Des mots à la pensée: Essai de grammaire de la langue française*. 7 vols. Paris: Bibliothèque du Français Moderne, 1932–1951.

Davidson, Donald. "What Metaphors Mean." In *Inquiries into Truth and Interpretation*, 245–64. Oxford: Clarendon, 1984.

Day Lewis, C. *The Poetic Image*. London: Jonathan Cape, 1969.

Descartes, René. *Meditations on First Philosophy*. Translated by John Cottingham, with an introduction by Bernard Williams. Cambridge: Cambridge University Press, 1986.

Deutsch, Helene. "Some Forms of Emotional Disturbance and Their Relationship to Schizophrenia." *The Psychoanalytic Quarterly* 11 (1942): 301–21.

Dewaele, Jean-Marc. "Is It the Corruption of French Thought Process that Purists Fear? A Response to Henriette Walter." *Current Issues in Language and Society* 6 (1999): 231–34.

Dubois, Jean, Francis Edeline, Jean-Marie Klinkenberg, and Philippe Minguet. *Rhétorique générale*. Paris: Larousse, 1970.

Dummet, Michael. *Elements of Intuitionism*. Oxford: Clarendon Press, 1977.

———. "Wittgenstein's Philosophy of Mathematics." In *Truth and Other Enigmas*, 166–85. London: Duckworth, 1978.

Feltham, Oliver. "As Fire Burns: Of Ontology, Praxis, and Functional Work." Ph.D. diss., Deakin University, Geelong, 2000.

Fink, Bruce. "Science and Psychoanalysis." In *Reading Seminar XI*, edited by Richard Feldstein, Bruce Fink, and Maire Jaanus, 55–64. Albany: State University of New York Press, 1995.

Fontanier, Pierre. *Manuel classique pour l'étude des tropes*. In *Les figures du discours*. Paris: Flammarion, 1968.

Freud, Sigmund. *Civilization and its Discontents*. In *Standard Edition*, 21: 59–145.

———. "The Dynamics of Transference." In *Standard Edition*, 12: 97–108.

———. *The Ego and the Id*. In *Standard Edition*, 19: 3–66.

———. *Fragment of an Analysis of a Case of Hysteria*. In *Standard Edition*, 7: 7–122.

———. *From the History of an Infantile Neurosis*. In *Standard Edition*, 17: 3–122.

———. *Group Psychology and the Analysis of the Ego*. In *Standard Edition*, 18: 67–143.

———. *Inhibitions, Symptoms, and Anxiety*. In *Standard Edition*, 20: 77–172.

———. *The Interpretation of Dreams*. In *Standard Edition*, vols. 4–5.

———. *Introductory Lectures on Psycho-Analysis*. In *Standard Edition*, 15–16.

———. *Moses and Monotheism*. In *Standard Edition*, 23: 3–137.

———. "Mourning and Melancholia." In *Standard Edition*, 14: 239–58.

———. *New Introductory Lectures on Psycho-Analysis*. In *Standard Edition*, 22: 3–182.

———. "Observations on Transference-Love." In *Standard Edition*, 12: 157–71.

———. "An Outline of Psychoanalysis." In *Standard Edition*, 23: 141–207.

———. "Some Psychical Consequences of the Anatomical Distinction between the Sexes." In *Standard Edition*, 19: 243–58.

———. "Psycho-Analytic Notes on an Autobiographical Account of a Case of Paranoia (*Dementia Paranoides*)." In *Standard Edition*, 12: 3–82.

———. "A Special Type of Choice of Object Made by Men." In *Standard Edition*, 11: 165–75.

———. *Totem and Taboo*. In *Standard Edition*, 13: 1–161.

Glover, Edward. *The Roots of Crime*. London: Imago Publishing, 1960.

Gover, John, Allen Mawer, and Frank Stenton. *The Place-Names of Devon*. Part 2. Cambridge: Cambridge University Press, 1932.

Grigg, Russell, Dominique Hecq, and Craig Smith, eds. *Female Sexuality: The Early Psychoanalytic Controversies*. New York: The Other Press, 1999.

Guéroult, Martial. *Descartes selon l'ordre des raisons*. Paris: Aubier, 1968.

Hintikka, Jaako. "*Cogito, Ergo Sum*: Inference or Performance?" *The Philosophical Review* 71 (1962): 3–32.

Hume, David. *A Treatise of Human Nature: Being an Attempt to Introduce the Experimental Method of Reasoning into Moral Subjects*. Oxford: Oxford University Press, 2000.

Jakobson, Roman. *Essais de linguistique générale*. Edited and translated by Nicolas Ruwet. Paris: Minuit, 1973.

———. "Results of a Joint Conference of Anthropologists and Linguists." In *Selected Writings*, edited by Stephen Rudy, vol. 2, 554–67. *Word and Language*. The Hague : Mouton, 1971.

———. "Shifters, Verbal Categories, and the Russian Verb." In *Selected Writings*, edited by Stephen Rudy, vol. 2, 130–47. *Word and Language*. The Hague: Mouton, 1971.

———. "Two Aspects of Language and Two Types of Aphasic Disturbances." In *Fundamentals of Language*, Roman Jakobson and Morris Halle, 67–96. The Hague: Mouton, 1956.

Jones, Ernest. "The Concept of a Normal Mind." *International Journal of Psycho-Analysis* 23 (1942): 1–8.

———. *Sigmund Freud, Life and Work*. 3 vols. London: The Hogarth Press, 1953–1957.

Joyce, James. *Stephen Hero*. London: Jonathan Cape, 1956.

Kant, Immanuel. *Critique of Practical Reason*. In *Practical Philosophy*. Edited and translated by Mary J. Gregor. Cambridge: Cambridge University Press, 1996.

———. *Groundwork of the Metaphysics of Morals*. In *Practical Philosophy*. Edited and translated by Mary J. Gregor. Cambridge: Cambridge University Press, 1996.

Katan, Maurits. "Schreber's Prepsychotic Phase." *International Journal of Psycho-Analysis* 34 (1953): 43–51.

———. "Structural Aspects of a Case of Schizophrenia." *The Psychoanalytic Study of the Child* 5 (1950): 175–211.

Klein, Melanie. "Criminal Tendencies in Normal Children." In *Love, Guilt, and Reparation and Other Works, 1921–1945*, edited by Roger Money-Kyrle, 170–85. London: Virago, 1975.

Koyré, Alexandre. *Entretiens sur Descartes*. Paris: Gallimard, 1962.

———. *From the Closed World to the Infinite Universe*. Baltimore, MD: Johns Hopkins University Press, 1975.

———. *Galileo Studies*. Translated by John Mepham. Hassocks, Sussex: Harvester Press, 1978.

Lacan, Jacques. "Comptes rendus d'enseignements." Notes from the seminar, *Problèmes cruciaux pour la psychanalyse*. *Ornicar?* 29 (Summer 1984): 9–12.

———. *De la psychose paranoïaque dans ses rapports avec la personnalité.* Paris: Éditions du Seuil, 1975.

———. "L'étourdit." *Scilicet* 4 (1973): 5–52.

———. *The Four Fundamental Concepts of Psychoanalysis.* Translated by Alan Sheridan. Harmondsworth: Penguin, 1979.

———. "The Function and Field of Speech and Language in Psychoanalysis." In *Écrits.* Translated by Bruce Fink, in collaboration with Héloïse Fink and Russell Grigg. New York: Norton, 2006.

———. "The Instance of the Letter in the Unconscious or Reason since Freud." In *Écrits.* Translated by Bruce Fink, in collaboration with Héloïse Fink and Russell Grigg. New York: Norton, 2006.

———. "Kant with Sade." In *Écrits.* Translated by Bruce Fink, in collaboration with Héloïse Fink and Russell Grigg. New York: Norton, 2006.

———. "Lituraterre." *Littérature* 3 (1971): 3–10.

———. "Metaphor of the Subject." In *Écrits.* Translated by Bruce Fink, in collaboration with Héloïse Fink and Russell Grigg. New York: Norton, 2006.

———. "The Mirror Stage as Formative of the I Function, as Revealed in Psychoanalytic Experience." In *Écrits.* Translated by Bruce Fink, in collaboration with Héloïse Fink and Russell Grigg. New York: Norton, 2006.

———. "The Neurotic's Individual Myth." *Psychoanalytic Quarterly* 48 (1979): 405–25.

———. "On a Question Prior to Any Possible Treatment of Psychosis." In *Écrits.* Translated by Bruce Fink, in collaboration with Héloïse Fink and Russell Grigg. New York: Norton, 2006.

———. "Ouverture de la section clinique." *Ornicar?* 9 (1977): 7–14.

———. "Présentation des *Mémoires* du président Schreber en traduction française." *Ornicar?* 38 (1986): 7.

———. "Presentation on Transference." In *Écrits.* Translated by Bruce Fink, in collaboration with Héloïse Fink and Russell Grigg. New York: Norton, 2006.

———. "Psychoanalysis and Its Teaching." In *Écrits.* Translated by Bruce Fink, in collaboration with Héloïse Fink and Russell Grigg. New York: Norton, 2006.

———. "Radiophonie." In *Autres écrits.* Paris: Éditions du Seuil, 2001.

———. "Response to Jean Hyppolite's Commentary on Freud's 'Verneinung.' " In *Écrits.* Translated by Bruce Fink, in collaboration with Héloïse Fink and Russell Grigg. New York: Norton, 2006.

———. "Science and Truth." In *Écrits.* Translated by Bruce Fink, in collaboration with Héloïse Fink and Russell Grigg. New York: Norton, 2006.

———. *Le séminaire de Jacques Lacan. Livre VI. Le désir et son interprétation, 1958–1959.* Unpublished.

———. *Le séminaire de Jacques Lacan. Livre VII. L'éthique de la psychanalyse, 1959–1960,* edited by Jacques-Alain Miller. Paris: Éditions du Seuil, 1986.

———. *Le séminaire de Jacques Lacan. Livre XI. Les quatre concepts fondamentaux de la psychanalyse, 1964,* edited by Jacques-Alain Miller. Paris: Éditions du Seuil, 1973.

———. *Le séminaire de Jacques Lacan. Livre XII. Problèmes cruciaux pour la psychanalyse, 1964–1965*. Unpublished.

———. *Le séminaire de Jacques Lacan. Livre XVII. L'envers de la psychanalyse, 1969–1970*, edited by Jacques-Alain Miller. Paris: Éditions du Seuil, 1991.

———. *Le séminaire de Jacques Lacan. Livre XVIII. D'un discours qui ne serait pas du semblant, 1970–1971*. Unpublished.

———. *Le séminaire de Jacques Lacan. Livre XX. Encore, 1972–1973*, edited by Jacques-Alain Miller. Paris: Éditions de Seuil, 1975.

———. *Le séminaire de Jacques Lacan. Livre XXIII. Le sinthome, 1975–1976*, edited by Jacques-Alain Miller. Paris: Éditions du Seuil, 2005.

———. *The Seminar of Jacques Lacan. Book I. Freud's Papers on Technique, 1953–1954*, edited by Jacques-Alain Miller. Translated and with notes by John Forrester. New York: Norton, 1988.

———. *The Seminar of Jacques Lacan. Book III. The Psychoses, 1955–1956*, edited by Jacques-Alain Miller. Translated and with notes by Russell Grigg. New York: Norton, 1993.

———. *The Seminar of Jacques Lacan, Book VII, The Ethics of Psychoanalysis, 1959–1960*, edited by Jacques-Alain Miller. Translated and with notes by Dennis Porter. New York: Norton, 1992

———. *The Seminar of Jacques Lacan. Book XVII. The Other Side of Psychoanalysis, 1969–1970*, edited by Jacques-Alain Miller. Translated and with notes by Russell Grigg. New York: Norton, 2007.

———. *The Seminar of Jacques Lacan. Book XX. Encore: On Feminine Sexuality: The Limits of Love and Knowledge, 1972–1973*, edited by Jacques-Alain Miller. Translated and with notes by Bruce Fink. New York: Norton, 1998.

———. *Television: A Challenge to the Psychoanalytic Establishment*. New York: Norton, 1990.

———. "A Theoretical Introduction to the Functions of Psychoanalysis in Criminology." In *Écrits*. Translated by Bruce Fink, in collaboration with Héloïse Fink and Russell Grigg. New York: Norton, 2006.

———. "The Youth of Gide, or the Letter and Desire." In *Écrits*. Translated by Bruce Fink, in collaboration with Héloïse Fink and Russell Grigg. New York: Norton, 2006.

Lakoff, George, and Mark Johnson. *Metaphors We Live By*. Chicago: University of Chicago Press, 1980.

Levin, Samuel. *The Semantics of Metaphor*. Baltimore, MD: Johns Hopkins University Press, 1977.

Lévi-Strauss, Claude. "The Structural Study of Myth." *Journal of American Folklore* 78 (1955): 428–44.

London Review of Books, Letters 23: 6 (March 22, 2001).

Lyotard, Jean-François. *Discours, figure*. Paris: Klincksieck, 1978.

Medawar, Peter. *The Limits of Science*. Oxford: Oxford University Press, 1985.

Miller, Jacques-Alain. *Cinco Conferencias Caraquenas sobre Lacan*. Caracas: Editorial Ateneo de Caracas, 1980.

Miller, Jacques-Alain. "Elements of Epistemology." Translated by Russell Grigg. *Analysis* 1 (1989): 27–42.

Miller, Jacques-Alain. "Notice de fil en aiguille." *Le séminaire de Jacques Lacan. Livre XXIII. Le sinthome, 1975–1976,* edited by Jacques-Alain Miller. Paris: Éditions du Seuil, 2005.

Miller, Jacques-Alain. "Le vrai, le faux et le reste." *La Cause Freudienne* 28 (1994): 9–14.

Milner, Jean-Claude. *L'amour de la langue.* Paris: Éditions du Seuil, 1978

———. *L'oeuvre claire.* Paris: Éditions du Seuil, 1995.

———. *Les penchants criminels de l'Europe démocratique.* Paris: Verdier, 2003.

Morel, Geneviève. *Oedipe aujourd'hui.* Lille: Association de la Cause Freudienne, 1997.

Perelman, Charles, and Lucie Olbrechts-Tyteca. *Traité de l'argumentation.* 2 vols. Paris: Presses Universitaires de France, 1958.

Popper, Karl. *The Logic of Scientific Discovery.* Rev. ed. London: Hutchinson, 1968.

Quine, W. V. O. *Philosophy of Logic.* Englewood Cliffs, NJ: Prentice-Hall, 1970.

Richards, I. A. *The Philosophy of Rhetoric.* Oxford: Oxford University Press, 1936.

Russell, Bertrand. *History of Western Philosophy.* London: Allen & Unwin, 1961.

Sachs, David. "In Fairness to Freud: A Critical Notice of *The Foundations of Psychoanalysis,* by Adolf Grünbaum." In *The Cambridge Companion to Freud,* edited by Jerome Neu, 309–38. Cambridge: Cambridge University Press, 1991.

Salecl, Renata. *The Spoils of Freedom: Psychoanalysis and Feminism after the Fall of Socialism.* London and New York: Routledge, 1994.

Scholes, Robert, and Richard M. Kain, eds. *The Workshop of Daedalus: James Joyce and the Raw Materials for* A Portrait of the Artist as a Young Man. Evanston, IL.: Northwestern University Press, 1965.

Schreber, Daniel Paul. *Memoirs of My Nervous Illness.* 2nd ed. Edited and translated by Ida Macalpine and Richard A. Hunter, with an introduction by Samuel M. Weber. Cambridge, MA.: Harvard University Press, 1988.

Silvestre, Michel. "Le Transfert." In *Demain la Psychanalyse.* Paris: Navarin, 1987.

Soler, Colette. "L'Expérience énigmatique du psychotique, de Schreber à Joyce." *La Cause Freudienne* 23 (1993): 50–59.

Strachey, James. "The Nature of the Therapeutic Action of Psychoanalysis." *International Journal of Psycho-Analysis* 15 (1934): 127–49.

Whateley, Richard. *Elements of Rhetoric.* 7th ed. Ithaca, NY: J. W. Parker, 1846.

Wright, Crispin. *Frege's Conception of Numbers as Objects.* Aberdeen: Aberdeen University Press, 1983.

———. *Wittgenstein on the Foundations of Mathematics.* London: Duckworth, 1980.

Žižek, Slavoj. *Enjoy Your Symptom!* New York: Routledge, 1992.

Žižek, Slavoj. "Kant with (or against) Sade." In *The Žižek Reader,* edited by Elizabeth Wright and Edmond Wright, 283–301. Oxford: Blackwell, 1999.

Žižek, Slavoj. *The Sublime Object of Ideology.* London: Verso, 1989.

Žižek, Slavoj. *Tarrying with the Negative*. Durham, NC: Duke University Press, 1993.
―――. *The Ticklish Subject: The Absent Centre of Political Ontology*. London: Verso, 1999.

WEB SITES

http://www.forumpsy.org/index.html
http://www.etatsgeneraux-psychanalyse.net/actualites/Dubernard.html
http://www.legifrance.gouv.fr/
http://www.senat.fr/cra/s20040709/s20040709H35.html
http://www.spp.asso.fr/Main/Actualites/Items/21.htm

Index

www.ingramcontent.com/pod-product-compliance
Lightning Source LLC
Chambersburg PA
CBHW020352270326
41926CB00007B/398